HOCKEY'S ORIGIN UNMASKED:

The hidden hand covering a Native source

by

Howdie Mickoski

Hockey Unmasked: The hidden hand covering a Native source

Copyright © 2023 howdie mickoski

All Rights Reserved

ISBN 978-82-691266-5-5

Cover design: Verushka Ettlin
Cover images: Hockey Cibils card in author's collection,
Istock image of curtain, credit: razihusin, Stock photo ID:610838846
Ice Photo by Bruce Christianson on Unsplash

Typeface- Baskerville 12 pt.

Table of Contents

DEDICATION

This book is dedicated to my mother. She died before any of my recent books hit the market, and as such never saw that I did in fact become an author and speaker. She only knew me in the period of working hard with research and failed early attempts at books. It took me a while, and a lot of challenging times, but I did make it.

It is also dedicated to four medicine people who were helpful in my life to learning Native culture and ceremony in their sweat lodges and conversations: Bruce Starlight, Doreen Spence, Dennis McKay, and Clayton Bunn. What they shared with me over the years has helped to have my eyes tuned to see the "old world" before 1900 in different ways.

I wish to thank the terrific Archive.org. Without their tremendous availability of resources (many removed from library shelves) much of the research into this book would have not been possible. The early hockey section of Sihrhockey.org was helpful for finding detail on every recorded Montreal game prior to 1883, and many statistics of early players.

DISCLAIMER

This work is my opinion on the subjects of history, sports and the 1800s, based on my research over several years. It is presented to promote debate, discussion and for others to ask further questions and do further research in these areas. Nothing in this work has the desire to lessen the "name" of anyone mentioned. I don't know any of the people written of in this book personally, I am just presenting the research as it was uncovered. I will leave the deeper details of what it all might mean up to the readers.

All images have been checked to be public domain images, and/or have received permissions for reproduction. Should it be brought to the attention of the author that an image is not in the public domain, it will be removed from future editions of this book.

Thank you to all the editors who helped with the text. After their edits I added some more material, and as such any errors that remain are due to my own late additions, not their time and work on the project.

Illustration 1: Hockey in 1894 at Victoria Arena (composite, 1893. Painter George Horne Russell, Object Number II-101415, McCord Museum)

---

[1] *Foucault's Pendulum*

INTRODUCTION

"The first step in liquidating a people is to erase its memory. Destroy its books, its culture, its history. Then have somebody write new books, manufacture a new history, a new culture. Before long that nation will begin to forget what it is and what it was. The world around it will forget even faster."[2] (Milan Kundera)

This book has surprised me. I thought it would be somewhat easy research, looking into a few odd co-incidences that I had found around the origin of hockey. This narrative tends to be presented as ball-and-stick games were played on ice for several centuries, until an indoor ice game was played, called hockey, at the Victoria Skating Rink in Montreal, Canada on March 3, 1875. This game was supposed to have been organized by James G.A. Creighton. But as I began to look again into all of this, I realized that three very important questions have never been properly answered. Why Montreal? Why 1875? Why James Creighton? Then I began to get into the research and found: outright lies, misdirection, pasted and doctored images, and everywhere I would turn in the story another secret or esoteric society would show up? What was going on? A whole new set of questions began to appear.

Where did hockey really start? You might think that answer has been solved. Not really. One problem is that when one looks into the origin of any sport, the narrative tends to present how the sport has "evolved" from earlier games and pastimes. I am going to suggest that there is another narrative, equally provable, that there was no start to hockey per se, but rather a hijacking and re-dressing of the long-standing ceremonial games of the Native Peoples of North

---

[2] Milan Kundera, *The Book of Laughter and Forgetting*

America. And that those games (for a variety of reasons) were to be presented as something new and unique. The simple history of hockey became a dive into the history of the 1800s.

What does seem clear is that in the 1870s the British elite in Montreal had problems. They were not seen as locals, but rather as foreign conquerors who were now everyone else's bosses. It had been such a problem that two rebellions occurred between 1837 and 1838. The average Canadian was very unhappy. The elite thus were looking for ways for staying at the top of the totem pole of control, but fooling the "lower classes" to believe all were equally "Canadian." Hockey was the tool that did this. There was a second problem, that being Canada had just become its own country in 1867, and the British military garrison had returned to England. This left no soldiers to defend Canada against the ever possible invasion from the USA (a country Canada had been at war with several times in the past). How to get the young men of the country to be trained as potential soldiers? Hockey was the tool that did this as well.

What these British gentlemen did in Montreal, was not to really "invent" a new ice sport. They followed the model of what they had already done in the 1850s with another Native Aboriginal game (bagattaway). There they took the game and by slightly modifying it and giving it a structure- all of a sudden a new sport called lacrosse appeared. With hockey they went a step further. The choice here was to hide its true origins, and proclaim themselves (the British) as the only evolution line in the creation.

But this standard narrative is full of holes. One obvious one is that until around 1900, the Mi'kmaq Natives of Nova Scotia were the only ones in Canada that knew how to make proper hockey sticks. Why did the colonists not make all the sticks if they were really the inventor of the game? Even odder, why are the Mi'kmaq Nation seemingly associated with the Knight's Templar, Ancient Egypt, and Scandinavian Vikings? Is it all just a co-incidence, or is it a clue to the origin of hockey?

Hockey became the plan of Canada's elite to generate an identity, for themselves personally and for the new country as a whole. In that end, they succeeded greatly. And there was a hidden hand behind it all. When I say the hidden hand behind the scenes I am referring directly to Freemasonry. The hand placed under a jacket is one of lodge's oldest symbols, and means they "control things without being seen."[3] Freemasons have been at the center of just about everything that has happened over the last 200 years; from government choices, banking decisions, wars, commerce, and societal changes. I will not be presenting that this organization is a fraternal brotherhood that one should join, nor that it is a nefarious organization that is controlling the world for its own interests. I can leave the decision process of what the purpose of this group is up to you. What I will be doing is revealing the co-incidence that just about everyone involved in the origin of hockey was a Freemason. As well, this group was involved in the genesis of every other major sport of the 1800s, with a few Theosophists thrown in.

A key early hockey image I want to address is a woodcut that was found in 2010 that seems to date to 1797, and might be the first image of a person playing hockey. The owner of the image would not allow it to be reproduced in this book, so please see the footnote.[4] As such I will have to explain it in a bit of detail here so those of you without the image can get a sense of what I am pointing towards. What appears is a young man in a top hat and long coat, on an ice surface wearing a type of ice skate, and holding a very hooked-like stick. In front of him is what appears to be a flat disk (certainly not a ball). To the right is a younger boy, dressed in blue, seated on a small island putting on some skates. There is no second stick to be seen. In the distance of the lake or river is an obelisk.[5]

---

[3] The Freemason gesture can be found at wikipedia page at
https://en.wikipedia.org/wiki/Hand-in-waistcoat

[4] The image can be seen on the cover of Houda, Giden and Martel's book *On the Origin of Hockey* which can be seen at their Amazon page or other booksellers. You can also Internet search with the words: Le Petit, 1797, hockey

[5] What is also interesting is that no one is really sure who the artist was. The suggestion is Dutch artist Benedictus Antonio Van Assen. claimed to have lived from 1767 to 1817. There is little other information on him. He made another drawing (portrait Daniel Lambert) in 1805 of a very large man (with the face of Napoleon) also making the hidden hand gesture. He also made a series of rather odd artwork of skeletons of death at the moment of plunging an arrow into living people, such as the work "dance of death." He made other esoteric pieces.

What no one before me seems to have noticed is that the man with the stick has his left hand hidden under his coat. The Freemason gesture! Why does the first image made of a hockey player need to have this gesture? As mentioned in the above footnote, the suggested artist is one who used this gesture and other esoteric symbolism in some of his artwork. However, I have found that he made no other depictions of sporting events besides this one. So why did he choose to create this specific sports image?

I have always seemed to have a different perception than others. One day twenty-five years ago, I had taken my then girlfriend to a Calgary Flames game at the Saddledome. After a few minutes I noticed that she was staring at me. I asked if I had something on my face?

She responded, "No. I am staring at your eyes. Everyone's eyes in this arena is looking one way when the play is going on, but yours are looking somewhere else. You are seeing a different game than everyone. Just once I would love to see a game of hockey through your eyes."

This book will be a journey to present the standard origin narrative, and then question it. To see it through my eyes. This research is not so much about what happened specifically, but who were the people involved in what happened? The biographies provide insight into what might have been going on prior to 1900. And to note the various organizations and secret societies that interconnected with everything. At some point it is no longer a coincidence.

This story must start in 1875 with a man named James Creighton. He is not only is credited as being the organizer of the first indoor game in Montreal; he also becomes the person who helps set up the Ottawa Parliamentary Team which includes the sons of Lord Stanley. This Ottawa team will be the force behind the donation of what becomes the Stanley Cup. Is Creighton a genius, lucky, or is something else going on?

1

INVENTION OR MISDIRECTION?
Montreal 1875

"Some say that no one ever leaves Montreal, for that city, like Canada itself, is designed to preserve the past, a past that happened somewhere else."[6] (Leonard Cohen)

Montreal between 1850 to 1880 is presented as the most innovative hotbed of sports in history. In just 20 years this city "invents" lacrosse, hockey, American football, and if James Naismith had continued teaching at McGill University one more year - perhaps basketball. What is the coincidence that four of the five major North American sports were all founded in Montreal in a thirty year period? And we know nothing about how baseball was really formed, so who knows, Montreal might be able to claim that sport also.

How is that possible? The obvious answer is that it wasn't. Nothing was "invented" in Montreal. That story is a big misdirection. So what happened in Montreal, specifically regarding the supposed "first game of organized hockey" in 1875? It becomes obvious with even just a little investigation that this is not the first hockey game played on ice, as many ice games are documented long before 1875 in England and Canada (as the excellent book *On the Origin of Hockey* by Giden, Houda and Martel shows). The 1875 game appears to be some sort of marker. One question to ask is, what is that marker, and who is doing the marking?

---

[6]Leonard Cohen in *The Favorte Game* https://www.azquotes.com/quote/1160200

*Illustration 2: James Creighton in 1902
(Creighton, J.G.A. Mr., Source: Library and
Archives Canada/Topley Studio fonds/a197799)*

Most hockey historians will claim that the "inventor" of modern hockey is James George Alwin Creighton, who organized the first recorded Canadian game in 1875.[7] Amazingly, he is NOT in the Hockey Hall of Fame. Let that sink in. The supposed inventor of the sport is not in its Hall of Fame! I find this omission to be very strange.

Creighton was born in 1850 in Halifax, Nova Scotia. His father was part of the shipping and wholesale food business. He received an

____

[7]Information on Creighton mostly from
http://www.biographi.ca/en/bio/creighton_james_george_aylwin_15E.html,
https://sihrhockey.org/__a/public/creighton.cfm

HBA from King's College in 1868 (later associating with Dalhousie University). Soon after he became a survey worker for Sandford Fleming (the engineer-in-chief for the Inter-Colonial Railway and known today as the inventor of everything). We will come back to Fleming's connection later; I think he's also very important to this story. Back to Creighton, he moved to Montreal in 1872, and became an engineer on such projects as the Lachine Canal and Montreal Harbour. During his time in Montreal he became a member of several clubs including the Victoria Skating Club. Beyond being a hockey pioneer, he later went to work for the Senate in Ottawa, and also "amazingly" became a part of the Rideau Hall Rebels, with the sons of the Governor General, Lord Stanley of Preston. This is the person who would create the Stanley Cup. Creighton's connection to the Stanley Cup tends to be overlooked. We will get to that also.

The claim is that he began to organize early morning games with his friends from McGill University as early as 1873 (perhaps bribing the caretaker to have access to the rink on Sundays). There is no direct evidence for this, only claims of the last surviving player, Henry Joseph in the 1930s. We do know that Creighton was a team captain in the 1875 game, and also for a few of the games in subsequent years. He himself never had anything to say about his involvement in these games. Part of the historical claim is that he took the ball-and-stick ice games of his youth from the ponds of Nova Scotia to Montreal. Generally this gets presented as meaning the games of the British colonials. The local Nova Scotia Mi'kmaq Natives and their ice games have been presented as having a connection to the origin of hockey, but few have really seen just how much that may be. Recall that for several decades the Mi'kmaq were the only ones in Canada that seemed able to make proper hockey sticks. They were likely using a flat wooden disk for their ice games for at least a century, and had been using bone skates long before the new iron and steel models began to appear in the 1800s. The Indigenous Peoples connection will demand an entire chapter to properly assess their part of the real origin story of hockey. Suffice to say, there is no proof of exactly what ice games Creighton played as a kid, or what rules he did or did not use for those games. So again why

Montreal, 1875 and James Creighton? And why for several years do only the sons of the British elite play in hockey games?[8]

The announcement for a new game to be played at the Victoria Skating Rink was made in the March 3rd *Montreal Gazette* newspaper, that was likely in fact written by Creighton himself (in the future becoming a writer for both the *Gazette* and several book companies):

> *"Victoria Rink - A game of Hockey will be played at the Victoria Skating Rink this evening, between two nines chosen from among the members. Good fun may be expected, as some of the players are reputed to be exceedingly expert at the game. Some fears have been expressed on the part of intending spectators that accidents were likely to occur through the ball flying about in too lively a manner, to the imminent danger of lookers on, but we understand that the game will be played with a flat circular piece of wood, thus preventing all danger of its leaving the surface of the ice. Subscribers will be admitted on presentation of their tickets."*

Both sides in the game had nine skaters, though no one can say why this number was chosen. If we take a look at the games that were played on ponds or lakes, open ice shinny or hurley could have as many as 50 players per side, so needed to be reduced given the confined space of the Victoria Rink. But why nine and not seven or fifteen? Fifteen would have made sense if this was supposed to be a winter rugby practice, as much of the legend suggests.

This announcement gives us a few key pieces of information. The first is that it is using the term hockey, and not giving any explanation of what the name means. Secondly it says that some of the players are "reputed" to be exceedingly expert, though it seems no one has ever seen them play. It would also indicate that even seeing

---

[8]Key sources for the examination of the early games in Montreal are at the SIHR.org early hockey database.

them, no one would be able to "rate their ability." The paper is thus suggesting that anyone viewing this ice game would have no idea what was going on. It also indicates that a flat piece of wood (the word puck not used in Canadian print until 1876) would be used, as a way to "avoid injuring spectators." The article is all about promotion, trying to draw a crowd, thus the flat disk is all about spectator safety, not its importance (over a ball) in the ice game being played.

If this first match was really about showcasing a new sport, as some have tended to present, then Creighton would have asked 14 or 15 players from Nova Scotia (where the game was supposed to originate), and bring them to Montreal to show off their top skills. What we have here instead are a bunch of Montreal elite, who were young, athletic, and soon to be rich, showcasing a sport that they possibly had little life-connection with. I don't really think this was some idea Creighton had to showcase a sport from his youth, this was more of a plan much higher up the ladder. Creighton was likely just the chosen front man to make it happen.

The game was played at the Victoria Skating Rink (seen in illustration 1), which had an ice surface of 204 feet by 80 feet. All arenas since 1875 have pretty much mirrored the definitions of the Victoria Rink, as if without even knowing it, enshrining the Victoria Arena as the "original temple of hockey." And I don't mean that lightly. I get the sense the Victoria Skating Rink was held in some sort of "religious esteem" prior to this exhibition game, and somehow elevated itself in the years that followed. Recall that in the near future, this arena would be the site of Lord Stanley's first view of hockey during the Winter Carnival of 1889, the first Stanley Cup playoff game in 1894, and was where the first telegraph wires would be set up to move play by play back to Winnipeg marking a new step in sport and technology in Canada.

It had been built solely as a skating facility for the wealthy, and was known for its many "fancy dress-type" ball functions. Its location at 49 Drummond Street (now 1187), put the arena into the area of Montreal known as the "Golden Square Mile," where Montreal's rich British businessmen lived. Other rinks for the "lower classes" would be built in other locations around the city. The arena originally had 500 gas lights to shine at night, while a band performed for the

15

skaters, but later it became the first building with electricity in Canada.
It was sold in 1925 after the building of the Forum (the new temple of
hockey), and the Victoria site was turned into a parking garage

*

The next day, March 4, came the first hockey game report,
again in the *Gazette*, and again likely written by Creighton:

> *"HOCKEY -- At the Rink last night a very large
> audience gathered to witness a novel contest on the
> ice. The game of hockey, though much in vogue on
> the ice in New England and other parts of the United
> States, is not much known here, and in consequence
> the game of last evening was looked forward to with
> great interest. Hockey is played usually with a ball, but
> last night, in order that no accident should happen, a
> flat block of wood was used, so that it should slide
> along the ice without rising, and thus going among the
> spectators to their discomfort. The game is like
> Lacrosse in one sense -- the block having to go
> through flags placed about 8 feet apart in the same
> manner as the rubber ball -- but in the main the old
> country game of shinty gives the best idea of hockey.
> The players last night were eighteen in number -- nine
> on each side -- and were as follows: -- Messrs.
> Torrance (captain), Meagher, Potter, Goff, Barnston,
> Gardner, Griffin, Jarvis and Whiting. Creighton
> (captain), Campbell, Campbell, Esdaile, Joseph,
> Henshaw, Chapman, Powell and Clouston. The
> match was an interesting and well-contested affair, the
> efforts of the players exciting much merriment as they
> wheeled and dodged each other, and notwithstanding
> the brilliant play of Captain Torrance's team Captain
> Creighton's men carried the day, winning two games to
> the single of the Torrance nine. The game was
> concluded about half-past nine, and the spectators*

The SIHR web archive has managed to find the first names of these players, as well as provide biographies of them: Charles E. **Torrance** (captain), Daniel **Meagher**, Thomas J. **Potter**, Edwin H. **Gough**, William M.S. **Barnston**, George W. **Gardner**, W.O. **Griffin**, Francis **Jarvis** and a fellow named **Whiting**. The other team was composed of James G.A. **Creighton** (captain), Robert **Esdaile**, Henry **Joseph**, Frederick C. **Henshaw**, William B. **Chapman**, Robert H.W. **Powell** and Edward S. **Clouston**, along with brothers Stewart **Campbell** and George **Campbell**. We will get back to these names in a moment.

The March 4 article says there was a very large audience, while other sources (such as Michael McKinley[10]) have suggested the actual number present was forty. Nowhere have I seen a verifiable number for the spectators present. The article says that the sport is "much in vogue on the ice in New England and other parts of the US." Does the newspaper mean that literally? That an ice sport, called hockey, was not just being played- but was popular in the Eastern United States? Most historians try to present that this reference in the article meant various games on the ice such as shinny, bandy, or ice polo- but given that Creighton was likely the writer of this article (or at least what we for sure can call the source), this should be taken as a direct pointer. The question no one was asking was, with which group was the sport popular with, and what happened to all this hockey in the Northeast USA? Granted several articles and books through the 1880s described an American stick and ball ice version known as Ice Polo that held great popularity (which was different from Canadian hockey in the sense of having a bigger outdoor surface, heavier sticks, a ball, and no offside rule as would come in Canada).

As for this game in Montreal, the newspaper report tells us very little about the rules. The article compared the game to lacrosse (already popular in Montreal), but claimed that the block must go

---

[9]*Montreal Gazette* March 4, 1875
[10]McKinley *Putting a Roof On Winter*

17

through flags (I would assume meaning poles frozen in the ice with flags on top. Why one needs flags is not really explained). The article compared the game more to shinty, the Scottish game. What is interesting is that it was not compared to hurley (the Irish game) which is supposed to be what early ice games in Canada were known as. A big part of this 1875 game was about "presentation," of and for, the Scottish-British contingent in Montreal. There are only English-Scottish sounding last names among the players. This would be the norm for most of the next fifteen years. Right from the beginning, the game's "official source" the *Montreal Gazette* is all about "creating an image." We will see that other papers (not focused on the image making) had a completely different report about this first game.

Also there is no mention of hitting in the game (or any kind of contact at all), just that players "wheeled and dodged." If there had been any hitting, I am sure the article would have mentioned this as it would have been a unique feature. A depiction of this game in the documentary "Hockey a People's History: Episode 1", showed a number of players being hit and smashed. But there is no such evidence that hitting of any kind took place. That is not to say it didn't, but there is no reference in the article, and it does not seem likely once one begins to understand what this March 3 game really was. I suggest that this game would have appeared more like a group of buddies going out to "shoot some hoops" after work. It would have been "competitive" in that they would like to win their contest, but not competitive enough that they would want to injure any of their fellow participants. These are all very connected men, all in the same elite clubs, and all going to same McGill University. This is not smash 'em up hockey as so many historians have wanted to present, which is another part of the legend origin story as years went on. However it seems someone did in fact get smashed at the first game.

Lets look at an article that appeared in another paper, the *Montreal Witness* on March 4 1875:

> *"Hockey in the Victoria Skating Rink-Last evening a game of hockey was played in the Victoria Skating Rink between two nines (lists the players). The game is generally played with a large rubber ball, each side*

trying to knock it through the bounds of the other's field. In order to spare the heads and nerves of the spectators, last evening, a flat piece of board was used instead of a ball, it slid about between the players with great velocity, the result being that the Creighton team won two games to one for the Torrance. Owing to some boys skating about during the play, and unfortunate disagreement arose, one little boy was struck across the head, and the man who did so was afterwards called to account, a regular fight taking place in which a bench was broken and other damage caused. It was the intention of the players to have another game, but this disgraceful affair put a stopper on it.[11]

So we find there was more to this game than the *Gazette* mentioned. Before we get to the incident, it tells little of the game itself. Just that the game is "generally played" with a large rubber ball. So where is it "generally being played?" And why does the article suggest it must be knocked through the bounds of the other's field? That is very strange language, with no mention of goals, posts or flags like in the Gazette. This sounds very much more like a field sport being compared with. If ice sports were so popular, as suggested in the standard historical narrative, then every reporter should have seen hundreds of examples of games on ice during their life to compare with. So why be so confounded by it? To be honest, it is almost as though whoever is presenting this report in the paper has no idea what they were watching. For Canada in 1875, that strikes me as very strange.

Then the *Witness* article described a "disagreement" with boys used to having the rink for their own skating. The article claims one boy was "struck across the head." Lovely gesture. Then seemingly a fight between the boy's parents and the players occurred. Another similar newspaper report has long been claimed in books to have come from the Kingston Whig Standard. I have looked through the paper for the month of March 1875, and did not find any such report. Again the SIHR came to the rescue and found that the paper

---

[11] *Montreal Witness* March 4 1875

who covered the story was in fact The Times of Ottawa who presented that "*A disgraceful sight took place at Montreal in the Victoria Rink over a game of hockey. Shins and heads were battered, benches smashed, and the lady spectators fled in confusion.*"[12]

What does seem certain here is that something did happen during the hockey game at the Victoria Rink, and there was some sort of fight between players and spectators connected to the skating club, which did cause the game to be stopped. And it sounds brutal; shins and heads were battered, benches smashed. Why does *the Gazette* not make any mention of it? This is a very important question. It will make more sense when you have read the upcoming chapter on the Snowshoe and Lacrosse Clubs of Montreal, for to realize that this "game" was not just a foray into starting a new winter sport, it was also a marketing tool to set up a Canadian identity, and also to give the "upper-middle class" an activity to identify themselves as Canadian.

There is a lot wrapped up in this 1875 experiment. Sports were taken at the time by the British as a means to learn proper adult skills. As written by Paul Kitchen "*Sporting competition promoted discipline, co-operation, fair play, gentlemanly conduct, resolve, respect for teammates and opponents, and overall proper behavior.*"[13] Thus anything that might shine a "bad light" on the players or sporting endeavors needed to be quietly ignored. This ignorance by *The Gazette* is one of the most important pieces to come out of this game, presenting that everything looked nice, when obviously it was a chaotic mess. But again, animosity was NOT between the players, who likely behaved in a very fraternal fashion with each other.

*

I looked into several of the names that appear in the listings as those who played in this first game and asked, what can we know about these people?[14]

---

[12]McKinley *Putting a Roof On Winter* p6, SIHR Origins reference database

[13] Kitchen *Win Lose or Wrangle* p13

[14]SIHR 1875 player biographies, and portrait plates found in the McCord Museum of Montreal

We start with the other team's captain, Charles E. Torrance. He had fought in the Fenian Raids of 1866 and 1870 (as many of the other early players had as well). His grandfather, John Torrance, was Director of the Bank of Montreal and "was one of the wealthiest men in Montreal," including having a 42-room stone mansion that included gardens, orchards, and wineries. Like just about everyone connected with all of hockey origins (including Creighton), Charles attended went on to study at McGill University. After graduating he became an agent importing tea from the Far East. Later he became President of the Victoria Skating Club.

On Creighton's team, we have Frederick C. Henshaw, who was also a Lt. Colonel of the Victoria Rifles, and sat on the Board of Directors for Montreal Street Railways, the Marconi Wireless Telegraph Co. and various banks. By 1888, he was Vice President of the Montreal Football Club, President of the Victoria Skating Club, and honorary President of the Victoria Hockey Club. Some reports have suggested that it was he (not Creighton) who was importing sticks and pucks from Nova Scotia, due to his wife being the daughter of Nova Scotia coalmine owner John McDougall. Henshaw was also the President of the St. George Snow Shoe Club in the early 1880's and later held the position Consul of the Argentine Republic.

Another member on Creighton's team was Edward Clouston, who was the president of the Bank of Montreal, an advisor to several Canadian finance ministers, and who went on to be one of the trustees of the Allan Cup and the Minto Cup. He is also claimed to have been the captain for the famous 1874 Harvard-McGill football game. His Wikipedia page is loaded with all sorts of banking and finance information, and how he was one of the first five Montreal residents to own a car, with no mention whatsoever about his "important" hockey background or being a part of this first hockey game.[15]

Another of Creighton's teammates was Henry Joseph, who apparently also played in that famous 1874 McGill versus Harvard

---

[15]   https://www.vernonmorningstar.com/community/first-hockey-game-was-played-in-summerland/

21

football game. What made that game famous is that there are claims that "the rules of the game were altered as the game continued, with Joseph's assistance." Also Joseph was claimed to be the founder of ice lacrosse in February 1875 (even though there is a listing of an ice lacrosse game played at the Victoria Skating Rink in 1871). So what luck, one of the players of the first hockey game was also a rules inventor in three "ball and stick" sports within a span of two years! And by the way, he also happened to have competed at one of the first US Open Tennis Championships. He was the last surviving member of the original group of players, and it was he who presented the information as to how Creighton had been the organizer of the entire first hockey game in an interview in Montreal Gazette (either in 1936 or 1943). But there is more. Joseph also became President of the Windsor Hotel, the very hotel where the NHL was founded in 1917. He finished out his life buying many properties in British Columbia in an area known as "Millionaires' Row."[16]

The rest of the players will be a brief overview: George and Stewart Campbell came from a Scottish line of wealthy landowners and also played football; William Chapman was a merchant and one of the founders of the Metropolitan Club in 1874 (that played in a key hockey game in 1877 that will later be presented); Robert Esdaile was a wholesale broker and one of the founders of the Montreal Corn Exchange, and also a founder of the Metropolitan Club; Robert Powell was a doctor, and not just any doctor but the personal physician for Canadian Prime Minister Sir John A. MacDonald in Ottawa; William Barnston and George Garner were stockbrokers; Henry Gough was a clerk at the Bank of Montreal; W.O. Griffin was known for his lacrosse play; while Francis Jarvis and Tomas Potter were book keepers. The player called "Whiting" in the newspaper still remains unknown.

This is the pedigree of the players listed as taking part in the first game. Why does this group of elite, soon to be rich, want to take part in a rough and tumble new sport of hockey? Unless, as I mentioned earlier, the game was not so rough and tumble and was

---

[16] https://www.vernonmorningstar.com/community/first-hockey-game-was-played-in-summerland/, Joseph football reference https://www.mcgill.ca/channels/news/date-history-first-football-game-was-may-14-1874-106694, McKinley Putting a Roof p6

very "gentlemanly" and refined. Yet if this was a type of fraternal ritual, even an initiation (not for the people involved but of a sport or an organization), it would all make much more sense.

There is one final name on the first hockey players list I have not discussed, that being Torrance's teammate Daniel Meagher. Granted there is not much to say about Daniel other than he was a medical doctor in Montreal. The connection is to his brother George, claimed to be the "magical" father of hockey EVERYWHERE in Europe. George Meagher (born in Kingston in 1866) was one of the world's first figure skating champions. He went to Paris on a figure skating exhibition in 1894 and was claimed to be "surprised" that the French were not familiar with hockey. By some freak chance, George just happened to have 12 hockey sticks with him on his trip. Because as you know, every figure skater who travels across the globe also needs to carry along a dozen sticks! While in Paris, he is claimed to have formed both the Paris Hockey Club and the Club des Patineurs de Paris (so each would have someone to play). The story might seem plausible if it stopped there...but alas it continues. He then went on to London, and formed a hockey league there, and then in Glasgow Scotland where he also did hockey exhibitions. He then did the same in Nuremberg Germany, and then in St Petersburg Russia where he explained, "Hockey is going to take here (St. Petersburg) as it has in other cities, it is exciting, scientific, and an excellent exhibition game, so why shouldn't it be popular."[17]

This magic origin story for how hockey spreads is going to turn up again and again to explain how hockey came to such places as Winnipeg and Toronto. Just by chance someone shows up "surprised" no one is playing hockey, and either has some sticks, or sends for some, and there goes the sport. But in each case, these stories will be shown as a type of fabricated myth. And when you see these stories of hockey's origins are a type of legend, then one can start from scratch with everything we think we know. What are the myths attempting to hide or cover over? And why does Meagher bring hockey to Russia in 1894, where he thinks it will become incredibly popular, but then seemingly no one knows anything about

---

[17]Shea, Kevin *Lord Stanley* p316, https://skateguard1.blogspot.com/2015/01/george-alfred-meagher-champion-figure.html

the sport again until 1946 (the country only playing bandy up to that point)?

George Meagher has more hockey connections. He wrote three figure skating books, including the 1895 Lessons in Skating, which somehow had Lord Stanley (yes that Lord Stanley) write the forward. But there is more. His older sister Mary married Montreal alderman William Farrell, And their son Arthur went on not only to be a star on the Stanley Cup champion Montreal Shamrocks in 1899 and 1900, but who was also inducted into the Hockey Hall of Fame in 1965. More so, it was Art Farrell who wrote the first book about hockey in Canada in 1899 (others had come out in the US previously) and has so many odd parts to it I had to include an overview of the book in a separate chapter. Meagher also ends up with an odd obituary (as men like James Creighton will also have) and whose burial certificate described him as an "artist."[18]

*

A second hockey game on March 16, 1875 was reported in the *Gazette*, this time between two named teams; the Victoria Skating Club and the Montreal Football Club. *The Montreal Gazette* presented that; *"the players will be in uniform this time, which will add greatly to their own comfort and ease, we should imagine, and will certainly lend additional picturesque attraction to the game."* This writing style sounds very similar to how Creighton wrote in his chapters in *Picturesque Canada* in 1882.

Creighton was presented as the captain of the Football Nine, and his side wore sweaters with red and black stripes while their opponents wore white shirts. A note about all the newspaper game reports from Montreal in the 1870s: while they do include a list of all the players and the final score, there is no information about who scored, how long the game was played (either by time or number of goals), nor if penalty infractions occurred. At the same time it has been found that in England, newspapers as far back as 1870 were reporting on games of ice hockey and bandy, which often included the names of goal scorers, and, in one case, even the times of the

---

[18]Shea p316

goals. The absence of not reporting who scored in the games played in Montreal seems odd.

As for the game itself, again the *Montreal Gazette* the day after that second game, was there to give its overview. After again listing all the players the paper claimed:

> *"Captain Creighton whose individual play deserves special encomium, did all he could to get his men together and make them play into each other's hands, but to no purpose. They seemed to have lost that organized system which distinguished their play at the beginning of the afternoon and the result was a well deserved victory for their opponents, who certainly did play exceedingly well and with remarkable science."*

This is an important article. Right away there is discussion of "team play" and systems, and by not playing as a team is the reason why Creighton's team lost. Most importantly is that the winning team was said to play with "remarkable science." We will see that this choice of key words, playing sports as a "science," will be an important component for the British colonialists to present the reason why they are the "inventors" of a previously unskilled and unscientific Native pastime. Their science and organization is what was needed before something can be called a sport. Many of the layers that will be brought out in this book about why and how hockey was "invented" in Montreal are already apparent in the newspaper reports of 1875. Please also recall that in another co-incidence of 1875, the Field Hockey Association of England was formed and put out its first set of rules on April 10. Hockey is magically forming worldwide, on ice and on the field, and within a month of each other.[19]

---

[19]The year 1875 was not an easy time for Montreal. A *Montreal Gazette* article on December 15, 1875 was discussing the continent-wide depression that was leading to starvation in the slums of Montreal. Earlier in the year two banks had collapsed, Montreal factories were shut down because no one was buying goods.*"The Protestant House of Industry and Refuge was bending under the strain of people seeking relief. Among them was a man long out of work who, to keep his children warm, had to leave all three of them bundled together in bed. "Others," the House of Industry reported, "were obliged to burn articles of their furniture to keep them from freezing."* It was leading to a case of civil unrest by the population against the mayor and the ruling class of the city, and 200 police were called in to control protesters at City Hall. I just mention that a city-wide depression and outrage of the working-class against the ruling class was occurring exactly at the time a

*

Now that the basis of hockey in 1875 has been presented, we can get back to the very co-incidental life of James Creighton.[20] A direct connection is to Sanford Fleming, who hired Creighton out of university and sent him to Montreal for his works projects. Often overlooked, but presented by hockey historian Paul Kitchen, is that *"Fleming was an excellent skater, and at his 25th anniversary he thought there was no better way to celebrate than to have a skating party at his personal rink at his Ottawa Sandy Hill residence."*[21] Thus the key backer of Creighton's professional life was also a skater from Nova Scotia, and likely would have had knowledge of any outdoor hockey games taking place in that province. Fleming also had a personal outdoor rink at his house in Ottawa, long before Lord Stanley's rink was being discussed. The two Nova Scotia skating enthusiasts do not stay geographically apart for long, as Creighton soon joined Fleming in Ottawa.

One of Fleming's key chroniclers was George Munro Grant, who wrote a best-selling book at the time about Fleming's crossing of the Rockies. I mention Grant as he later also connects with Creighton, as Creighton will be one of the writers of Grant's historical book series Picturesque Canada in 1882. Fleming would work together with Grant in the 1880s as Chancellor and President of Queens University in Kingston (even though he quit school at the age of 14). Fleming became a Freemason in 1854, and was later fully knighted into the order of St. Michael and St. George, the same order that both Creighton and Grant would also gain access to, as companions but not full knights. One must ask why Creighton (whose accomplishments are nothing compared to Grant and Fleming), winds up in the same British Knight class, unless it is to include his hockey origin background? However it seems Creighton never spoke

---

few young men from McGill decide to "market" a new sport Starvation stalked the streets of Montreal John Kalbfleisch • Special to the *Montreal Gazette*

•https://montrealgazette.com/sponsored/mtl-375th/from-the-archives-starvation-stalked-the-streets-of-montreal

[20]Key detail of Creighton can be found in Bill Fitsell's article at http://www.biographi.ca/en/bio/creighton_james_george_aylwin_15E.html on his brother's death in the Montreal Witness July 11, 1881, and various articles on the SIHR.org website

[21] Kitchen, *Win Lose or Wrangle* p.8

to anyone about his being the founder and organizer of hockey. His name doesn't even appear in print connected with hockey until after he is dead, that being the Henry Joseph interview that claimed Creighton was the 1875 game's organizer. In another co-incidence, Sandford Fleming is buried in Beechwood Cemetery in Ottawa, where many of the founders of hockey, including James Creighton, are also buried.[22]

Creighton was also an early football player, and he was a key member of a meeting in Toronto in October 1875 to organize an inter-provincial association. The previous year (1874) he wrote a testimonial for spring skates for the Starr Manufacturing Company of Dartmouth. By 1880 Creighton had finished his McGill law courses, and joined a law firm in Montreal. On March 3, 1882, he accepted a position as a law clerk of the Senate in Ottawa, where he preferred to be known as Aylwin, his middle name. Creighton became the parliamentary counsel to the Senate in 1909 and stayed in the position until his death in 1930. His initial appointment to the Senate was March 3 1882, the same day (March 3) he is supposed to be "founding of hockey" in 1875. That is not some freak co-incidence, it is a hidden message to those that can see it.

James Creighton was also an author and historian, and wrote two chapters in the 1882 Munro Grant book Picturesque Canada: The country as it was and is. Creighton's two chapters were titled, "French Canadian Life and Character" in volume one, and "The History of the Lower Saguney," in volume two. So he seemed to have claimed quite a knowledge of French-Canadian history. Which he might have well had. The chapters were well written, with plenty of praise for the habitant farmer, and much detailed presentation of nature and scenery. The question I have is how exactly did a man only in Montreal for less than ten years, with a background in law and engineering become such an expert in the history, thoughts and ideas of the French-Canadian farmer? Creighton also wrote the book Origins of the Northwest Mounted Police, as well as some fishing and outdoors pieces in other magazines and books of the period.

---

[22] Biographi.ca articles on both men,
https://freemasonry.bcy.ca/biography/fleming_s/fleming_s.html

However what does get our attention is the chapter that follows his in the first *Picturesque* volume, which is about the city of Montreal. Oddly Creighton did not write this chapter, but it was written by Reverend A.J. Bray and John Lesperance. In that chapter they described the Winter Sports Scene in Montreal:

> *"But Montreal is more interested in outdoor sports and in organizing amusements than in art. The Victoria Skating Club, whose famous rink on Drummond Street, one of the first erected on this continent, has been the scene of many brilliant fancy-dress entertainments, which Royalty and nobility have graced. These 'carnivals' on the ice were first instituted here, and have since become popular elsewhere. There are three curling clubs- the Caledonia, Montreal and Thistle-with a Canadian branch of the Royal Caledonia curling club of Scotland...snow-shoeing has been reduced to an art."* (The author then gives a long discussion about how much he enjoys snow shoeing). *"Lacrosse is the 'national game' of Canada, and in that character it had its birth in Montreal. Four or five years ago, a select team make the tour of England, and had the honor of playing before Her Majesty at Windsor...There is also a golf club established in 1873, a bicycle club, foot-ball club, and a chess club, which numbers among its members some of the strongest and most brilliant players in the country."* [23]

The chapter also discusses that there are also clubs for the protection of fish and game, one society to prevent cruelty to animals, as well as clubs for boating, bicycling, and yachting. Meanwhile page 130 has a plate that is labeled "Government house from the skating pond" with three couples together skating on the ice, each consisting of two parents with two children.

So what is missing in that description? If you said hockey, you win a prize. Here is a chapter touting the greatness and innovation of

---

[23] *Picturesque Canada*, Volume 1 pgs 129-130

Montreal, its finest chess players, great curling rinks, even saying it was the founder of lacrosse...but the article does not once mention that a new sport was recently invented in that city. A bicycle club is mentioned, but not hockey. Creighton himself did not write the article, but he was associated with the book as an author, and he was an obvious well-known sportsman in the city; you would think the Reverend and Creighton might have met once or twice. I just find it a very odd omission when the chapter is all designed to present the "specialness" of Montreal, and lists EVERYTHING about Montreal sports- with the exception of hockey. Not even a mention that games like hurley or shinny on the ice had been played by "thousands of young sports minded folks" for many years. Stick-and-ball games on the ice seemed to just not exist in the mind of the book writers.

But James' Creighton's hockey luck is not done yet. He became a founding member of a new hockey team in 1889 in Ottawa that included the two sons of Governor-General Lord Stanley. It is through this team, The Rideau Hall Rebels, that not only will hockey be barnstormed and grown across the Province of Ontario, but in just three years the Governor-General would purchase a new hockey challenge trophy that would later become the Stanley Cup. Thus, Creighton was also directly involved with the person that created the Stanley Cup. But his Ottawa hockey connection raises a couple of questions.

He moved to Ottawa in 1882, and the following year the Ottawa Hockey Club started, again very co-incidental to Creighton's arrival. The story claims that the team formed after two or three young men from Ottawa watched games played at the Montreal Winter Carnival. Creighton was not one of them, nor was he part of the organization on their return to Ottawa. Why was Creighton not involved with the first hockey team? He would have known about its creation, he was in the same clubs as the founding players, and the team was discussed in the various city newspapers. Many of those players (as I will show in a future chapter) turned out to be transplants from McGill University to Ottawa, and as such they all should have known Creighton personally. Why is he not involved? Something is odd with the presentation that he is nowhere to be found around the formation of hockey in Ottawa. However when the next "big thing" hockey-wise is rolled out, there he is front and center. This new 1889 parliamentary team nicknamed "the Rebels," has many oddities surrounding them, and they will be examined in chapter six.

Also co-incidentally, James Creighton was a cousin of famous Canadian folklorist Mary Helen Creighton, another (of course) McGill graduate (in music). She was born in Dartmouth, Nova Scotia in 1899, and lived for one hundred years. Using grants from the Rockefeller Foundation, "*She collected over 4,000 traditional songs, stories, and beliefs in a career that spanned several decades, and she published many books and articles on Nova Scotia folk songs and folklore. She received numerous honorary degrees for her work and was made a Member of the Order of Canada in 1976.*" There was later criticism of her work by historian Ian MacKay in his book *Quest of the Folk* who claimed Helen was creating a type of "Scottish commodification" to connect the upper elite with the working class by appropriating older folk songs. In a sense making people believe that Nova Scotia really is "New Scotland" and not a conglomerate of Native Peoples, French Acadians and British colonists. It is an interesting criticism that just as well may be leveled on the elite in Montreal sports.[24] I bring this up as a discussion point, that perhaps James Creighton was less an inventor, but more of an archivist like Helen? Was he bringing something "back from the long forgotten past?"

There is another famous Creighton historian in Canada. That would be Donald Creighton, born in 1902 in Toronto, and might have links to our story. His most famous book was published in 1937 titled *The Commercial Empire of the St-Lawrence, 1760–1850*. It was a study of "the English merchant class in relation to the St Lawrence River in Canada." Recall this is the same area of historical subjects, the southern part of Quebec, that James Creighton also wrote about in *Picturesque Canada.* That Donald's best known historical work is about the British elite of Quebec in early 1800s is also coincidental. Wikipedia claims that Donald became a criticizer of the ruling Liberal Party in the 1940s for "undermining Canada's link with Great Britain and moving towards closer relations with the United States, a policy which he strongly disliked." This again seems

---

[24] www.helencreighton.org Creighton Folk "Alliance Lifetime Achievement Award Winner 2017" video, and Wikipedia page on Helen Creighton

remarkably similar to very reasons I am claiming (in chapter two) that hockey would be taken by the British and used to create a unique (non American) identity for Canada. In 1944 Donald wrote *Dominion of the North- a History of Canada,* quite literally becoming the go-to work for history in many schools. Donald claimed he was writing his history to combat against "the so-called "Liberal Interpretation" of Canadian history that would ultimately lead to Canada being absorbed into the United States."[25]

James Creighton lived in Ottawa until his death in 1930, a member of the Skating Club and the prestigious Rideau Club. Any comments that have been written about him by fellow people who knew him were all exemplary. His funeral was attended by former Prime Minister Robert Borden. Creighton's obituary lists his recreations as "exploration, salmon fishing, angling and skating." There is no mention of hockey. The guy who formed the sport, and might have even been the one who directly created the Stanley Cup, has no mention of hockey in his obituary. Is that not strange? Some have suggested that he lived as a very "modest man who didn't want the fame or publicity." Maybe. But there might also be something more going on with this story.

His Beechwood Cemetery grave had been unmarked until *The Society for International Hockey Research* had it marked in 2009. The explanation for a lack of a monument had been because he and his wife Eleanor had no children. Maybe? I have been to many cemeteries in my life and seen many grave sites marked for people who died without children. He worked as a high official for the Canadian Parliament, had a former Prime Minister at his funeral, was close friends with at least one Governor-General, was a member of the most elite clubs in Ottawa, a city where he had been an excellent community member for 48 years, and buried in the elite cemetery of not just the city but the entire country. Yet, no one "marked" his grave? Trust me, something is very odd about this; as will be the case for another hockey founder, James Stewart of the Montreal AAA, who will also be later buried in an unmarked grave in Seattle.

---

[25]https://en.wikipedia.org/wiki/Donald_Creighton

I hope you will start to see that James Creighton was not just some Halifax shinny player who wanted to keep the McGill rugby team fit in the off season as has long been presented. I think that is what many in the early years wanted people to believe. We saw that not only was he a writer, but likely the very one doing the writing in the newspaper for the early games. He could have thus been an organizer, player and promoter all in one package. I will show he may have also been a cog in a much larger system started in the early 1840s, after the Rebellions of 1837 and 1838. The cog being to tie Native Aboriginal and French Canadian culture together, and then "British them up" by adding organization and structure in order to create something seemingly new. An "invention." It is my suspicion that he was just a "front man" for a much bigger story going on behind the scenes.

Canada was a new nation after 1867 and needed in a sense to build itself a national identity and psyche. A big part of this building process was through sports. What we have come to think of today and define as "Canada" and "hockey" was purposely being constructed in the period 1850-1890. As such, the sport of hockey did not evolve from British pastimes (the usual suggestion), nor was it some type of accident. It was likely a planned operation. The question becomes, if so, who planned it, and why? If I had to guess, I would say that Sandford Fleming might have been the key to it all, and his connection will be looked into deeply in chapter nine.

But we have to take a step back, and look prior to Canada's formation as a country in 1867. Not to early newspaper reports about stick-and-ball games on ice (that is what most would expect in my book now). No, actually we have to investigate some Montreal elite clubs, particularly the Snow Shoe and Lacrosse Clubs, which were part of a template which would also be used on hockey in the 1870s. And the historical political unrest of the period, which was a main fuel for the entire operation.

2

SNOWSHOES, LACROSSE, and HOCKEY
Montreal's Plan

> *"Moreover it is suggested that the snowshoe and lacrosse clubs created a 'myth of origin' which linked members back to 'their' history in Canada, but in the process, effectively erased the histories of real Canadian Natives."*[26] (Gillian Poulter)

> *"The earliest clubs were constituted to provide social outings for the Anglophone elite in the community rather than opportunities to demonstrate physical skills in a competitive situation."*[27] (Alan Metcalfe)

There were several problems for the British colonial elite in Montreal at the beginning of the 1870s, but three stand out. First, Montreal was for all intents and purposes, the capital of Canada. Yes, the actual capital had just been made Ottawa, but Montreal was still the home of all big business. Therefore, the home of the elite. The problem is that all of those elites were from England, and even if their children were born in Canada, they still looked, dressed and talked as if they were in Edinburgh or London. They did not "fit in" with the local populations of either the First Nations People or the French Francophones. Most of the regular workers in Montreal were Francophones, and they resented that the new British conquerors were their bosses. Actually, those sentiments would still exist almost a hundred years later in what became the Richard Riot of 1955. This

---

[26]Gillian Poulter, *Becoming Native* pg 5

[27] Alan Metcalfe, "Organized Sport"

chapter is now a discussion about the Victorian elite of Montreal in the 1870s, and the constant threat of revolution against them. This is a very important chapter for understanding the hows and whys behind the elite's creation of the sport of hockey. I am just giving an overview of rather complex historical events. If you have an interest, I would recommend you look deeper into the situation around the Canadian rebellions of 1837 and 1838, and read Gillian Poulter's excellent book *Becoming Native in a Foreign Land.*

A second problem was that Canada had just become a new country in 1867, and thus the previous garrison of British soldiers had gone back to England. Canada was now in charge of its own army, and preparing the country for the always-possible invasion from the United States. Canada had been invaded three times in the last hundred years. A question was being asked in very high circles of how to get the young Canadian male population ready to be soldiers. Thirdly, a new country needed a new national identity- one that was unique and not American, nor British. Sports would become a key step in attempting to solve these three problems.

Gillian Poulter claims that "the British colonists 'improved' Native skills by imposing their own notions of science and order upon them. Therefore, these skills were transformed into uniquely new organized sports, governed by rules, which ensured discipline and 'fair play.' This intervention justified the colonists' claim to have invented the sports, and legitimized their claim to be native Canadians."[28] Snowshoeing was the first attempt at appropriation, setting up the club system. Next came lacrosse, which laid out the groundwork that would be later followed by hockey. In many ways, there are great similarities between George Beers (father of lacrosse) and James Creighton (father of hockey).

This ideology can be traced back to around 1840 when Lord Durham took over as the new Governor-General following the huge rebellions of 1837 and 1838. The rebellions took place in both Upper and Lower Canada, the original names of Ontario and Quebec, as the population was demanding political reform. Some

---

[28]Poulter 52

historians have speculated that the rebellion's ideology was similar with those that had started both the American and French Revolutions. Without going into great detail, the people wanted much more input in the decisions governments would make on their behalf, and a call for equal rights. The lower classes felt they were not getting any acknowledgment, from the heads of state or from the local political leaders (mayors and town administrators) who were linked to the elites and who were controlling them behind the scenes. All this while a recession swept the country, hitting farmers the hardest, who were also dealing with nation-wide crop failures in 1836, and were being hounded from lawsuits from merchants trying to collect old debts. At the same time, banks and the financial system collapsed, pushing the lower classes further into poverty. Feeling they had no other option to get attention for their demands, they chose armed rebellion.[29]

The rebellions began in Lower Canada with the highly oppressed French, led by Louis-Joseph Papineau, Robert Nelson, and others (called the Patriotes). "In an era that espoused a hereditary monarchy, rights of conquest, aristocratic privilege, and monarchical government, there was nothing more revolutionary than principles that challenged the legitimacy of the state and the social order." William Lyon Mackenzie, the leader of Upper Canada's abortive insurrection, drafted a constitution in 1837 that recognized "civil and religious liberty," and provided guarantees against excessive bail costs and cruel and unusual punishments. The republicans then drafted Lower Canada's "Ninety-Two Resolutions," which became a demand for freedom of religion, physical security, and due process of law. Patriote leader Robert Nelson issued a declaration of independence in 1838 that explicitly referred to religious freedom, free speech, trial by jury, and the right to vote and speak in French or English in all public matters. Both rebellions were quashed by the British military. And that is when things got even worse, with Canada becoming a "defacto" police state.

The British colonial government responded by declaring martial law, and legislators were replaced by Special Councils. The

---

[29] Information on the rebellions found at https://historyofrights.ca/encyclopaedia/main-events/1867-confederation/

Councils "suspended habeas corpus" for people who were accused of treason or of possessing knowledge about treasonous activities. It passed the Lawless Aggression Act, which facilitated the confiscation of property as well as the prosecution of rebels by enabling juries to be selected outside the jurisdiction, putting individuals on trial in absentia, and allowing regular courts to hear felony cases...The legislature also passed a law empowering constables and justices of the peace to disperse any unlawful meeting or assembly and to arrest or detain the participants."[30] They even put civilians into court martial proceedings. One consequence of such trials was execution or exile. Newspapers were shut down, and reporters jailed. Free speech was taken away. Needless to say this created even more divison in the people, and more demands for freedom.

This was the mess that Lord Durham was taking over in 1840. The rebellions had created fear for the ruling British. They knew they had to make some major changes or Canada would likely go the way of the United States into full-on revolution. All of the choices made for the next several decades by the British elite in Canada all revolved around finding ways to be sure another rebellion did not start.

Durham's "Report on the Affairs of British North America" and "the Act of Union 1840" were the responses by the British to find some way to control the local population in new ways. It would be the stepping-stones to the Confederation of 1867, and more influence by the people in the political system (or at least it would appear to be so). However, Durham was coming up with other "behind the scenes" plans as well. He was looking for a way to end the interior conflict, and integrate the Native and French communities with the British "bosses." By the 1840s, the French had been in Canada for hundreds of years, and they had already incorporated much of the Native ways into their own culture, like wearing snowshoes and Native buckskin clothing. To the British there was no difference between the Native and French, because they appeared the same.[31] That became the most logical first step; to start to look like a "Native Canadian," whatever that actually meant.

---

[30]https://historyofrights.ca/encyclopaedia/main-events/1867-confederation/
[31]Poulter 48-52

Of course, one could suggest that the British could have really become a native Canadian, by honestly being with and connecting together with the Native and French populations, and by granting them the same rights, privileges and opportunities that the upper classes had. But of course, if the elites directly "associated with the savages," they would lose their civilized Victorian perfection. The Native and French were being seen as inferior by the British Victorian in the now widely-believed theory of evolution, greatly presented during the late 1800s period World Fairs. The Fairs of the time always contained "human zoos" to showcase savage primitives in their natural habitats for the rich Victorian visitors to gasp at and be thankful they were of the correct racial stock, and social class. The Smithsonian laid out the skulls of the primitive African and North American tribes, as well as criminal skulls (all of course shown as small and poor-brained) beside a large Victorian skull. The exhibit leader would measure the skull of the fair-goer to show "where they fit in the process of evolution" based on their skull size. Were they an Aboriginal, criminal, or did they have the properly evolved white Victorian Skull? This is the type of thinking that was at the core of the men who would be inventing North America's sports in the 1800s.

Montreal had the biggest problem in Canada for the elites. In Toronto or Halifax, one would mostly be surrounded by other English lower classes but in Montreal they were surrounded by the French. The best way to integrate then was to seem like one of the regular French people, though not speaking the language nor learning any of their customs, the idea being to just "look like one" from the outside. This started a process of using sports as that appearance creator.

Games and pastimes that were generally held on holidays and special occasions, and inclusive to all races and classes, have always been a part of any society, from Ancient Egypt right through to English society in Britain. However, as Gruneau and Whitson pointed out:

> *"By the 1850s, a growing class of anglophone businessmen and professionals- with many of the members now Native-born rather than transplanted from England-began to modify the older paternalistic*

traditions...and place greater emphasis on organization, regulation, competition and values of self improvement. Prominent businessmen and professions would struggle to apply those values to create new forms of sporting recreations in the image of their own cultural ambitions."[32]

England started a process of what could be called "organized sport" in the 1850's. It was set up in such a way that the lower class was not allowed anywhere near these specialized events. Just as the lower class was all but excluded from attending the great spectacles of the day such as the World Fairs, so too were they excluded from organized sports. This was not due to the famous argument presented that only the rich had leisure time for games. The poor played games as well, but a new aspect was created to govern who could participate in anything that could be called "sanctioned." They had to belong to a club. These clubs were more than just meeting areas, they were screening places. A sports club was in a sense no different from a Freemason or Shriner lodge. They were fraternal societies where one had to be "allowed" entrance. The already "enshrined" could determine if one was worthy.

The period of 1837-1875 was vital to the creation of hockey. It did not happen in a vacuum, it happened in the midst of incredible political turmoil, revolution, thoughts of class,—evolutionary superiority, and the need to control entrance to any area of importance via the "club system." And all this while there was an ongoing attempt by the average person to gain some measure of human rights. Of course, the original Native Peoples had already lost most of their rights, but that is a story we will get to much later in the book.

*

Snow Shoe Club

[32] Richard Gruneau *Hockey Night* p 40

I present this odd announcement from the *Quebec Daily Telegraph* of February 7, 1880 (just one year after the Quebec hockey club was founded): "*A match will be played this evening at the Quebec Skating Rink between two teams chosen from the Quebec Hockey Club and the Waverley Snow Shoe Club...we hear that the Quebec club will play St. George's Snow Shoe Club of Montreal, in that city, some day next week.*" At first glance you may think that it seems odd that a new hockey club in Quebec wants to play against snow shoe clubs rather than hockey clubs. That is until you understand that snow shoe clubs are part of the hidden story of the real origin to hockey.

The first Montreal Snowshoe club was founded in 1840, just as reports on the Rebellions came out), and by the 1880s there were over 100 such clubs in Canada. The choice of this being the first foray was that the snowshoe had been a key element of Native Aboriginal gear. The first French fur trappers, then later French-Canadian Habitant farmers, adopted the snowshoe as a key tool to navigate the Canadian winter. For whatever reason, perhaps because the snowshoe was seen as a part of both Native and French-Canadian culture, it was the one that the Montreal elite decided to appropriate first. Prior to this, Montreal British sports clubs had been in the areas one would expect: cricket, curling, golf and rowing. But now the idea was to make a direct historical connection to the time before the British conquest of Canada."[33] Granted the act of snowshoeing, which they called tramps, was just one part of the club's activity (the physical part). A second part was to afterwards go to the Têtu Café on St. James Street for food and drinks. It seems that a lot of drinking and socializing, songs and rituals accompanied the snowshoe tramps.

---

[33] Poulter and Don Morrow "The Knights of the Snowshoe"

*Illustration 3: George Beers, "father of lacrosse," in his snow shoe outfit.
(Montreal, QC, 1881, Photography studio Notman & Sandham Object Number II-60469. McCord Museum)*

In theory, anyone could join a club. The problem was that it was set up as any fraternal organization of the day. You would first have to be vouched in by two existing members. Thus, it kept its elite and private status as any other gentleman's or Freemasonic club of its day. After being "vouched," one would then have to pass a voting round by the senior members. Only those with the proper status and class would be given acceptance to join, thus making it almost impossible for anyone of lower class,-French, or most certainly Native to be in the club. The clubs chose a very specific uniform, which was very much a copy of standard Native and French-Canadian clothing, while adding flags or emblems that indicated a their British origin.

Interestingly, Gillian Poulter showed that this specific snowshoeing image is what was presented in newspapers around the world as to "this is what a Canadian looks like."[34]

Beyond just an appearance, they also generated what could be called a "revised history" of snowshoeing to suit their goals. One, which became known as Dawson's Supplement, attempted to show that their tramps (the name given to very long snow shoe hikes) had first begun in "the expedition under de Courcelles in 1666, during which the regular soldiers (from France) suffered much, but of the Canadians (those born in Canada), not a man was frozen." This is an amazing document. First they presented that the first "tramp" was in 1666 (and note the three sixes chosen for the date marker), and thus slyly inferred that all Native Aboriginal snowshoeing prior to that date no longer mattered. It also inferred that the French soldiers from France could not handle the climate. Thus to snowshoe effectively and handle the cold well, one could only be a local born Canadian.[35] This similar method of destruction of the early roots of anything (especially Native) is going to be seen again with the other appropriated sports- lacrosse, baseball, basketball, football, and hockey.

---

[34]Poulter p 59
[35]Poulter p 119

*llustration 4: A snow shoe club "bounce"
(composite, 1886, Artist Wm. Notman & Son (1882-1919), Painter Eugène L'Africain (1859-1892), Object Number VIEW-2425, McCord Museum)*

The snow shoe club became fully organized in 1843, with its new president Colonel Charles Ermatinger. He set up a common law of "Snow Shoers," whatever that is supposed to mean. The majority of members would be high connected Englishmen who lived and worked in the area of the city known as Montreal's Golden Square Mile. One element of the snow shoe club is what is called "the bounce" (as depicted in illustration 4). All of the photos depicting this activity are not really photos but paintings made to look like a photo. In all of them, it is very unlikely that the one being bounced would have the photo taken the exact moment of stillness. Anyways as the history goes, this bounce was a type of initiation ceremony, where new members, snow shoe race winners "or special guests," were constantly thrown in the air and caught. It sounds like a very odd ritual for those who walk across the snow. Just as an aside, Lord Stanley was "bounced" at his first day at the Montreal Winter Carnival in 1889, claimed of course because he was a guest. It could also have been either a public initiation, or something else with some sort of significance that I haven't yet figured out.

It did not take long however to see that the snowshoe club by itself was not going to answer the issues of integrating the elite into Montreal's lower classes. Another rebellion was taking place in 1849, however this time, by the elites themselves.

*

Montreal Fire 1849

Another key Canadian event stems from the Rebellions and that is the fire of the Parliament Building in Montreal on April 25, 1849. The rioters were Torries, mostly British Anglophones who supported more economic ties to England, while the main force in government was now more highly French-Canadian and supported breaking away from England to become their own country. The upset "a protest against the Rebellion Losses Bill (linked to amnesty to those involved in the 1837 rebellions, but not the 1838) while the members of the Legislative Assembly were sitting in session. There were protests right across British North America. The episode is characterized by divisions in pre-Confederation Canadian society concerning whether Canada was the North American appendage of the British Empire or a nascent sovereign nation."

The crowd which became the riot was put together through a quickly printed Montreal Gazette article, the key English newspaper of the city (and the one that will promote hockey in the 1870s) which published, "The Disgrace of Great Britain accomplished! Canada Sold and Given Away! The End has begun. Anglo-Saxons you must live for the future. Your blood and your race will now be supreme." A very unique choice of words and sentences. The article called for a mass gathering that night at 8 PM, which turned into a the storming into the Parliament and the riot. While inside a fire started by opening the gas mains, most of the treasures and library books were lost, but you will see in the final chapter our co-incidental friend

Sandford Fleming was not only there, he acted a superhero to save a painting and a few other treasures. The riots continued for two days, rolling into the streets of Montreal. In response to the riots, a special police force was created to hold off the rioters. Due to these riots, the capital of Montreal was relocated to Quebec City.[36] It should be no surprise to see that the aftermath of another rebellious explosion in Montreal was to find another avenue to get the population focused on. This was a sport, what we now call lacrosse.

*

Lacrosse

The examination of lacrosse becomes important because this was the first attempt of the Montreal elite to transform an actual sport (as opposed to an activity). Even today, not many doubt that lacrosse has a Native origin, known around the Montreal area at the time as "baggataway." This fact could not be hidden from the population, who would have witnessed the Native games, as well as early "friendly matches" between whites and Natives. These exhibitions took place until the forming of the Montreal Lacrosse Club in 1856. To no surprise, many snowshoe club members also became lacrosse members.

George Beers[37], a local dentist, became the man "chosen" to make lacrosse a British-Canadian "invention." To do so, he would need to upgrade the seemingly unorganized Native sport into an organized sport "through the imposition of rules and regulations which encapsulated the British ideology of order and fair play." This upgrade would be called an evolution, which was a key concept for the Victorians, even more so after the publishing of Darwin's *Origin of Species* in 1859. Just as the Victorian had come to believe that they

---

[36] https://www.thecanadianencyclopedia.ca/en/article/montreal-riots
https://www.canadashistory.ca/explore/politics-law/parliament-in-flames
https://en.wikipedia.org/wiki/Burning_of_the_Parliament_Buildings_in_Montreal

[37] Beers had been one of many of the professional elites that were involved in all of these early origins of sport, to have fought against the invaders in the Fenian Raids of 1866 and 1870. This is another period to keep in mind at the formation of all of these sports in Canada, that the country had been invaded again, this time by the Irish Republican organization, with the idea of freeing the Irish in Canada. Amazingly Beers is credited with being the one to establish the Victoria Rifles of Canada during the raids.

were the pinnacle of all humanity, any sport which they "created" had to be the best possible sport. The primitives played crude games, while the Victorians were the inventors of true sport, organization, rules, and science.[38]

In 1860, lacrosse took a new step when the first written rules were presented in a pamphlet titled "The Game of Lacrosse," written by Beers under the pseudonym Goal-keeper (he was a goalie). The rules included such things as the exact size and material of a rubber lacrosse ball, the lacrosse stick size, the length of the field–being 200 yards (180 m), the size of the goal and goal crease, that there were twelve members on a team, and the duration of a match. Interestingly, this pamphlet of rules came out during a big exhibition match that occurred–during a visit by the Prince of Wales. In 1877, there was also a "ceremonial event" that co-coincided with the publication of the rules. As Michael A. Robidoux mentioned in his article of how the British viewed things, "*Modern sport is not a random pursuit but rather a highly organized event played within specific boundaries and performed with uniform rules maintained by leagues and organizations.*"[39]

In 1867, Beers created the Canadian National Lacrosse Foundation, and in 1869, he published the book *Lacrosse: The National Game of Canada,* which not only gave a history and rules of lacrosse, but also presented what might be called the correct moral qualities that any player should strive to achieve. Thus, we see a similarity to Creighton. Beers is the presented inventor, writer, and promoter of lacrosse. Beers also added instructional photographs in his -book, however only featuring white players, thus, "presenting the white Montreal elite as the real experts of lacrosse, and in a sense subliminally inferring that it is a white Canadian game, not Native."[40] In 1876, Beers organized a team of Canadian and Native players to tour England, Scotland, and Ireland, during which Queen Victoria called the game "very pretty to watch." Interestingly with the Queen commenting on the game, it led to a rise of young English girls to take up the sport in the 1880s. Beers would take another tour in 1883.

---

[38]Poulter p 211

[39] Michael A Robidoux, "Imagining A Canadian Identity"

[40]Poulter p 234

The first question one might be asking is that out of all the sports and pastimes of the Natives, which there were hundreds, why was lacrosse the one chosen by the Montreal elite? To start with, this sport had a clear Native origin, thus could not be thought of as somehow American. However as Poulter suggested, by "taming" lacrosse, the British colonials were also symbolically "taming" the Natives themselves. They had civilized and modernized the savage people, and everything associated with them.[41] Beers wrote, "*The Indians' old fierce baggataway has shared the fate of the Indian himself, in having become civilized almost out of recognition into a more humane sport. It has lost its wild and wanton delirium, and though restless under regulations, has become tamed into the most exciting and varied of all modern field sports.*" He also wrote, "just as we claim as Canadian the rivers and lakes and land once owned exclusively by Indians, so we now claim their field game as the national field game of our dominion."[42] Thus to Beers and his associates, by being the winner of colonialism, they took ownership of everything. The land, the people, their customs, and their games. The only element really needed was a subtle change to the sport, and just enough so that no one would confuse the white version from the Native version. Once done, the takeover would be complete.

After an exhibition match in 1886 between a traveling Irish team and Montreal, the *Montreal Daily Herald* wrote that during the banquet, J.J. Curran presented (as the *Herald* termed it) a "*history of lacrosse from the time it was adapted in a crude state from the Indians to the present when it had been brought to perfection by the Montreal Clubs. He concluded by expressing the hope that Ireland would one day enjoy the same advantages as Canada.*"[43] Lacrosse by the Natives is crude, as opposed to the set up by the superior elite British "perfection."

---

[41] This is a key point, as what was being done to the Natives for the previous several hundred years, was destroying their culture, way of life, and ideals. The idea was to turn them into Christian Victorian people. I will go into this more in the final chapter of the book to share some of the stories surrounding these concepts shared to me by the medicine men that I learned from while I was in my 30s.

[42] Robidoux p 215, Poulter p 211-212

[43] *Montreal Daily Herald* Aug 14, 1886 pg 5

Certain cores of the game needed to be kept so as not to appear "too new," along with streamlining it. The game of baggataway was played in a giant field, with hundreds of players and could last for several days. As Michael Robidoux points out, Beers had a problem with westernizing the sport, because "baggataway was not really a sport. It was "spiritual and religious occasion, often having healing or prophetic significance."[44] I will go more into the ceremonial aspects of Native sports in chapter five; I just mention this here as a problem, to take what is essentially a ceremonial and religious activity and turning it into a sport.

I previously mentioned, the Native game was streamlined. Now a game that had few rules needed some strict regulation. From the size of the field, to the regulated number of players, to the specific duration requirements. To the British, common rules were an underlying element to make the sport scientific and universal. It is via these rules that they could claim ownership and present that, prior to the rules, it was all a chaotic and primitive mess. Poulter reminds us that early portrait photos of white lacrosse teams needed to show order, uniformity, and symmetry. Often when Native teams were photographed, they made the arrangement chaotic, with varied clothing on the players to present the ideas of being primitive and un-structured. All to remind the viewer that lacrosse was not baggataway. *"The fundamental difference between the 'primitive' Native game, and the 'modem' white game was, Beers claimed, the diligent application of 'science.' This was a crucial concept because it ultimately legitimized the gradual exclusion of Native players from the game on the grounds that it was only "the whites-who can develop its science."[45]* Now, whenever Natives and whites would play, it would be the new "white rules only" that would be used. As such, Natives would now have to learn to adjust to play this "new game," and not the one they had in a sense truly invented and played for thousands of years.

When Beers took Native teams to England for exhibition games with his club in 1876, he forced the Natives to wear very "Indian-style costumes" (the while teams wore white), and prior to

---

[44]Robidoux p 215
[45]Poulter pg 215, 222, 229

47

games, they were to wear feathers while participating in–dances and pow-wows. Again, to in a sense shock and contrast the primitive version with the Victorians version. As Don Morrow added about these exhibitions, "James Fennimore Cooper (writer of Last of the Mohicans) could not have contrived a more colourful image of stereotypical Indian-ness for these early 'Harlem Globetrotters' of lacrosse."[46]

For a while, the Natives were still needed by the clubs, as exhibition matches to showcase the best of the sport, as they themselves had not reached a high enough stature of play. However as white players' skills evolved, they needed the Native presence less and less. As such, new club rules came in play to bar them from playing on white teams, or being involved in any championship events. They found all sorts of ways to deem the Native players "professionals." Still, teams tried all kinds of ways to bring in Natives with light skin to pretend that they were a new British immigrant from another part of the country.[47]

The lacrosse clubs were run no differently than the other clubs. They both included sponsorship and voting. I should mention that many young French-Canadians at the time felt that they were forbidden from joining sport, not just due to the exclusion of the British club system, but also partially due to the attitude of the Catholic Church who presented it was best not to participate in any sports at all. This attitude would not begin to change until the 1890s.

As it all turned out, lacrosse failed to catch on across the country, and greatly declined after World War I, only being popular in the major cities. Gambling, professionalism and violent play were all listed as reasons why the game never fully caught on with the general public. However, the astute reader will recognize that those three elements were very much part of hockey. So why did hockey take hold and not lacrosse? Perhaps one reason is that hockey was a winter sport, and thus would have no real competition during the snowy months. Another reason might be that the creators of hockey

---

[46]Morrow, Don "Case Study of"
[47]Poulter 248

made sure to make it SEEM like hockey evolved from very white, jolly old England, and not the Canadian Natives as was obvious

*

A Manly Sport

> "*The task of defining a national identity is a creative process that requires constructing a shared history and mythology that best suit the identity "imagined" by those few responsible for responding to this task...By the turn of the 18th century, sport in Britain was being realized as an excellent means of social control and conditioning.*"[48] (Michael A. Robidoux)

This opening two quotation is very important to present where this chapter must take us. That is, to the concept that sport is just not some simple set of pastimes that people partake in. Sport is one of the key ways in which cultures can be defined. America and France showed differences in their ideologies based on the most popular sports that they played. The narrative of sports is a narrative of creating identity, and, realizing this, if you want to control what the identity of a country is , one must also control sports. Control for the elite via that identity. As Alan Metcalfe wrote, "*Sport is not peripheral to society; indeed it is central to life and reflects the dominant social and political concerns.*"[49] (Alan Metcalfe)

Originally, hockey had been a game for the members of various elite sports clubs. One of the duties of those clubs was to teach polite behavior. Sports for them was a shaping tool, but rather than violence or military training, it was how to be strong physically and mentally and also how to be very gentlemanly. Fighting or violent play would not be in line with the strict club concepts. To them, this is how they showed they were one-step above the fighting and rabble rousing lower classes.[50] The way to show one's manliness was not through handling physical play, but rather through self-control. Sports

---

[48] Michael A Robidoux, "Imagining a Canadian Identity" p 210

[49] Metcalfe p 12

[50] Poulter 239-240

49

was more than just places to test their physical skills and gentlemanly conduct. It soon began to be set up to encourage females to come and watch the events, so that the men could in a sense "show off for them." It was the influx of female spectators that caused sports to grow, and require the need for larger stadiums and venues for those watching the contests.

> *"Sport in Canada during the late 19th century was intended to promote physical excellence, emotional restraint, fair play, and discipline; yet these ideological principles were consistently undermined by the manner in which Canadians played the game of hockey."*[51] (Michael A. Robidoux)

In Canada's case, there was more going on than just a rich British merchant class finding some new way to fit in. Now, there was a need to build an army. Up until Canada's Confederation in 1867, the country had been garrisoned and defended by British soldiers. Of course, some born Canadian would join and be a part of these regiments, but the majority would be from Britain. After 1867, with the British soldiers now gone, the question arose of how to defend the country. Canada and the USA had been directly at war six times by 1871 in the American Revolution (1775), War of 1812 (1812-14), Rebellions (1837-38), Patriot War (1838), Pork and Beans War (1838), Pig War (1859), and the Fenian Raids (1886 and 1871). In addition, there was great concern that Canadians (especially now becoming more urban and less rural) would not be at all ready if the US cavalry attacked across the border. Kevin Shea brought this up in his Lord Stanley book, "Nineteenth century military life and organized sport of the same era are inextricably tied that it is hard to determine where one stops and the other begins," and "Social theorists, church leaders, politicians, the aristocracy and even the Queen perceived a strong link between sport and war, and enthused about how useful sport could be in preparing a young man for military life."[52]

---

[51] Quotes are from , Michael A Robidoux, "Imagining A Canadian Identity"

[52] https://www.history.com/news/7-times-the-u-s-canada-border-wasnt-so-peaceful, Shea pg 89-90, *A website on the UK military presented similar, "The British Army has long believed that sport prepares soldiers for combat by increasing fitness, channeling aggression, and focusing the mind. Sport serves to strengthen the ties between troops, instilling discipline and readiness to serve a common cause*

At first, the sport that may have been thought to fill this preparatory role was lacrosse, but there were a number of reasons why ~~that~~ it never fully met all the requirements. Remember that it was not the British who first found lacrosse in Canada, it was the French missionaries. Unlike the British, the French needed the Natives and their survival skills when they first arrived. There was more interaction, and the missionaries often lived in Native villages for long stretches of time. Even though there was a destruction of the Native population occurring, there was also at the same time a connection between them. It is somewhat hard to explain. However, in this Native game, the missionaries termed lacrosse; something which was recognized by the young French Canadians. They appreciated an alternative model of masculinity from what they had known in France, "The young Voyageurs struggled to copy in the Indian's stoicism in the face of adversity and their endurance when confronted with hardships, deprivation and pain...French males found the liberated sexual attitudes of the young Indian women before matrimony as attractive as the missionaries found them repugnant."[53] Beyond just the need for Native activities and skills to make their daily lives easier; such as the canoe and the snowshoe, the French were drawn to their stick-and-ball games like lacrosse.

With lacrosse not fitting the bill, a shift began to happen in the 1870s to focus on a new sport, one which had a long history in Canada, England, and likely Scandinavia. In one form or another, ice games; like hurling, shinty, rickets, hockey, and ice-polo which were all known to the white European colonists. Where those games in Europe originated is up for question.

Yes, the Native versions of lacrosse could become violent. Yet, just because there were violent actions at times in the Native games; does not mean they were some type of free-for-all as suggested. For the Natives, while taking winning the contest very seriously, an important element was that the teams were equal. Not just in the number of participants, but also in the overall skill level. It would not be a contest if one side would be an obvious winner beforehand. If conflicts between Native players did arise, they were

https://www.nam.ac.uk/explore/sport-and-preparing-troops-war
[53]Robidoux p 213 and Millar 54

51

left to deal with it themselves, and not slow down the play of the main game. To British eyes, it would have seemed "un-gentlemanly," but actually, it was very honest. However, it did not take long for lacrosse to become a violent sport in the white community, especially once the "lower classes" began to make it onto the teams, which led to fierce rivalries playing out between Scottish- Irish, or upper and lower class. It is claimed that the violent nature of lacrosse is why it could not really take on as Canada's national sport. We know that is nonsense as hockey was just as violent. So what was that-difference?

Hockey was as violent as lacrosse. Perhaps hockey being played on skates so the players moving with more speed than lacrosse which would lead to more frequent collisions, and allow-the spectator to accept that a few fights were alright. As Art Farell wrote in his 1899 book, "hockey is a game for men, strong, full blooded men. Weaklings can not play in it."[54] Likely it was this element of skating, an extremely unique skill not a part of any other stick and ball game that may have been the determining factor for hockey taking the lead in Canada. The reason hockey became the preferred game to define Canada had to be that it was a winter sport played on skates. The skate thus becomes the symbol of the choice of this sport.

At the beginning while hockey was still an "amateur sport" (a pseudonym for "only elites are allowed to play"), the violence was kept to a minimum. No bank owner wanted to see his son seriously injured in a hockey match, merely tested, but still ready for work on Monday morning. It was not until the rich elite began to realize that their place was no longer as the players of the sport, but could move into their anticipated positions as: owners of teams and administrators of leagues; so the sport could fundamentally change. After this, the playing of it could be turned over to the working classes. It did not take long for professionalism to take hold, as the game then become one of money and the need to win. Given the need to sell out arenas, the violence would increase. The players could then become more like Roman gladiators, and the violent game sold (especially in the tough mining towns). Toughness was being added to the Canadian youth, just what the 1870s elite had wanted. Hockey began to be seen, first all through Canada and then worldwide, as a Canadian invention

---

[54]Farell, Art *Hockey Canada's*

and the thing that distinguished Canada from all other countries. An identity; just as the elites had wanted. It also soon became a professional business that made a very small minority (the rich British elite) a lot of money. Just what the elite had wanted. Perhaps no sport has served the originators of a country the way hockey has for Canada.

In some way, it was BECAUSE of hockey's rough and violent play that the sport began to be embraced by the local population. They did not want to be seen as the white-shirted British cricketers, they wanted a rough and tumble game that matched how they saw their nation. Hockey gave the population something uniquely their own. As Michael Robidoux wrote, "*Hockey displayed men who were perceived to be stoic, courageous, and physically dominant: precisely the same images of masculinity valued in First Nations culture, and later by early Canadian settlers, an image outside of the standard British Victorian framework.*"[55]

But, as written in other histories, hockey was supposed to start as a pastime on the lakes and ponds of England, then transplanted to Canada via colonists and soldiers. Is that narrative correct?

---

[55]Robidoux p 220

3

**HOCKEY PRE-1875
Who is telling the truth?**

This chapter will be short. Not because there is not lots to discuss, but other books have done a great job at looking at this line of evidence. Specifically, there is a long history of a game called hockey being played on ice prior to 1875, in Canada, USA and Europe. There are even newspaper accounts of games in England that provided lists of players, and often who scored the goals. For more complete details of this "pre-1875 Canada-Europe story, I suggest the excellent book *On the Origin of Hockey* by Giden, Houda and Martel.[56] The question will become the "direction of the flow of the sport." Was it really from Europe to North America, as the standard story suggests, or could it have been from North America to Europe?

Various stick-and-ball games were played on fields for many centuries. There is a relief in a Middle Kingdom Egyptian tomb of Kheti at Beni Hassan that has what look like two players in a field hockey "bully" (a type of face-off). Peter Piccione, professor of comparative ancient history, found a wall relief in Hatshepsut's temple at Deir-el-Bahari where Thutmose is seen holding a ball in one hand and a long stick in the other. Ancient Greece has reliefs from 600 BC that present a game with the possible name kerētízein, with similar ball-and-stick players that appear at the Parthenon in Athens.

---

[56]Suggested further reading is *Hockey's Captains, Colonels and Kings* by Bill Fitsell from 1987 to show which is some of the first resarch into the origin events of hockey in Canada.

I found an odd article from April 10, 1912 in several US newspapers. It discussed that hockey was Arab in origin. I present the article as it appeared.

> "The oriental origin of hockey is proved by the fact that it is often mentioned by Arabian writers in the earliest days of Islam at a time when France and England had no national existence. They speak of it as koura and describe it as a game in which the ball is struck with a curved stick, called a mibdjan or sanladjan. The latter word is Persian, which seems to indicate that the Arabs learned the game from their neighbors of Iran, who first taught them civilization." [57]

I looked up all of the words in the article and found none of them listed anywhere online, or if they did, they seem to have no connection to a sport. I have no real idea what the purpose of this is, or why it could have gotten into several US newspapers without anything that could be seen as a reference for the article's view. I present it simply as another oddity in this research.

*

Soule and the Vikings

---

[57] *Lexington Gazette* April 10, 1912 pg 6

   https://chroniclingamerica.loc.gov/lccn/sn84024716/1912-04-10/ed-1/seq-6/#date1=1900&index=3&rows=20&words=Hockey+hockey+origin&searchType=basic&sequence=0&state=&date2=1963&proxtext=hockey+origin&y=0&x=0&dateFilterType=yearRange&page=1

*Illustration 5: From 14th century illuminated manuscript
(Smithfield Decretals (Decretals of Gregory IX), British Library/Science
Photo Library)*

A French sport played with curved sticks known as "choule (soule) a la crosse," is found in the 13th century French book *Speculum Maius*.[58] Something similar is depicted in the *Decretals of Gregory IX*. This does not seem to be a sport for the ruling elite or clergy, but one for the working farmers. Some claim that the sport was closer to modern golf, others to hockey. Traditional sports site claims, "The main feature of this game is the struggle, often violent between two groups, and the spontaneous and public pleasure of the confrontation. The spice of the meeting could also be the settlement of certain grievances between two villages or small towns. Soule was the tournament of the poor, with its heroes, its wounded and .... its dead !"[59] As you will see, this overview of the game is almost EXACTLY the same as to what the reasons are behind playing the ceremonial Native sport of lacrosse. Are we seeing the parallels? Could "soule a la crosse" and "lacrosse" be the same game? Was lacrosse truly named by early French missionaries because it resembled the game soule a la crosse, involving a stick (crosse)? Or is

---

[58] https://www.rollerskatedad.com/history-of-ice-hockey/

[59] http://www.traditionalsports.org/traditional-sports/europe/la-soule-a-la-crosse-france.html

56

the game of soule a game that was brought back from North America after early explorers saw the sport played? There were a group of colonists in North America that many historians attempt to ignore, the Scandinavian Vikings. Historians will claim that they spent some time in Newfoundland, but few are willing to suggest they made it further to the North American Eastern seaboard. A few, such as Barry Fell, did indeed find evidence of a Viking presence all throughout the east coast. As such, the early Vikings could have come over, appreciated the various stick-and-ball games of the North American Natives, and brought the sport back to Scandinavia with them.

So how would such a game wind up in France you ask? The game of soule is claimed to originate in Normandy and Picardy, which were Viking held areas. Normandy is named after the Normans, which is an Anglicized word for Nordmans, the name for the Scandinavian Vikings. Given that the Irish sport of hurling comes from another key Viking held area, we might have some ideas as to the origin of stick-and-ball field games. The Vikings themselves have a very particular ball game that has made it through the annals of their famous myths and sagas.

That Viking ball game was known as Knattleikr. It was presented as being played on ice in their mythological tales, *Sagas of the Icelanders* (first recorded in print around 950 AD). What the texts present is that there was a specific stick-and-ball game that players played, disputes and injuries occured, many spectators watched, though few specific rules were provided.[60] The sagas indicate that the games were played near ponds, and ice is involved in the stories. There is a question as to whether the games were played on the ice covered ponds themselves or on ice covered shorelines beside the ponds. Teams of players lined up to face each other, and perhaps there was a "pairing" of similar skilled players on the two teams. Or it could be more thought of the way modern hockey is played, the left wing on one team is matched up against the right wing of another. Again, what appears in the Sagas is not complete.

---

[60] Key Icelandic saga sources are Gisla's Saga cp 15, 18, Grettis Saga Ch 15, Egils saga ch 40 and Eyrbyggja's saga cp 43. They are found in *The Sagas of the Icelanders: A Selection* (2000 Viking New York),
http://www.hurstwic.org/history/articles/daily_living/text/knattleikr.htm

A couple of quotes from the Sagas about the game[61]:

> *"One day, a great crowd came to see the game ... the more people arrived to watch, the greater the eagerness to compete ... Bork made no headway against Thorstein all day, and finally he became so angry that he broke Thorstein's bat in two. In response to this, Thorstein tackled him and laid him out flat on the ice."*

> *"[Gisli and Thorgrim] played ball games at Seftjorn pond and there was always a large crowd...Gisli brought [Thorgrim] down and the ball went out of the play." "Gisli tackled Thorgrim so hard that he could do nothing to stop falling. His knuckles were grazed, blood rushed from his nose and the flesh was scraped from his knees."*

One last piece to ponder regarding a possible Scandinavian origin for the integration of the sport to Europe is the presence of a grave marker known as the "Gallowglass (a type of mercenary soldier) Gravestone." Originally found at Clonca Church in Inishowen Ireland, this gravestone can now be seen at GAA Museum in Croke Park. On it appears a hockey stick and what most call a ball, but it could just as easily be a flat disk. The museum site states that the stick is a hurling stick and suggests "that Magnus was famed for his skill at what was called winter hurling, a form of the game played in the north of Ireland and in Scotland."[62] Scotland was very much a Viking stronghold, and there is much similarity in the ancient sites I have explored in Scandinavia and the Northern parts of the British Isles. What might be seen as Scottish (and the originators of the first games in Montreal in 1875) were of course really long-time descendants of the Celts, who were descendants of the early Scandinavians. Thus, the games of hockey in Montreal could have been some sort of genetic

---

[61]Presented on the site https://timothyrjeveland.com/did-vikings-play-ice-hockey-a-history-of-hockeys-origins/

[62]https://100objects.ie/gallowglass-gravestone/, Houda pg 263

revival of the Scandinavian games of the long ancestral past brought back to life. I will return to the subject of the Vikings in the final chapter.

*

English Field and Ball Games

Most writers who look into hockey history focus on the evolution aspect, because generally researchers believe this can be the only way hockey came to be in 1875. They attempt to show a progression from games and pastimes played by youths, to games played by adults, to the eventual "moderniztion" of organization and systems, creating a narrative of how something moved from pastime or physical activity into a "sanctioned sport." No other way is presented as possible. Before a new narrative might be researched, the current one needs to be known.

The main games usually presented as precursors of hockey are the sports of shinty (Scotland), hurling (Ireland), bandy, and field hockey. All are played with hard wooden balls, though cork bungs started to take the place of balls sometime in the 1700s (as found in the 1797 Le Petit engraving mentioned in the introduction). The bent or curved sticks used in bandy are similar to those used in early versions of cricket and golf. Many paintings by Dutch or Flemish artists in the early modern period depict the game of "kolf" (an early version of golf) played on ice with skates and using bent sticks. The most famous is "The Hunters in the Snow" (1565) by Pieter Bruegel. To me they appear to be more in a golf like activity as opposed to hockey.

Yet, there have been a wide variety of ice games of hockey that have been recorded long before 1875; Lincolnshire 1838, Cambridgeshire 1857, Wiltshire 1859, Aspatria 1861, Berkshire 1864, Worcestershire 1870, Hertforshire 1871, Huntingstonshire 1871, and Lincolnshire 1871.[63] Many of these reports not only list the names of all the players, but also include the goal scorers, and even the times of the goals. Because of these findings the book *On the*

---

[63] Giden, Houda, Martel pgs 36-44, 58-74

59

Origin Of Hockey asks, why then must Montreal 1875 be labeled as the first real hockey game? There were many similar seeming games occuring earlier in England.

Hockey information also appeared in several English books and gives details of how one should play (simplified rules). These books include the 1773 *Juvenile Sports and Pastimes*, the 1849 *Boy's Own Book's* which stated, *"With a group of skilled skaters, this game offers fine sport, but naturally is best played on ice surfaces."* and 1850 *Boys Book of Sports Games. The Boy's Handy Book,* which was published in London in 1863, noted that "Hockey is a winter game, and is often played on ice, and also by skaters." Though the authors went on to say that playing hockey on ice was not recommended for safety concerns because "falls against ice are extraordinarily hard."[64]

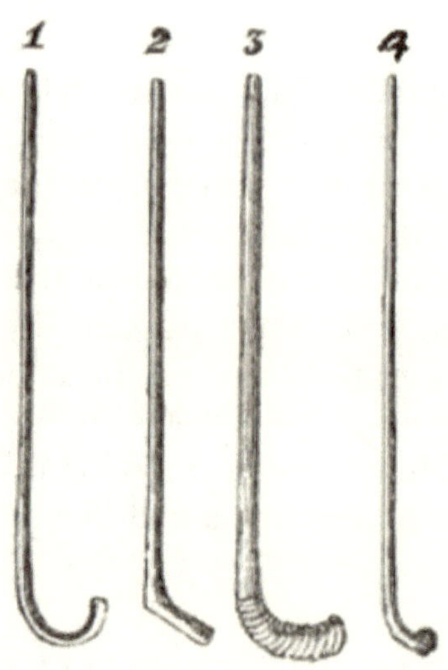

Il

lustration 6: Sticks seen in Every Boys Book: A Complete Encyclopedia of Sports and Amusements p.265

Another possibly revealing book is *Every Boy's Book A Complete Encyclopedia of Sports and Amusements.* The section on

---

[64]Giden, Houda, Martel pgs. 48-49, https://www.rollerskatedad.com/history-of-ice-hockey/

hockey (the Gutenberg free copy I found was published in 1869)[65] gives an account of hockey so good that one would think it was written recently. I put the entire section into the appendix, but I wanted to share a couple of key observations here. *"In all the general principles, hockey bears a great resemblance to foot-ball, the game consisting in driving a ball through a goal. The ball, however, is of much smaller dimensions, even where a ball, and not a bung, is used; and it is impelled, not by the foot, but by certain sticks, or clubs, called hockeys, or hookeys, because the end with which the ball is struck is more or less hooked."* This is referring to the name hockey being given to the stick and not the ball-bung object being hit. Four sticks are illustrated, and the second above looks about as much like a modern hockey stick as we can know. So here we have "proof" that sticks that look much like the one we are accustomed to were used in England at least in the 1860s. And that type of stick is not the best for hitting an object on a field, but for moving specifically a flat disk-like object on ice. That does not mean these sticks "invented" in England, only that what we may call a hockey stick (as opposed to curved hurley or bandy sticks) were in use there. We will find similar looking sticks in the Native Aboriginal games of shinny in North America.[66]

There were many letters written by people about hockey in their youth such as in 1853 by Charles Darwin. Yes that Charles Darwin, who wrote his son William Erasmus at his boarding school, "Do you have a decent pond to skate on? I used to enjoy playing hockey on skates very much."[67] It is interesting that Darwin, the one who developed the evolution theory, has his name added to this discussion- as if the idea of an evolution of the sport is almost implanted in the mind when Darwin's name is added. Darwin played it, the game evolved, he is part of the narrative's creation of the step by step process of hockey. But there comes a question, just what is hockey?

*

Name of Hockey

---

[65]https://www.gutenberg.org/files/42172/42172-h/42172-h.htm#Page_265

[66]Giden, Houda, Martel pgs. 86-129

[67]Giden, Houda, Martel pgs. 48-49

The Canadian Encyclopedia states that Richard Johnson's *Juvenile Sports and Pastimes* from 1773 is where the word "hockey" first appeared in print. Chapter XI is titled, "New Improvements to the Game of Hockey," which suggests the sport and the name had to be around for some time in order for there to be improvements. The chapter describes the game using the word "hockey" to refer to the barrel plug used to play, and not the stick. This seems to refute the older accepted theory that the word "hockey" is derived from the French term "hoquet," which means "shepherd's staff.'" However, the term "Hockie sticks," written that way, was mentioned in the Irish Gallway Statutes of 1527. Another interesting reference is in the 1805 *Book of Games* in its description indicated that the object used (a bung not a ball) was called a "hockey" and the sticks used were called "hockey sticks." This seems to indicate that the idea that the sport is named for the stick is not correct, the stick is just referring to a specific type of stick that was used in the a game involving a bung, but when a ball was being used the stick (and game) were called something else.[68] So what does the name of hockey really indicate? To be honest no one is really sure. When looking into dictionaries for the word hock, I find that it means to "pawn an item," or can mean "the back side of a horse or calves' lower leg", and written as hawk can mean the "falcon-like bird." Though in Germanic languages, the word hok, is linked to the word keg, indicating a type of curved wood or metal. And thus is linked in such way to the english word "hook." In the Norwegian language one of the words for hook is "hake" pronounded "hawk-eh." Which sounds very similar to hockey, and so we are back to is the word generated for the type of object used in the game, or for a specific hooked stick that was used in the game?

Historians Giden, Houda and Martel suggest that the term hockey may have come from the use of barrel bungs, which are flat and round corks that would be later cut down to size, called "hockeys," due to them coming from hock-beer barrels. "Hock ale" was a beer brewed for the festivals at Hocktide (a festival on the second Monday and Tuesday after Easter) that came in barrels with the bungs. At times, they claim that, the word "hockey" (sometimes

---

[68] Poulton p.24, Giden, Houda, Martel pgs. 93-97

"hocky") was used not only to refer to the beer itself, but also as a synonym for "drunk."[69] James Murray's 1901 *A New English Dictionary* claimed that the hocktide festival was called hockey, hawkey or horkey.[70]

*

Bandy

According to bandy historian Charles Goodman Tebbutt (the one claimed to have also formulated the rules for bandy), people were probably playing bandy on ice since the mid-1700s in the Fens of Eastern England. He and his brother Arnold wrote a book in 1896 called A *Handbook of Bandy or Hockey on Ice.*" Even in the 1890's, English Bandy players felt that there was no difference between ice bandy and ice hockey. For me hockey begins to became to be seen as a uniuqe sport at some point due to the flat disk being used. All the other sports, be they bandy or hurley or shinty or ice polo, all used a ball.

Even though we will see bandy matches mentioned in English papers in 1857, there is what is called "the original bandy match," held in 1875 at The Crystal Palace in London. Given that the site of what is called the "first modern bandy match" is held at a temple-like site, here at the site of the 1851 World Fair (the first of the modern era) I do not think the choice of the location is by accident. Of course, it is a co-incidence that the TWO ICE games of England and Canada both have their mythological first games in 1875, and both at what might be seen as "temples." The official rules were not published by Tebbutt until 1882.

---

[69] Giden, Houda, Martel pg 230

[70] "Beginner's Guide to British Folk Customs,"
https://www.efdss.org/learning/resources/beginners-guides/48-british-folk-customs-from-plough-monday-to-hocktide/3389-hocktide, and Giden, Houda, Martel pg 235

Illustration 7: Charles Tebbutt, father of bandy, with an obvious pasted on head. (Fotografering – 1889, Reprofotograf (F) Anno Domkirkeodden, identifier 0401-02823, DIMU-CODE 011012742927)

I found some photographs of Tebbutt. One is an obvious early attempt at "photoshop" of putting one head on a different body. The head is not the right size, and the skin tone of the face does not match the arms at all. A second photo appears from this "shoot," and while the head paste is better, it can still be seen as a cut-and-paste head. Why would someone need to create this?[71] If this was really the father of bandy, there should have been lots of opportunities to take

---

[71]Photos can be found at wikipedia for Tebbit and also at
https://digitaltmuseum.no/011012742927/england-bluntisham-charles-goodman-tebbutt-1860-1944-var-en-engelsk-skoyteloper/media?slide=0

photographs of him. Whenever there are doctored images one always has to start to question the narrative. You don't create fakes for something obviously true. In chapter eight I am going to look at this strange phenomena of cutting and pasting heads onto other's bodies, and other anomalies of early hockey photographs.

*

Canada

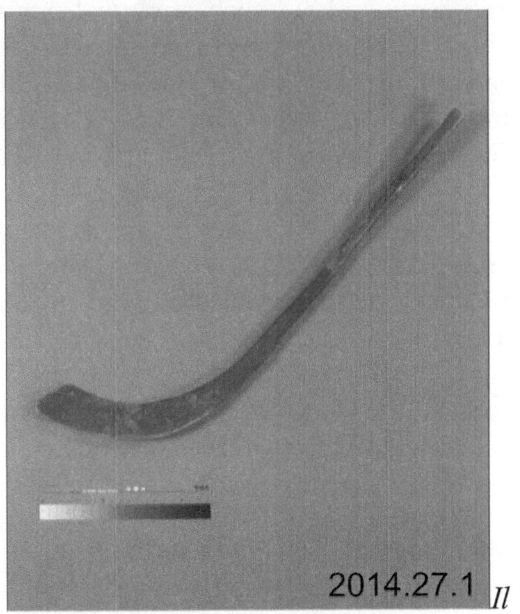

Illustration 8: Moffatt Stick, 1836 (courtesy of Canadian Museum of History, 2014.27.1, IMG2016-0253-0027)

Above is a photo of what is now known as the "Moffatt Stick," found in the Canadian Museum in Gatineau, Quebec. It is made out of sugar maple, and was likely created sometime in the 1830s, and was in the collection of the Moffatt Family of Cape Breton, Nova

Scotia for over a century. The initials WM are carved into the blade, suggesting it was for William Moffatt. What I find most interesting about the stick is how short it is (certainly nothing like what we will see in the late 1880s) but also the blade, which is rocked but not fully crooked like a hurley or shinty stick. This stick looks like a type of cross that between the two types of sticks. I would assume such a stick could propel either a wooden puck or a leather ball on the ice.

As mentioned previously, Canada had gone through its exploration trying to pinpoint an EXACT origin point (a specific place) for the start of hockey. The problem is that this seems not to be possible, with too many origin stories that it becomes impossible to choose one over another. One such story is from Deline in the Northwest Territories, based on letters written by Sir John Franklin in 1825, during one of his attempts to find the Northwest Passage. Another is from the Niagara Region in 1839, as Sir Richard George Augustus Levinge, a lieutenant of a light infantry unit stationed in Niagara, wrote in his memoirs, "Large parties contested games of hockey on the ice, some forty or fifty being ranged on each side." Kingston, Ontario, puts its claims in the diary of Sir Arthur Freeling in 1843, then a first lieutenant stationed in Kingston. Michael Vigneault's article "Out of the Mists of Memory" discussed a few more early games, the Dorchester Club vs Uptown Club held in Montreal in February 1837, one in Halifax 1851, and one in Ottawa 1852 (with a shinty medal as will be discussed in chapter six). There is also a painting from the 1850s done in Montreal titled "Skating on the Harbour Ice," with a group in the back with either hockey or lacrosse sticks.[72] Again with all of these games listed, the standard response is always something like, "but with no guarantee of how many players, what the rules were, if referees were used, or even what the score was, all that can be said is ice games did occur, but not how organized the games were." It often tends to be a focus that one can not label any sport official, until there is some sort of British organization, rule and league structure, specific note taking of scores, and all being published in newspapers. That puts a very small box around what is "allowed" be qualified as an "official sport." Of course

---

[72]Vigneault "Out of the Mists of Memory, Montreal 1875-1901" Total Hockey 1998, Giden, Houda, Martel chapter 1

only the elite parts of society would be able to take any pastime and fulfil all of these requirements.

Windsor, Nova Scotia looks to a passage put forth in a book titled *The Attaché, or, Sam Slick in England* by Thomas Chandler Halliburton as proof that the game was born on the place called Long Pond. Halliburton's book refers to playing "hurley on the long pond on the ice." He had been a schoolboy at King's Collegiate School, from which he graduated in 1810. Similarly, an anonymous letter to the editor, published in the Windsor Mail in 1876, describes the author's years (1816–18) at the same school, including a reference to "hurley" as well as skating. However, the evidence is still debated, and it is unclear whether a game resembling ice hockey was played on the "long pond" at this time. This was the focus of Nova Scotia historian Garth Vaughan. Part of his justification is by adding James Creighton into the mix, claiming that since he was from Nova Scotia, and that the sticks were from the Mi'kmaq, and the skates (Star Skates) were from Nova Scotia, this had to be the sport's real origin. I think this is true, but not exactly as Garth saw it.

So who is Tomas Haliburton? Not many hockey historians have looked into the story of the man who by wrote just one paragraph in a book in the 1840s, which then became the rallying cry of one city in the hockey birthright sweepstakes. Thomas Chandler Haliburton[73] was an author, judge, and later a political MP in England. He came from a rich Nova Scotia family, and his father was also a lawyer and political figure. Haliburton attended the University of King's College in Windsor, from which he graduated in 1815. He wrote a number of books on history, politics, farm improvements, and a series of adventures involving a character named Sam Slick. He wrote his first history book in 1829, *An Historical and Statistical Account of Nova Scotia,* which was estimated by M. Brook Taylor to be about 70% copied (plagiarized) from other sources. When examining his historical writing, Ian McKay described him as "proudly identified with the civilizing mission of the British Empire, (and that for him) the real history of Nova Scotia began in 1749 when

---

[73]http://www.biographi.ca/en/bio/haliburton_thomas_chandler_9E.html

67

the Empire made its first substantial investment in the colony by founding Halifax."[74]

Both of his sons became lawyers, one later Secretary of War in England (and Knight of Bath) and the other (Robert) an anthropologist. Robert was a part of the very strange Canada First Movement. What Wikipedia says of it: *"Haliburton and like-minded authors that made up the Canada First Movement saw that the milder southern climate was said to lead to "degeneration, decay, and effeminacy." The harsher northern climate they argued was said to produce the most Canadian of characteristics, "the inclination to be moderate. The Canada First Movement saw the French Canadian and Métis cultures as dead weight that was holding the advancement of English Canada back."*[75] That movement has similarities to the mindset I am suggesting in this book for who created the sport of hockey. Thomas was a relative of James Burton, the early Egyptologist, whose original family name was Haliburton. However, at some time prior to 1800, he dropped the Hali from his last name for no apparent reason. Thomas moved to England in 1837 to stay with James, where they traveled together and looked into various family backgrounds. James Burton is a very strange figure as well, with an extremely odd life. You can look into him as well if you wish.

While Thomas Haliburton is never openly cited as a Freemason, one such masonic site did present that they found a number of Freemasonic references in his novels.[76] On digging a bit further, I did find a clear connection. That involves what has become known as the Masonic Stone of 1606, found at Port Royal in the Annapolis . Basin of Nova Scotia where French explorer De Champlain set up a settlement. In 1827 the stone was found, and is claimed to be early evidence of Freemasonry based on specific carvings that had been placed onto the stone. One account of the stone's finding is made by Thomas Haliburton in his 1829 book *History of Nova Scotia*. The stone is described by Haliburton as "about two feet and a half long and two feet broad, and of the same kind as that which forms the substratum of Granville Mountain. On

---

[74]McKay, Ian *In the Province* p38

[75]Wikipedia, Robert Haliburton page

[76] https://freemasonry.bcy.ca/fiction/haliburton_t.html

the upper part are engraved the square and compass of the Free Mason, and in the center, in large and deep Arabic figures, the date 1606." A second account by Boston chemist Dr. Charles T. Jackson in 1856 claimed that Haliburton was the one who now had the stone.

In 1887, Halliburton's son Robert, gave the stone to the Canadian Institute of Toronto (founded in 1850 by Sandford Fleming) with "the understanding that the stone should be inserted in the wall of the building then being erected for the Institute. Sir Sandford Fleming wrote that he received the stone from Mr. R. G. Haliburton in order that it might be properly cared for."[77] So this very unique stone, perhaps with the oldest masonic inscription in all of North America, was placed inside a new building (which is a masonic ritual) in Toronto, and the stone has connections to both Thomas Haliburton and Sandford Fleming. So is it not interesting that for a long while, the number one source cited for the existence of British settlers playing hockey in Canada is from Thomas Haliburton? I leave all this out there for you to ponder again the strange co-incidences with this story every part you turn towards.[78]

*

The Nova Scotia origins group has presented various evidence of newspaper, book and diary reports of games (generally referred to as hurley on ice) in the province going back to the 1820s.[79] The *Acadian Recorder* of January 22, 1853 spoke of the problems of ice players on Sundays, while everyone was to be at church, but:

---

[77] https://www.masonicworld.com/education/articles/Freemasonry-In-Canada-before-1750.htm

[78] Of course when I look at the stone I see I606 not 1606, but that is whole story unto itself about true dates of history and what a I or J prior to a date means As I mention in Exposing the Expositions, dates prior to 1800 are generally written not with a 1 as a place holder but a J or I. A J623 would be "the year of Jesus 623." There seems to have been a "fast one" pulled on the world when a new calendar came out that by replacing the J or I with a 1, they had just added 1000 years to the calendar. You can read that book for further reference. Why is it important? If correct it would mean that most of history is a false narrative rewrite to fit a new calendar system, and that what we call the 600s might be the same as the 1600s and change how all of history really happened.

[79] Gerald Owen "Origins of Hockey"; Paul Bennett "Re-Imagining" p11

> *"Not so was it in the vicinity of the Town, on Sunday last. The Lake above Mr. Hostermau's was literally covered with skaters, with their hurleys...to great peril to those upon it. The road leading in that direction was filled with persons of all ages, going towards the place of sport, and we regret to add, that well dressed females were to be seen in considerable numbers on the shores, enjoying the scene- while the vile effluvia, from hundreds of cigars, polluted the pure atmosphere of heaven for a considerable distance around. All this too, during the hours of Divine Service...in old times the whole of the Sabbath, and not only the small part, sent withing the Church doors, was considered holy. Then, Parents and Masters and Dames used to look after the young fold, and catechise them, and keep them around them."*[80]

Another article is from the *Boston Evening Gazette* from November 5, 1859 in an article titled "Ice Hockey in Nova Scotia," which I have presented in full in the Appendix. The article speaks of the popularity of skating in Halifax, and information about an ice game called ricket. The ricket is the goal area, and hurley sticks were used to propel the ball. The article ends with the suggestion that "It might be well if some of our agile skaters would introduce the game. It would be a fine addition to our winter sports, and give a new zest to the delightful exercise of skating. We have sent down for a set of hurleys preparatory to its introduction." If this article is correct, why were there no winter stick-and-ball games being played in Massachusetts in the 1850s? You would think that there would be some who would have taken the field sports from England and transplanted them onto the ice as was being done in Nova Scotia. What makes Nova Scotia so unique for putting these games to ice?

A much later book from 1898 by JA Tuthill *Ice Hockey and Ice Polo Guide* also gives some useful information about the differences between Ice Polo (played in the USA) and hockey. Historian and author, David Jones attempts to show that a recorded

---

[80]https://archives.novascotia.ca/newspapers/results/?nTitle=Acadian+Recorder

game of ice hockey took place at Dartmouth's Oathill Lake on February 18, 1867. He shows that the game was mentioned in the following day's *Halifax Reporter* "Two well contested games of 'ricket' were being played. At the upper end were a number of young men from Dartmouth and the City, playing their 'hurleys' and 'following up' the ball, while the center was occupied by a number of officers of the Garrison and fleet, in a match game called hockey i.e. ricket."[81] Again, the game was called ricket and the sticks used were referred to as hurleys, which should cause us to ask "what game was being played?" How are all of these various named ice games supposed to link up to Montreal in 1875? And how is someone to devise criteria to determine what a game of "hockey" is and is not. Society for International Hockey Research attempted to define hockey in a 2002 paper, but even then it became very muddled to claim that what took place in Montreal in 1875, was really much different than was played and reported on in England in 1871, or was happening on the ice prior to that?

*

Halifax Rules

That brings us to a final topic of the pre-1875 discussion that must be looked at. This is the so-called Halifax Rules. While most are in agreement that youngsters had been playing various games of hurley, bandy and proto-hockey on the ponds of Nova Scotia, no one had written down the rules. Since they didn't write rules, they must not have had them. Then in the midst of the hockey origin debate came a newspaper interview in the *Halifax Daily* in October 1942 of a Col. Byron Weston, who told his stories to sportswriter James Power.[82] The interview should be taken as a possibility, and not guaranteed fact. Weston claimed to have played ice hurley/hockey type games with local men as well as with the Mi'kmaq Natives. He also claimed that there were specific rules, presented to Power as:

The game was played with a block of wood for a puck.

---

[81]   https://halifax.citynews.ca/remember-this/remember-this-beer-band-and-hockey-canadas-first-fully-reported-hockey-game-860245/

[82]Weston article found in entirety on https://birthplaceofhockey.com/hockey-history/hockeyists/nova-scotias-hockey-ambassadors/col-byron-weston/

71

The puck was not allowed to leave the ice.

The stones marking the place to score goals were placed on the ice (at right angles to those at present) Parallel to the sides of the ice surface.

There was to be no slashing.

There was to be no lifting the stick above the shoulder.

When a goal was scored, teams changed ends.

Players had to keep 'on side' of the puck.

The 'forward pass' was permitted.

All players played the entire game.

There was a no-replacement rule for penalized players.

The game had two thirty-minute periods with a ten-minute break.

The goal-keeper had to stand for the entire game.

Goals were decided by the goal umpires, who stood at the goal mouth and rang a handbell.

Col. Byron Weston was another of the elite, having graduated from Harvard University in 1873. How exactly does a man from Windsor, Nova Scotia get into Harvard in the 1870s? Perhaps due to the fact that Weston was actually born in Maine and moved with his family at the age of nine, when his father was in charge of building the first marine railway in Nova Scotia. That would put a Maritime railway connection between Weston and Sandford Fleming. Interesting how his name keeps connecting to everyone in this story. Weston became a lawyer (no surprise) and was instrumental in founding the Eastern Trust Company.

As for the rules, there are so many strange attempts by the proponents of the Windsor story as to the legitimacy of these rules, such as the comment by Garth Vaughan, "Players then, as today, know the rules by heart, and usually saw no reason to write them down. They were interested in playing the game. Other matters concerning the game were left for management and academics."[83] Vaughan even tries to claim that James Creighton must have used these Halifax Rules in his 1875 game. But there were no listing of any rules in Montreal until the presented "iceified" field hockey rules in 1877. If they really had these rules in Halifax that had been used for

---

[83]https://birthplaceofhockey.com/hockey-history/origin/rules/

decades, why all of sudden in 1877 would the Montreal group go get a field hockey rule book to make their rules?

Granted it has been shown that early hockey teams in Nova Scotia did play by different rules than had been formed in Montreal. In 1889 when Dartmouth Chebuctos played exhibition games in Montreal and Quebec City, there were no offside rules enforced and the goal markers (two curling stones) were placed parallel to the sides of the rink, instead of facing the end for the games under "East Coast rules." But after these exhibitions when the Nova Scotia team returned home, they too adopted the Montreal rules, stopped forward passing, and put the net posts square to each other as in Quebec.[84] Why they chose to do this has not been explained, nor has it ever fully been explained why exactly their rules were so different from what was used in Montreal. The newspaper story of Col. Weston is likely just an attempt to explain this oddity, but never going into detail of where these rules emerged, or why they were so quickly dropped, would be the real important parts of the story to find out.

At the same time, a few articles in the newspapers were also appearing from the local native community, such as one from a Mi'kmaq historian known as "Old Joe Cope." He was a former prospector that I will look at in chapter five. In 1943, he sent a letter to a Halifax newspaper after hearing of the city of Kingston's claim to be the Canadian hockey capital. In the letter he wrote that, "*Long before the pale faces strayed in this country, the Micmacs were playing two ball games, a field game and an ice game, which were identical in every way.*"[85] The Dictionary of the Mi'kmaq has words for their original ice game called Oochamkunutk, but when they played with the white colonists they called that game Alchamadyk.

Jerry Lonecloud, another Mi'kmaq, described in 1913 a traditional Mi'kmaq game called Duwarken, played on the ice. I hear some of you say, "it would be too difficult to hide such a thing as a Native origin to hockey." I beg to differ. Even though the 1920s are a bit past the focus of this book, I want to share one story that may help to reveal the many ways this omission of a Native game might occur.

---

[84]Fitsell, Bill "The Halifax Rules, fact or fiction", *SIHR Research Journal*

[85]Complete letter can be read at https://boomer649.wordpress.com/at-last-joe-copes-full-letter/

In Hardy and Holman's book *Hockey: A Global History*, they discuss the Cree and Ojibway hockey tour of 1927-28. This book describes two Northern Ontario brothers, Joe and Willie Friday, who were hunting and fishing tour operators. To promote their business, they decided to put together two hockey teams, made up form the main tribes of the North (Cree and Ojibway), and take them to play a barnstorming series of exhibition games in the Northern United States (where the majority of Friday's clients would be found). Sometimes the two tribes played a game against each other, while other times played as a combined team against one from the city they were visiting. They wore jerseys of buckskin, and also wore head dresses in the warm up. When not playing hockey games they put on pow-wows, canoe paddling demonstrations and other events showcasing "Indian" skills. In a sense, not much had changed since the 1870s lacrosse tours of England, as the Natives were there to "put on a type of stereotype show."

But the newspapers of the day made some rather interesting comments that tend to be overlooked. The *Global History* book stated, "Amid this commentary was an assertion that Indian hockey was authentic hockey, that these teams offered a glimpse of the modern sport's ancient forbears. White sportsman, reporters and promoters wanted to believe that when they played it, Natives played the original game." That is quite the statement. Perhaps in the 1920s there was still a sense of memory, especially in the Northern United States where it had not been as important to take control of hockey as a national identity (for they had already done that with baseball). Could the fact Americans had a sport identity with baseball mean that they could examine hockey more objectively than was "allowed" in Canada? The *Cleveland News*, reprinted in the *Toronto Globe* on January 31, 1928 claimed, "Canada is home of hockey and the Indians of that country were the first to play it...it was taken up by the French and English settlers of the Dominion and gradually developed into the king of winter sports." Perhaps this paper's writer was more on the mark than anyone might have guessed!

Yet the newspapers then go to the next level, presenting why "Native hockey" cannot be called "modern hockey." Here is where the whitewash of history continues. Generally speaking, the news reports would praise the skills, speed, and checking of the Natives, but the reporters would always find a way to claim the Natives were missing the "science of hockey." The white teams would win because of their "organization," "combination," "team play," and "aggressiveness." What these reporters were saying is that hockey as a sport is Native in origin, but that the original game was long gone. The British game, as seen in the NHL and other professional leagues, is the "way the game is supposed to be played," and anyone playing a style that is not matching this, could not be classified as playing "modern hockey."[86] But is that really correct?

*

Hockey Cards

The basic story is that "Montreal-style" hockey did not make it to Europe until George Meagher's "magical" journey of 1894, where he traveled with hockey sticks and "brought the sport to Europe." But we have seen games called hockey on ice have long been listed in England. Can some early hockey cards tell us anything?

Did you know that there were several hockey cards made prior to 1900? I didn't either until just recently. None it seems were made in Canada. Several come from the ice skating series known as Bufford Litho Cards out of Boston. One is number 903 of a young boy with a hockey stick over his shoulder while carrying a ball, which is dated to around 1880. But there are other cards depicting games on the ice. Another Bufford card comes dated from 1887, and features longer sticks but the usual ball being used. A similar card from 1888 is listed from the Great Atlantic and Pacific Tea Company. This is another card featuring a ball in play. Another card from the era is from the Royal Dutch Cocoa Company, and has three young boys and girls with bandy sicks and a ball. If they are on the internet still they can be found here.[87]

---

[86]Information on the Cree-Ojibway tour from Hardy and Holman, *Hockey a Global* pgs 260-264

[87]https://www.reddit.com/media?url=https%3A%2F%2Fpreview.redd.it %2Favpbla8zu4s51.jpg%3Fwidth%3D1080%26crop%3Dsmart%26auto%3Dwebp%26s %3D7cfc6c68fef5515f72799c7d203fe811e57c3360

https://prewarcards.com/2016/09/10/1888-great-atlantic-and-pacific-tea-company-hockey-trade-card-set-and-checklist/

Illustration 9: Diamantine card, unknown date (photo courtesy of Glory Days Collectibles, Toronto Canada)

Diamantine — mit Sparsieb — Allerfeinster Schuhputz
Diamant in Tuben, Gläsern u. Dosen für feinfarbiges Leder
Diabona Edel-Bohnerwachs
Bei Sammlung und Einsendung der unseren Artikeln und Packungen beiliegenden Gutscheine gewähren wir Prämien:
40 Stück 1 Diamantine-Poliertuch oder 1 Glanzbürste
80 „ 1 Sammelalbum f. Diamantine-Serienbilder
120 „ 1 Spiel oder Bilderbuch oder 1 Gerstenkornhandtuch oder 1 Serviette
200 „ 1 pa. Teelöffel, 90er versilb. od. 2 Handtücher
Bei mehr Gutscheinen weitere wertvolle Prämien.
Rud. Starcke G. m. b. H. Melle i/H. (Gegr. 1879)

Wintersport.

4. Eishockey.

Hockey ist dem Fussballsporte ähnlich und wird gewöhnlich auf der Rasenfläche betrieben. Auch die Regeln sind fast dieselben. Im Winter aber verlegt man den interessanten Sport auf die blanke Eisfläche. Es bedarf einer grossen Geschicklichkeit, dass sich die Spieler nicht gegenseitig zu Fall bringen oder mit den langen Schlaghölzern einander Schaden zufügen. Ist ein Tor gewonnen, so herrscht natürlich die gleiche Begeisterung wie beim Fussballspiel. Rücksichtsloses Verhalten, das sogenannte Holzen, kann bei diesem Sport unter keinen Umständen geduldet werden.

Illustration 10: Back of card to the left

I begin with the card above by Diamantine Shoeshine Company in Germany. Such cards were in a sense advertising

---

https://glorydayscollectibles.com/products/c-1880s-vintage-diamantine-hockey-card-very-rare-hockey-image-german-issue-1

https://hockeygods.com/images/13385-Bensdorp_s_Royal_Dutch_Cocoa_Hockey_Trade_Card_1880

https://www.ebay.ca/itm/234336629268

https://glorydayscollectibles.com/products/1885-vintage-ciblis-hockey-trading-cards-early-hockey-imagery-1?_pos=1&_psq=1885&_ss=e&_v=1.0

business cards for the company. On the front of the card we have what would be a standard look of hockey in Europe in the 1880s, played with a ball, though the sticks are much longer than standard bandy-hurley sticks. The German word Eishockey appears on the front of the card, while the back gives a unique description of the sport translated here:

> Wintersport4 Eishockey Hockey is similar to soccer and is usually played on the grass field. In winter, however, the interesting sport is moved to the bare ice surface. It requires great skill so that the players don't trip each other up or damage each other with long bats. If a goal is won, then of course there is the same enthusiasm as in a soccer game. Reckless behavior, the so-called lumbering, cannot be tolerated in this sport under any circumstances

Some try to date this card to 1879, which I feel is incorrect. There is an 1879 date that appears on the back of the card, under the abbreviation Gegr. That is a short form for the German word Gegrundet, which means "founded" in English. The date on the back of the card is the founding date for the company, not necessarily the card itself. The cards of this "set" (which include similar backs) are suggested by card experts to be from the 1880s. Given the look of the players I would have to say that the card is prior to 1900. These cards were made by companies to be given away in specific areas of the world, thus the image on the card has to be recognizable to the place that they are giving the cards away to. In this case, they felt this image was very understood by the people in Germany. Interestingly though is that the players appear to look very "French-like" as opposed to German.

Illustration 11: Diamantine Card, unknown date (photo courtesy of Glory Days Collectibles, Toronto Canada)

A second Diamantine card is listed as being from 1880, but I doubt that date as well. Can you spot the reason for my questioning the date of 1880? It is the goal net to the left of the card. Nets were not supposed to have been added to posts in the ice in Canada in the 1880s. The first recorded use of a net with the posts is from 1890-1891 at Storrs Agricultural School (Now UCONN) (photo of the net can be found at the footnote). Spalding New Cage Hockey Goals were sold starting in 1895, though I have been unable to find an image of one of them. A new steel cage net (similar to what is seen in the above hockey card) was invented in 1897 by Quebec Bulldogs goalie Frank Stocking. Interestingly Stocking was not Canadian, but from New York, so might have come across nets in the United States early in his career.[88] In 1899, Halifax, Nova Scotia began to use a new Box Net. For some reason Montreal teams did not start using nets until 1899.[89]

Thus the card above can be said to date no earlier than 1895. Also curious is that this is obviously bandy, with a large ball and short

---

[88] https://tedtalkshockey.com/2020/05/04/the-history-of-the-hockey-net/,

[89] https://forums.hfboards.com/threads/the-history-of-hockey-nets.1660325/

bandy-like sticks. Yet they are using Canadian hockey nets. Also interesting is that usually the word used on similar cards in Germany was Eis Hockey, while here it is just Hockey. In case you were wondering, the first listed game of hockey in Germany was a game on February 4, 1897 between Akademische Sport Club versus Berlin in Charlottenburg (the famous palace in West Berlin).

Illustration 12: Cibils German Card, unknown date, in author's collection

This brings us to a very unique card. This card is from the French Cibils meat extract company. Four other versions of this card exist, but they are in French and have the title "Le jeu de hockey." This card is in German, made for a German audience, and the image reads "Das Hockey Spiel." There is nothing on the back that would indicate the date of the card. There are several card sources on the Internet that date this card to 1884 or 1885. An expert in the Cibils cards I consulted suggested to me a date of 1900. A similar, and more well known meat extract company of the time was Liebig, and they began producing similar looking cards in 1872.[90]

---

[90] https://en.wikipedia.org/wiki/Liebig%27s_Extract_of_Meat_Company

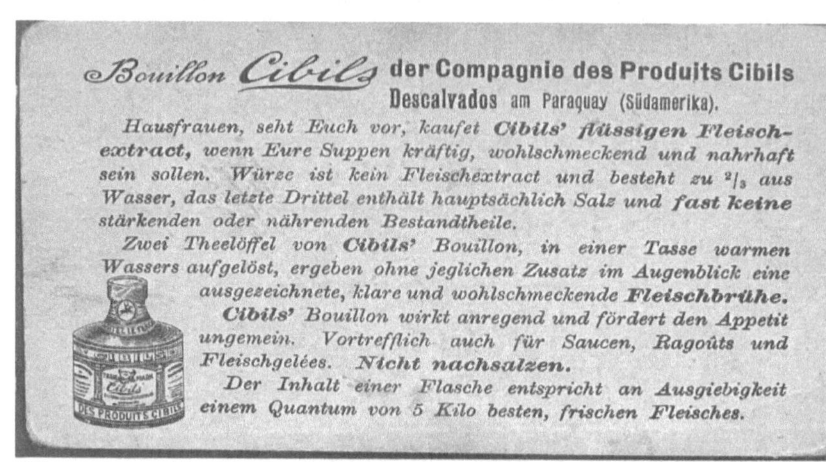

Illustration 13: Back of German card above

The date of the card is very important for this research. If the 1884 date is correct, as some card sources suggests, it throws the origin hockey wide open. Even if the date of the card is 1890 it still does the same for two reasons. The first is by looking closely at the image we notice that the game is being played with a flat wooden disk. In all the other cards of the era, it is always a ball that is being shown. Secondly, we see the two large posts placed in the ice, just as was being done in Montreal. No other cards are showing posts in the ice. We also notice far longer sticks being used than the bandy sticks of the era. This is almost a perfect representation of hockey as it is claimed to look in Montreal prior to 1890. The players themselves look French, this version of the card is meant for Germany, there is only one German card in existence compared to four French, indicating that the likely main audience for the image was France.

Perhaps a Cibils company artist traveled to the Montreal Carnival sometime after 1883, saw the hockey games played there, and then depicted it on the card. The images on the cards were made to be specific for those regions, to be instantly recognizable to the people living in that area. So whether the artist of the card was copying hockey in Montreal or was depicting hockey that he saw in Europe, the company had to feel that the image being presented on this card would be as easily recognized in France and Germany. At what time was hockey recognizable with a puck in Central Europe? The true date of this card is important, and I am still looking into a way to verify it. If I can do so I will post an update on the hockey section of my website. One last oddity. When searching for the Cibils meat extract company on the Internet nothing shows us, save for various information about the trade cards. The company itself is pretty much missing. For the Internet, and the popularity of the various cards for sale, that seems like a very strange omission.

Illustration 14: Women on Ice in St. Moritz pre-1893
(Courtesy Lizzie Le Blond and Martin and Osa Johnson Safari Museum EMLB 002_089)

Illustration 15: Bandy game with no uniforms pre-1895 (Courtesy Lizzie Le Blond and Martin and Osa Johnson Safari Museum EMLB 004_042)

I have a few more images to discuss regarding this subject of when Montreal hockey was played in Europe. These come from the collection of Lizzy Le Blond, kept at The Martin and Osa Johnson Safari Museum.[91] Le Blond was a famous female mountain climber, and sports enthusiast (her photos include skating, curling, bobsledding, and hockey.) The images she took were carefully documented at the time of their taking, in St. Moritz, Switzerland. The first image is from a series of photos listed as 1890-1893, the second from 1894-95. The game appears to be very bandy-like, and includes a ball. Note that both men and women appear in the photos playing the game. T caption for the images says that they are from a series of photos "From the Negatives of Cyril Cunard." The museum archivist looked into some records and suggests the man is Cyril Grant Cunard from Nova Scotia, a friend of Le Blond. Things just

---

[91]I want to thank Safari Museum archivist Jacquelyn Borgeson Zimmer for providing detailed information on the photos in the collection.

got interesting as Nova Scotia entered the European hockey landscape.

I looked into Cyril Cunard. He was born in Halifax in 1867, died in London 1914. He seems to have lived in Europe most of his life, and had a daughter, Veronica, born in St. Moritz in 1902. His parents were William Cunard and Laura Charlotte Haliburton. Can you guess who Laura's father was? Yes, Thomas Chandler Haliburton, the very person who linked hockey to Nova Scotia in his 1840s book. Does that not seem like an odd coincidence? The grandson of the first Canadian to use the word "hurley on ice" in print, is playing hockey games in Switzerland prior to the standard narrative of the arrival of hockey to Europe. More so that the captions of the Le Blond photos are all titled hockey, not bandy, even though these first set of photos are showing a bandy-like game.

The Cunard family links to their family head, Samuel Cunard, a shipping magnate from Halifax, who created the Cunard Shipping Line. This was the first scheduled steamship connection between England and North America. His son William (Cyril's father) took over the business in the 1840s, as father Samuel chose to spend most of his time living in England.[92] The point is, that we have a type of ice sport being played in St. Moritz in 1890-95 (the dates listed for the series of hockey photos above) connected with the son of a shipping magnate of Nova Scotia, whose mother is the daughter of Thomas Haliburton! The question we then must ask. If he is from Nova Scotia, and Nova Scotia is the foundation of hockey, why are they playing bandy? Should they not be playing the game known from Nova Scotia? Or is this game known from Nova Scotia? Or are they playing bandy because that was the most popular ice sport in Europe at the time? Is is true that Montreal-style hockey did not appear in Europe until 1894-95? Or is there some other reason?

---

[92] https://www.ancestry.co.uk/genealogy/records/cyril-grant-cunard-24-zlpf9k
https://en.wikipedia.org/wiki/Samuel_Cunard

Illustration 16: Hockey in December 1896 St. Moritz (Courtesy Lizzie Le Blond and Martin and Osa Johnson Safari Museum EMLB 6_204)

That leads to the second group of photographs from a series listed as December, 1896, one of which appears above. These images clearly has a more Canadian game look to them, with large posts placed into the ice for goals. However, the players still seem to be using bandy sticks, and I can not discern from the photos if the object being used is a puck or a ball (the object never seems to be in any of the photos. If the posts are linked to the new Canadian game brought by Meagher on is 1894 trip, why are the players not using the Canadian sticks and puck that he also would have brought? Also note that the players in the image above are now wearing matching sweaters, while previously they were in their standard day-wear clothing. These images show something has changed since the first two photos, but it hard to tell just how much. Even more interesting is that Le Blond is recorded as having made a film about hockey in 1898 titled "Hockey on St. Moritz Lake." The film seems to be lost.

The finding of this film might shed light on the true origin of hockey in Europe.

When looking into the history of hockey in Switzerland, the claim (recognized by the International Ice Hockey Federation) that the fist ice hockey game played in Europe was an exhibition match in 1885 was played in St. Moritz between English schools Oxford and Cambridge. However, there is no specific evidence the game took place, and those that do present the date as accurate state that it was really a bandy game. Besides, why would the first hockey game between the two universities in England need to take place in Switzerland? The reason has shown that games with the name hockey had been played in England well before 1875. It could make sense that the universities just wanted one of their regular matches played overseas in 1885 for a bit of a vacation added to the match.

No other games are listed in Switzerland until 1895, with games happening between Davos and St. Moritz in January, with only English players being used. The Davos team in 1895 is claimed to have used cricket player Teddy Wynyard, speed-skater Charles Edgington, and Sir Arthur Conan Doyle, author of Sherlock Holmes. Now Sherlock Holmes is getting thrown into the origin stories. George Meagher returns to the story, as it is claimed he played in the Davos-St. Moritz game on January 16, 1898 and helped organize another game between the two sides that December. These games are said to be a cross between bandy and hockey.[93] However the Le Blond photo archive shows that hockey, albeit played by a number of English elites and very bandy-like, were playing games on the St. Moritz ice as early as 1890.

1894-95 is an important date in hockey origin stories in Europe. 1894 is the date of the magical Meagher trip, and 1895 is the year that is claimed to be when Lord Stanley's sons returned to England, and brought the Canadian game with them. Do you find it odd that no one prior to 1895 decided to bring Canadian hockey to England, either as a test game or at least let them know what was going on? How many Canadians must have been traveling to England

---

[93] Swiss hockey information found at
,https://web.archive.org/web/20020320214131/http://www.ouihc.org/historybeg.asp and
https://internationalhockey.fandom.com/wiki/Early_Swiss_Hockey

85

between 1875-1895? How many British business people and merchants must have been doing the same? None of them mentioned this new growing sport of hockey that was supposed to be taking over Eastern Canada at that time? Some young sports enthusiast should have wanted to try out the new game. Lacrosse exhibition matches has been staged to huge crowds in the 1870s all through England. Why did no one want to do the same for hockey? There are lot of people that like to make a buck, and the chance to be the first to show off the new game and make some money should have been in several people's minds in the 1880s. Why does it take George Meagher in 1894 (the same year) to come to Continental Europe, and by magic just have a bunch of hockey sticks with him? Something again just appears to be an attempted misdirection with these dates and events with the hope that no one will think and ask questions. I'm asking.

With the state of the hockey in the world presented, there is one other element of the time frame that needs to be properly examined. How much are the Native tribes of Canada associated with the true origin of hockey? What detail does their oral and mythological history, specifically for the Mi'kmaqs of Nova Scotia, about ball-and-stick games played on ice provide?

4

A NATIVE CEREMONY
Mi'kmaq Ice Games

"For many years, present day NS was part of the Milkmaid, the land of the Mi'kmaq. People have lived here for at least ten thousand years. Nevertheless, most history books only focus on the last four hundred of them. This seemingly arbitrary choice proceeds from an initial error: when Europeans landed on these shores, they fancied themselves occupiers of a virtually uninhabited land."[94] (Ian McKay)

"The invaders also anticipated, correctly, that the Europeans would question the morality of their enterprise. They therefore prepared quantities of propaganda to overpower their own countryman's scruples. The propaganda generally took standard form of an ideology with conventional assumptions and semantics. We live with it still."[95](Francis Jennings)

Standard history likes to present that real history did not start in North America until the arrival of the colonists. Yes, of course, there were Native Peoples all over North America, but they were mostly a nuisance and in the way of the Europeans and the great wonderful

---

[94]McKay, Ian *In the Province* p 22

[95]Lowewen, James *Lies My Teacher* p 93

expansion (take over of the continent) they wanted. The Europeans became the winners of North America, and the winners write history, always in their own favour. This required an altering of history, in an attempt to lessen the true impact of the culture that had been living in North American for tens of thousands of years. One that had built pyramids, mounds, and come up with universal types of transport. Most likely, the Iroquois tribal council was the model for the structure of the American government, and was the culture that invented some of the most important sports in history. Historians began to give the word "settler" to the Europeans. Actually, it should be the Native Peoples who were the ones who "settled" in North America, and the newcomers are better labeled "invading colonials." The Aboriginal population were a vast civilization, perhaps 10 million or more. Most would be killed, while tens of thousands were sold into slavery. Moving the Natives onto reservations came much later.[96]

An entire culture and its ideals were nearly wiped out; children were even beaten for speaking their Native language. That anything of North American Native culture survived to this day is a miracle. Medicine man Bruce Starlight of the Tsuut'ina tribe, who I spent time with, told me, "What we have now (healing and knowledge) is but a fraction of what we use to have." Another medicine man, Dennis McKay, after noticing he was doing some exercises with his feet, I asked him about them. First, he asked how I knew what they were. Once he understood my Qi Gong background, he told me, "there are many things I will share with you, but there are some things we cannot share with white people. They have stolen most everything we once had. This is one of the last things of our culture still has."

I contend that hockey is another one of those things that were stolen.

*

Cultural Games

> *"Sports were very important in Indian culture, and at times took up parts of their day, but it must be kept in*

[96]Lowewen, James *Lies My Teacher* chapter 4

context with their culture, not ours."[97] (Joseph B. Oxendine)

This section is going to look at the various views of the Native Tribes towards sports, their ceremonial aspects, and some of the myths and legends associated with them. Ice games will end this chapter. First will be an overview of the field games such as lacrosse and stickball as the understanding around them will apply to their "hockey" games.

One of the best books written on the understanding of the Native views towards sports is the 1988 book *American Indian Sports Heritage*, by Joseph B Oxendine. That book will be a key research tool for this chapter, along with the 1907 book *Games of the North American Indians* by Stewart Culin, as well as various art paintings by George Catlin. Catlin traveled among numerous tribes on the plains for eight years in the 1830s, and published his travels in 1841.

First, as always, we should look a bit at the three men who are going to form the basis of this chapter's research. Joseph B. Oxendine was the chancellor of Pembroke State University and the University of North Carolina at Pembroke from 1989-1999. Oxendine was a native born of the Lumbee Tribe of North Carolina. He moved to Detroit at age 17 to make money for university by working in an automobile factory. He then attended Catawba College and played many sports, including three years in the minor league baseball system of the Pittsburgh Pirates (batting over .330 in his final season). He received a PhD from Boston University in 1953. He played an integral role in intercollegiate sports as a professor at Temple University as well as while president of the Indian Rights Association.[98]

The second source comes from the 1907 book by Stewart Culin, who spent over ten years traveling around the Western part of the USA documenting the games being played. Born in Philadelphia, Culin became interested in the Chinese culture. Somehow he got himself a job (one of the few salaried staff) at the Penn Museum as an

---

[97] Joseph B Oxendine, *American Indian Sports Heritage* p xiii

[98] https://www.uncp.edu/news/uncp-mourns-loss-former-chancellor-dr-joseph-b-oxendine

anthropologist (though he had no education in that field), and by 1890 was appointed Secretary of the Board, as well as Curator of the Asian Section. In 1892, he became Curator of the General Ethnology and American sections. He became assistant curator of historical exhibits for the 1893 Colombian Exposition in Chicago. For me that is a red flag, as everything I have studied about these Fairs is now up for question, as well as everyone's involvement in them. Culin took as his anthropological focus: games, and his first book on the subject was about Korean games in 1895. [99]

George Catlin also has a very unique life. He was born in Wilkes-Barre in 1796. His mother, Polly, was captured by the Iroquois at the 1778 Battle of Wyoming in Pennsylvania. Supposedly, the tales she told of her time with them inspired George (along with the stories of various trappers and explorers) and made him want to go west. Though first, he became (you guessed it) a lawyer and practiced for two years before dropping his career and going west to be an artist and record on canvas the Native Americans as they were. He made numerous trips around 1830, visiting with almost fifty tribes, including many who up until that time had experienced very little contact with Europeans. After creating his artwork, the then traveled all around the US and Europe with his paintings. His entire body of work is now part of the Smithsonian American Art Museum's collection. Interestingly, he became a key researcher of the period on the Native technique of nasal breathing, as opposed to mouth breathing. He wrote a book on the subject *Shut Your Mouth and Save Your Life* in 1862. It has many similarities to the ideas of Taoist Qi Gong. He claimed that the Natives "believed that mouth breathing made an individual weak and caused disease, while nasal breathing made the body strong and prevented disease."[100]

---

[99]Information from Alessandro Pezzati, "Stewart Culin and the Study of Games," *Expedition Magazine 58.1 (2016): n. pag. Expedition Magazine. Penn Museum, 2016 Web. 29 Apr 2023 https://www.penn.museum/sites/expedition/stewart-culin-and-the-study-of-games/*

[100]https://en.wikipedia.org/wiki/George_Catlin

Illustration 17: Ball Players (George Catlin, Smithsonian American Art Museum, 1966.48.68)

When it comes to Native sports, it is important to know that there were games for children, games for adults, and larger events that were for community ceremonial purposes. Both men and women competed in the sports, but with different expectations. Partially, sports were used to benefit the health and fitness of the mind, body and spirit of both the participants and the community as a whole. Their sports, while not having what could be called "standardized rules," did have expectations of sportsmanship and fair play, and that art and beauty should be expressed in the game. Just because fair play was a key part of the sports attitude does not mean that the games were gentle. They would be hotly contested affairs and could have rough play (that generally the few referee medicine men let the players take care of themselves). In fact, Oxendine suggests, "if not for a great sense of sportsmanship and individual responsibility, the games could have easily deteriorated into chaos."[101] Johnathon Carver

---

[101]Oxendine p.3-4, 16

91

discussed Chippewa lacrosse games in 1796, "They play with so much vehemence that they frequently wound each other, and sometimes a bone is broken, but notwithstanding, these accidents there never appears to be any spite or wanton exertions of strength to affect them, nor do any disputes ever happen between the parties."[102] The games were partially as much a test of physical prowess of the contestants, as a test of their courage.

The referees of most games tended to be elders, seen as impartial, and who often spent several hours prior to the game in prayer for wisdom and fair judgment. George B Elden described a game of shinny among the Dakotas in 1871 and said, "no one thinks of disputing the judges' decision, and there is no appeal." With so many players participating, and very few officials, the players took it on themselves to assure the play was fair. This is the opposite of modern professional sports where the players feel it is up to the referee to control them from all ways of cheating they would partake in if "allowed" the freedom.[103]

Some games were to bring rain, heal a person or community, encourage crops to grow, or to send prayers to the Spirit. Players felt there was a spiritual connection in a victory, which brought a gift from the gods and pushed away evil spirits, thus players while friendly and fair with each other, took the winning of the game seriously. Most of the games had sacred elements to them. While a few were there as simple contests, most were ceremonial at least to begin with. In time though, as Black Elk described, "there are only a few of us today who still understand why the game is sacred, or what the game originally was long ago, when it was not really a game, but one of our most important rites."[104]

The games were not standardized, but could be adjusted depending on the number of players available, the size of the field used, or what would be needed to determine a win. Europe wanted documented specific rules to be used all the time, while the Natives

---

[102]Oxendine p 17
[103]Oxendine p 17-18
[104]Oxendine p5

were willing to adjust any game as was called for at the time of its playing. If instead of 50 players there were 100, then you would just double the size of the field. There were no coaches, nor even really "leaders," but more like a particular player who would take a responsibility for the team, acting as a type of team spokesman. Things were open and flowing for the players, "the hard dictatorial leader is a western invention, and a type of war controller."[105] The game was also art, and as such, decorative costume and paints were used by the players.

While winning was considered to be important, how great the margin of the win was not. A 1-0 win was the same to them as an 11-5 win, thus there was no need to compile records, keep track of who did what, or who scored the most goals in a game or career. Allen Guttman in 1978 claimed that record keeping in sports seems to have had its beginning with the Romans who kept a "numeration of achievements, detailed records of chariot races and other sporting events. In contrast, the Ancient Greeks, despite their creation and promotion of the original Olympic Games, were as indifferent to record keeping as were the American Indians."[106] Record keeping only came to North America with the colonial invaders.

While there were many types of games and contests in Native society, the main ones seem to be team games (lacrosse, shinny, double ball, stickball, and longball). We can use lacrosse and George Beers as an example as to what was done to appropriate Native sports. Although Beers never disputed the Native origin, he was presented as the father of lacrosse for putting the sport into the box of British ideology. Thus to Beers, "real (recorded) history began with the adoption of the game by white players in the 1850s."[107] Of course, what was really being done was to erase the long, long Native history of lacrosse from the minds of white people, who began to see the sport as starting in 1850, having "evolved" from old pastimes. This is the structure that will be followed for all other sports like baseball, football and hockey.

*

---

[105]Oxendine 27

[106]Oxendine p16

[107]Poulter p 269

93

Ceremonial Aspects

Much has been written about the various ceremonial elements of the game of lacrosse, which could also be called "the game for the Creator." One of the only key rules was that the hands could not touch the ball. However, there was always a ceremonial element to it; a specific reason for the game to be taking place. Jean De Brebeuf in 1636 wrote of how games of lacrosse might be used when a villager was sick and near death. If it was an entire village or area that was sick, then several villages might participate in a large game. Games could take place to settle disputes between villages (and thus avoid any real war), playing out the problem on the field (or ice).[108]

Prior to any game of ritual, there were several ceremonies that would take place. Medicine men and women would all have specific roles and duties for putting together not only the setup of the game, but the spiritual elements that would then become a part of the sport the participants would partake in.[109] Often it was suggested that the ceremonies before key stick-and-ball games were the same as those that happened before going to war. This is because the big team sports were not a game, pastime, or something fun to do, they were a component of a spiritual ceremony. To that end, players tended to decorate their bodies and sticks with paint and/or charcoal. As with any spiritual event, there were specific food requirements or fasting that would occur. Several rituals would often take place before the game could commence. One of those was that most everyone (participants and spectators) would make some form of wager (items such as knives, or horses, or personal items). This wager was not seen as gambling to Western eyes (as a way of betting to earn something) but instead I believe as a way to have each non-participant inject something of themselves into the contest, and as such, keep their energy and attention for the ceremony at a high level.

The sacred meaning behind any Native stick-and-ball game was not understood by the colonists, who saw it only in terms of recreation or tests of physicality and manhood. Gillian Poulter commented,

---

[108]Oxendine 6

[109] see Oxendine pgs11-13 for details

"Given these functions (ceremony), it is significant that whites would want to take this symbolic ritual over for themselves. British colonists saw themselves in the role of national leaders, and one of the prime purposes of playing lacrosse and other indigenous sports was in order to influence the representation of the Canadian climate and environment abroad. Of course, it would have been unthinkable for respectable Victorian Canadians to play a game tainted by pagan associations, hence the disavowals. In effect, the erasure of the game's religious functions by the colonists was an aggressive act of possession and secularization, because Native people were affected by the changes made to their ritual and its cultural meaning. Playing lacrosse against white teams was a form of employment for talented Native men, but it necessitated playing by white rules and this broke the bond between the ritual and its sacred meaning...Over time, then, Native players were forced to accept the Western game and consequently lost touch with the sacred ritual meanings of baggataway. This de-culturation of the game had deleterious effects on Native society...and the very game vanished."[110]

*

Native Stick Games

Here I will describe a few of the key stick-and-ball games of the Natives (not including lacrosse) before a more detailed explanation of the field-ice sport called "shinny" in English cultures. It is shinny that will be the foundation of what we know of as hockey today.

One game was called stickball, which can still be observed in the Midwest and the Southeastern U.S. The Chocktaw Natives called

---

[110]Poulter p 272

this game "Little Brother of War," and it was, at times, considered to be more violent than lacrosse. In this sport, it seems that players held two sticks (one in each hand), which could be called smaller versions of lacrosse sticks. One of the sticks was for catching the ball, while the other was for throwing and carrying. Posts were placed on either side of the field, and the goal of the game was to hit the post with the thrown ball, or touch the stick with the ball in it against the post.[111]

Then there was the sport known as longball, in which a leather ball was hit by a long slender wooden bat, very similar to baseball. What is unique about the Native game is that the ball is not thrown "to" a batter, but rather it is thrown up in the air where it is meant to be hit when falling back to the ground, which makes it similar to the game of Pasepo in Finland. I very much wonder if the Finnish game had its origins long back in the past and not the in 1920s as suggested. As for the Native longball game, it gets a standard explanation that prior to the white's arrival they had a very "simple" stick ball hitting game, and then "borrowed" new ideas from the white settlers when they saw their baseball games in the early 1800s. Few are willing to realize that the evolution of baseball likely went the other way, in which white colonists took a Native game like longball, and then made a few adjustments for their own game. If you look for it, you will see this happening repeatedly with just about any of the modern sports.

Here is a simplified rule explanation from an article I found on the native game. A line is drawn across the playing field, with a base at the starting point for the hitter. Two lines making a V are sent out from there, which set up the hitting boundary. Equal teams are chosen, with nine players being preferred. The first side to score 21 points wins (as early baseball games often had 21 as their end point). Teams have only three batters, the others are runners. One must run when the ball is hit to the far end point of the first line drawn, and back to the main base. A caught ball is an out, and the teams then change sides. Again similar to early baseball. The runners are either out when being hit by a thrown ball, or touched by it if they are closer. The run that has to be made is a long one, so there is much

____

[111]   https://www.montessoriphysicaleducation.com/new-blog/native-american-sports-shinny-lacrosse-and-stickball2019/4/24

excitement as runners try to avoid batted balls being thrown at them by the fielders.[112]

Eastern tribes had a sport very similar to European soccer, however, the whites held themselves superior to them. William Wood in 1634 claimed, "One white person could beat 10 Indians." Meanwhile on the West Coast, there were games more similar to American Football. Culin describes a game from the Nishinam Natives of California in which a ball twelve inches in diameter was used, players were allowed to run with the ball in their hands (very unique for any ball sport), and rough play along with interference (what we would call blocking) was permissible. What is most unique for me is that there is no way someone could say that this sport was somehow the natives copying the British early rugby games. California was mostly under Spanish control until the mid- 1840s, and even by the 1890s when Culin was traveling, many areas would have rarely even been visited by the English whites. This was a traditional game-almost like modern American Football, which had gone back centuries.[113]

*

Shinny

> "Shinny was strikingly similar to modern field hockey and ice hockey, and may have been the forerunner of both of those games."[114] (Joseph B. Oxendine)

> "*Shinny was practically universal among tribes throughout the United States.*"[115] (Stewart Culin)

I will now discuss the specific stick-and-ball game most similar to hockey, which is now referred to as shinny. This is not the same word as taken today to mean kids on an outdoor sheet of ice playing hockey without organized rules. This is a term used for similar Native

---

[112] https://www.onondaganation.org/culture/sports/longball/

[113] Oxendine 61, 62, Culin 703

[114] Oxendine p54

[115] Culin p 616

97

games, most of which were played by women. It would be interesting to see how many men today would feel about their sport if they knew in Native tradition that it was mainly a feminine activity. Some tribes though had young men playing it as well, such as the Oglala Sioux, in which Walker in 1905 called it "their roughest and most athletic game." The difference between lacrosse and shinny is that it does not seem that shinny had as much ceremony attached to it.[116] That may be true, that lacrosse was more of a ceremonial and healing game, but on examination of the number of myths that link to shinny, it might be a sport that is more played to somehow invoke a myth or you might say, energize a location with the very elements of the origin of creation.

Illustration 18: Lacrosse on Ice, 1859 Edmund C. Coates (Yale University Art Gallery, ID 6261)

---

[116]The bulk of this research can be found in Culin and Oxendine (pages 50-61)

In 1612, William Strachey wrote that the Native People around Jamestown, Virginia were playing a similar stick-and-ball game as in England, "A kynd of exercise they have often amongst them much like that which boyes call bandy in English, and maue be an auncient game."[117] He also suggested that Powhatan's favourite wife, Winganuskie, and the Princess Pocahontas played during the winter. The key phrase is Strachey describing that the Native game might be "ancient." Why exactly would he make that distinction, as he says it is similar to bandy but not the same. Either something about what the Natives were doing, or how the game was structured, indicated to him not just that it was not only different from what was being played in England, but somehow linked to a much more ancient time.

In 1832, *The Eaton College Magazine* (for the boys-only boarding school) published an article "On Eaton Games," which discussed the playing of foot-ball and hockey. Of hockey, it claimed, "Hockey we believe to be a very old and indigenous game, never heard of beyond the channel, and almost forgotten even in England..."[118] This small passage opens up a number of questions. Again is the suggestion that the sport is believed to be an ancient one, as well as that it had an indigenous origins. Who are these indigenous early people of the British Isles that the article is referring to? Celts? Druids? Someone else?

The article then makes two odd statements; the first stating that hockey was never heard of beyond the channel. This must mean the English Channel. How would the writer know if the game exists in the Americas, or Africa or Eastern Europe in the 1830s? Secondly, it makes another key point, that the game is "almost forgotten even in England." Most will miss the first part of this is statement. The second part is that it seems almost forgotten in England, even though we are presented with several articles and drawings from pre-1832 that had the words hockey, bandy or hurley in them. How is it thus forgotten if people seem to be playing it? The other part of that statement is that by writing the phrase "forgotten even in England," indicates that the sport is also forgotten in many places of the world as well. How many places? How long has it been forgotten? On the other hand, maybe it

---

[117]Houda p 228, I looked through the original text of Strachey (all handwritten) and was unable to locate it for further examination of what else was being written about the sport.
[118]Houda pg 98

99

is not so much the game itself that is forgotten, but something else. Games of hockey might still be going on, but the reasons behind it, the ceremonial or religious aspects of what the sport was and why it was played, are what might be claimed to be forgotten.

Why the name shinny was given by anthropological researchers to various Native field hockey games is not known. There is no such word in any of the Native languages. Each tribe has its own word. The Chumash call the tikauwich for the Chumash, while the Cheyenne call it ohonistus, and gugahawat is used by the Arapaho. One website makes the very unique presentation that many of the early Native sticks that have been discovered resemble (by just coincidence to the writer) "golf clubs, hockey sticks, shinty sticks, hurling sticks, shepherds' crooks, and spears."[119] Of course, it is just by "co-incidence" that the sticks look the same as those used in Europe at the same time. The Natives cannot possibly have influenced anything in Europe. That is the standard historical narrative that is not supposed to be questioned. Except here in this book.

What has been left to us about these shinny games is that they were played on a field, between two teams, using a ball (made of buckskin, wood or bone) with curved sticks (though in the photos from Culin's book you will already notice that it is much more of a flat ended bottom as opposed to the curve-like cane sticks of England). What we call a modern hockey stick is far more closely adapted from Native sticks than from Europe. This stick examination will become important. One other interesting point is that often the sticks were brightly painted and marked by the owner, thus very much personifying the player by the stick itself.

One unique element of the Native sport was that games were often first begun not with a standard "face off," but by the referee (medicine man) digging a hole in the center of the field and placing the ball in it, on which players would attempt to dig it out with their sticks.[120] This gives much more symbolism of the game itself coming "out of the earth," or directly connected with the earth in some way.

---

[119] https://healthahoy.com/ancient-sports/native-american-shinny-hockey/
[120] Oxendine 42-43

Other referees might throw the ball high in the air to begin the game, and have the players go and chase it. The game was organized so that some players defended the goal, others played in the middle, while others tried to score. It was a player setup similar to modern soccer.

In Northern areas, these games were transferred to ice in the winter, sometimes on foot, and other times on bone skates. A few interesting observations are made in an online article by James Dylan Laverance. He presented that the Kiowa used rib-bone skates and the Lakota used buffalo-bone skates, while the Nova Scotia Mi'kmaq tied jawbones to their moccasins to play the game in the late 1690's. Also interesting, was his suggestion that the lake at the bottom of Mount Rushmore was used by the Natives for sport, indicating that what is now a giant tourist attraction was previously a sacred site for shinny games. There are several suggestions that the current presidents' heads at Mount Rushmore were really "re-carved" from earlier Native carvings of some of the great chiefs or gods.[121]

*

Native shinny specifics

Culin's 1907 book is a good overview of all Native stick-and-ball games, including shiny. He has drawings of over 100 sticks that exist in museums all over North America, which just for that alone makes it is an interesting book for this research. He describes the various games of many tribes, as well as a few of the myths that go along with the games. I will share a few of them with you here to get an overview of the spiritual aspect that could be behind what we know today as hockey.

A. W. Chase in "Overland Monthly" in 1869 vol. 2 issue 5 (May) p 433 wrote, "One of the National games is extremely interesting. It is generally played by rival tribes and is identical with that in vogue amongst our school-boys called 'hookey.' Sides being chosen, each endeavors to drive a hard ball of pine wood around a stake and in different directions. Stripped to the buff, they display great activity and strength, whacking away at each other's shins if they

---

[121] https://jamesdylanlaverance.wordpress.com/2015/05/14/ice-hockey-begins-to-take-shape-2/

101

are in a way with a refreshing disregard of bruises. The squaws assist in the performance by beating drums and keeping up a monotonous chant."[122]

George A. Dorsey in *Wichita Tales* explains their tribe's myth of how the first man, Darkness, who began to get power to foretell things after the creation of people, told a woman Watsikatsia (made after his image) a story. He said that when a certain being, Man-Never-Known-on-Earth, reached down his left side with his right hand, he brought up a ball. Then he reached down with his left hand at his right side and brought up a belt. Then he reached down in front, touched the ball to the belt, and brought up a shinny stick. He took the ball, tossed it up, and struck it with the stick. As the ball flew, Darkness went with it. Thus guided, he went to the place where he expected to find Man-- the object of his visit was that power be given him so that there should be light on the face of the earth. He tossed and struck the ball again, but not arriving at the place, he knew he could not depend upon the ball, and so took his bow and arrow and shot an arrow and flew with it."

The myth says that he shot four arrows, and then ran 12 times when he eventually arrived at a village where he began the first game of shinny. "The crowd came and he told them they were to have such a game as shinny ball. He showed the people (how to use the ball and stick) then commanded the people to gather outside the village at about evening time, and then he set the time of play. They went as he told them. When they were all there, he tossed the ball towards the north and traveled with it. It went a long ways, and where it landed would be the goal. Then he struck it back with the stick to the south, and where it landed would be the other goal. Then he divided the men into two parties, and placed one at each goal. Between these two parties and in the center of the field he placed two men, one from each of the parties. He gave one man the ball and told him to toss it up. As the ball was tossed he told the other man to strike it towards the south....now they played, and the north side drove the ball to the south goal and won. Then they changed goals and the other side won. Then Darkness said they had played enough." Another Wachita story explains how the first shinny ball and sticks were given to the people

---

[122]Culin 623-24

by the first man Having-Power-to-Carry-Light, and taught that young boys should get a ball just after they are born, to observe it and watch it roll around.[123]

This is another myth, again related to the Navajo. I find it interesting that there are so many myths about the origins of Shinny from Tribes in the American Southwest. In this myth "a stranger challenged a Navajo god to a game of shinny in order to free Navajo slaves. Free men and slaves lined up and an agreement was made, the terms of which was as follows. If the Navajo god won, the free men would become slaves, but if the slaves won, the slaves would be free. Then a bird came to the stranger and said that if he were to hit the ball lightly the bird would take the ball across the line (commonly known as a goal). The god went first and hit the ball as hard as he could. It did not make it to the line, so the stranger went next and hit the ball lightly. The bird then took the ball and flew across the line. The slaves were then free men and hopped across the line to greet their relatives." Similar stories can be found in Culin's Book, especially the myths of the Tewa and Yuma tribes of New Mexico[124]

*

Mi'kmaq

An excellent source to look into how the Mi'kmaq viewed this world, and their relationship to it, can be found in Trudy Sable and Bernie Francis' 2012 book *The Language of This Land, Mi'kma'ki.* The book shows the Mi'kmaq's entire way of being to "mirror and express their unique relationship they have with the landscape they they call Mi'kma'ki. As an example, let's take a look at a conversation between a Mi'kmaq elder and French missionary Chestien Le Clereq in the 1670s. Upon learning how the French wanted to set up one permanent location in which to live, the elder responded, "...an Indian could find his living everywhere, and that he could call himself the seigneur and the sovereign of his country, because he could reside there just as freely as it please him with every kind of rights of hunting and fishing, without any anxiety, more content than a thousand times in the woods and in his wigwam."[125] It is important to keep this in

---

[123]Culin 626-27,

[124] https://www.hokejovysen.cz/en/ipha/history/, Cullin 627-644 for other myths

[125]Trudy Sable and Bernie Francis *The Language* pgs 17-18

mind that the Native populations of Canada had a completely different belief structure about just about everything as compared to the colonists: where to live, how to live, ideas of ownership, ideas of nature, ideas of religion and mythology, and ideas surrounding the use of games and sport.

I can now somewhat certainly say that hockey likely is a Canadian invention, and had nothing to do with British colonialists James Creighton or Lord Stanley. It was a sacred ceremonial game of "shinny" played in a unique way by one group of natives, the Mi'kmaqs of Nova Scotia. While the area around Windsor, Nova Scotia now gets all the attention, I do not think that is the only place this game was being played. The Mi'kmaq people lived all along the East Coast of the Canada and the USA, all the way through Maine and Massachusetts. In each area, local Mi'kmaq peoples were playing their own version of the unique ice game. In various areas, new colonists saw the game, and often adapted it, altered it or played it as is. This could be why slightly different versions of the sport (hockey, ice polo, a form of bandy) were developed in different areas of the East Coast. That is because each Mi'kmaq tribe played its own unique, slightly modified version. It is just the one from Nova Scotia that happened to become the chosen game to become Canada's national sport. It is even hard to know what trees were used to make the hockey sticks of the various Mi'kmaq tribes as different sources claim the sticks were made from different trees: hornbeam, spruce roots, and darkened yellow birch.[126]

The 1894 book *Legends of the Micmacs* made a clear distinction between the hurley played by the settlers (called Alchamadajk by the Natives), and the winter game they played which the Micmacs called Oochamkunutk. The colonists sometimes joined the Native games, while at times the Mi'kmaqs joined the colonists' game. The Indians often wore only moccasins on the ice, but were still faster than the settlers on their skates. Thus, there was a distinction between the winter games in the early stages of

---

[126] Paul W Bennett "Re-Imagining the Creation:"

colonization, but not between the races of the participants as they played together in relative harmony.[127]

A Mi'kmaq elder, Dr. Jerry Lonecloud described on October 8, 1913, a traditional Mi'kmaq game called Duwarken, played on the ice. Lonecloud recounted that Duwarken was played with "a round stone was hit on the ice" by a stick, most likely "a spruce root" which was called "Duwarkenaught." The stone ball was hit by a striker, causing the round stone to roll along the ice, which was then chased down by other players. The other players tried to interfere with the stone carrier and take it from him before it was returned to the striker. The player who returned it safely was permitted to hit the ball next.[128] This of course does not sound much like the current game of hockey we know now, only that he is describing a ball and stick game played on the ice.

Joe Cope of the Millbrook Indian Reserve sent a letter in 1943 to Halifax newspapers discussing how the Mi'kmaq had long been playing hockey prior to the white's arrival.[129] There is a red flag for me though in Cope's letter, and that is how he ends it by saying that he remembers seeing Col. Weston playing games with the Natives. 1943 is a very significant year in hockey origin examinations. That is because it was the first push back from other parts of Canada on the "Kingston is the birthplace of hockey" message. EM Orlick had published his articles in the Montreal Gazette in September, and then shortly after came the Nova Scotia interview with Weston about his remembering of "Halifax Rules." Joe Cope's letter seems to be a response to the Weston article. What I had hoped would be in the Cope letter would have been some discussion about these "so-called rules." Could he recall whether they did exist when he was young, or whether the rules were something that Weston was making up? Of course all of these interviews in the 1940s are up for question, given we do not know the real reason behind their presentation.

---

[127] Fitsell, *Hockey's Captains* pp.24, 26; Vaughan *Puck Starts* p.21, 29,

[128] Found in *Henry Piers Ethnology Papers* and reference in Paul Bennett p7

[129] http://www.backsportspage.com/the-forgotten-indigenous-roots-of-hockey/ ,https://boomer649.wordpress.com/at-last-joe-copes-full-letter/. https://acadiensis.wordpress.com/2019/01/18/reimagining-the-creation-the-missing-indigenous-link-in-the-origins-of-canadian-hockey/,

The best information I found on Joe Cope comes from a prospecting website, and like all the people in this story, he has a very unique story. When he died at age 91 in 1951, the *Chronicle-Herald* called him, "one of Nova Scotia's best-known citizens" It seems he prospected for various metals all over the province, and discovered tungsten in 1918. Cope is also claimed to be the first Mi'kmaq who was a photographer by profession, taking many portraits of local Natives.[130]

Another important piece of evidence of the Mi'kmaq origin comes from a paragraph in a 1948 book *Halifax: Warden of the North*, written by Tomas Raddell. The book indicates that the Mi'kmaqs were playing ice games, perhaps in the area called Tuft's Cove near Halifax. He wrote, "*It is a fact little known in Canada, but a fact none the less, that ice hockey, Canada's national game, began on the Dartmouth lakes in the eighteenth century. Here the garrison officers found the Indians playing a primitive form of hurley on the ice, adopted and adapted it, and later put the game on skates. When they transferred to military posts along the St. Lawrence and the Great Lakes they took the game with them and for some time afterwards continued to send to the Dartmouth Indians for necessary sticks.*"[131] A. D. Fisher wrote a letter to Raddell in 1954 after reading the book to ask for more detail on his sources of Nova Scotia Mi'kmaqs being the originators of hockey. Raddell responded, "In my research for the Halifax book, I came across several references to hockey played on the ice in the latter 18 and early 19th centuries. These references were in letters and newspapers, but I did not make exact note of the sources because the point did not seem of historical value, and I invariably came across them in looking for something else."[132] He did provide a few known sources, such as the 1894 Rand Book *Legends of the Micmacs* and the 1943 Joe Cope article. Cheryl Maloney, who made a documentary about the Mi'kmaq hockey story, suggested she found evidence of a mention in a 1749 British military

---

[130] https://notyourgrandfathersmining.ca/prospector-joe-cope

[131] Raddell, *Halifax* p 264

[132] https://findingaids.library.dal.ca/uploads/r/dalhousie-university-archives/1/2/b/12b726faf0d0ec779a877f1e063de7b67a4d96a5c0370a5373212fa4ea1dde88/MS-2-202_41_14_access.pdf

diary of the combination of British shinny with the Mi'kmaq ice game.[133]

I now get the sense that there are two key features when defining if there is an ice hockey game going on (obviously, beyond the ice and skates). One is the flat disk object. As long as a ball is used, it is not hockey, as a ball requires a different kind of stick to hit it with, such as the more cane-like objects seen in British images. The flat puck object requires a more flat-bladed stick. To test the game played, we can look closely at the sticks used. We have no early pucks from the Mi'kmaq, but several times tribal historians have suggested their use in ancient times. This was discussed by Gerald Gloade in Cheryl Maloney's documentary, that the puck was cut from a spruce tree (due to the hardness of the tree resin), just above and below a branch wall to make it very strong.[134] Another reference I remember reading in an old hockey book from the 1980s was that the Mi'kmaq puck was made out of black cherry wood so as to stand out on the ice. I have no specific reference for that, only my memory.

The most important element is the stick. That is because the Mi'kmaq were the only hockey stick makers in Canada for some time. An image of the Mi'kmaq making sticks can be found at[135] , and clearly shows that they were making "modern-like"sticks, similar to our current stick- longer and bigger and with a more flat blade, compared to the English hurley sticks. The English sticks are only good for striking a ball, not for moving a flat disk on the ice. These type of sticks appear with Native tribes in North America, though as show in chapter three, such a stick did appear in the *Boy's Book*.[136] This can be inferred in the images of English ice sports prior to 1875, all of the players are seen "whacking" at the object on the ice, which is the way you propel a ball. Doing this with a puck is futile. However there is evidence that cork bungs, a type of puck were used in England. Why did more flat-bladed sticks not develop to help propel that unique object on the ice? You can see the photo in chapter eight of the Barrie Women's Hockey Team of 1889, to see that all of those

---

[133]Cheryl and April Maloney *The Game of Hockey- A Mi'kmaw Story documentary*

[134]Cheryl and April Maloney *The Game of Hockey- A Mi'kmaw Story documentary*

[135] https://en.wikipedia.org/wiki/Mic-Mac_hockey_stick#/media/File:Mikmac-hockey-sticks.jpg

[136] https://boomer649.wordpress.com/2021/12/04/762/

107

players are using what would we would call a "modern" stick. If one of the first women's teams were using these sticks in Barrie, Ontario-why would the top men's teams in the country all not be using the longer, flat bladed sticks in their games?

Most historians try to present that the modern stick must have evolved from hurley, shinty or field hockey sticks. It is supposed to be an English sport, so the sticks as well must have evolved to prove its origin. The problem is, if the British invented the sticks, and could make the sticks, why did they need the Mi'kmaqs to make the sticks for many decades? In fact, it was only when a new two-piece stick was invented after 1900 (which was much easier to manufacture) that the Mi'kmaq stick business finally went under. The British wanted the Mi'kmaq sticks because they were better than their own.[137]

*

Glooscap

The Mi'kmaq have their own myth of shinny-hockey, and that is one of the myths of the great hero, Glooscap (who will be discussed in the final chapter). This myth[138] is connected to a wizard named Winpe. However, in Emelyn Partridge's book *Glooscap the Great Chief,* he presents the same tale in "How Glooscap Conquered His Enemies." While most of the following tale is in this account, there is nothing about a ball-and-stick game, only that Glooscap made himself even larger than Winpe the giant, and as such, the giant gave up. I am looking for an original source for the ball game, though it is one of the parts of the story that originally might have stayed fully in the oral tradition, and kept away from early white chroniclers.

"Winpe was a powerful giant, cheerful but quick-tempered, who delighted in games and tests of magic." However, when he heard of Glooscap's wizard like prowess, Winpe challenged him. Originally, Glooscap informed him that his focus was caring for his people and

---

[137] More stick information can be found at hockeystars
'https://boomer649.wordpress.com/2021/12/04/762/

[138] Found at Indigenous Peoples' Literature Return to Indigenous Peoples' Literature Compiled by: Glenn Welker https://www.indigenouspeople.net/winpe.htm

as such did not have the time for games. Therefore, Winpe stole his (Grandmother) Noogumee and friend Marten in a canoe. Glooscap chased after them." The Hermetic number three appears many times in this story related to such things as the chaining of dogs, or days of paddling canoes. This Hermetic number indicates that secret knowledge is placed in the story.

After a long journey to reach Winpe, a contest was set up, with "three"challenges that, if Glooscap could win, would get his friends back. For the final of the challenges Winpe, "brought forth two long sticks with webbing at the ends, and gave one of them to Glooscap together with a stuffed moose hide ball. This is a game I call tokhonon. As you see, I have set up two posts at each end of my cave. We must strike the ball back and forth, never touching it with our hands, and who ever first drives it between the other's goal posts, wins!" Glooscap nodded his understanding, and the match began." They played for three days, and when thinking of his people back home, Glooscap was given new energy, enough to hit the ball with enough force to drive it through Winpe's goal. Winpe acknowledged that Glooscap was the winner of the game, and asked him to choose his winning prize. Glooscap asked for the stick and the game, and as such brought back the tokhonon stick and game back to the Mi'kmaq people.

Granted, this myth is not a story of hockey, but lacrosse, it reveals a Mi'kmaq tale of their ball sport origins. As I mentioned, though, I have been unable to find an original source material, but that does not mean it hasn't survived in oral tradition. Perhaps even being hidden from the white researchers. It could also have been the early white researchers who might have taken the myth "out of circulation" in order to not have Canadians believe that there could be any connection between the "new" 1875 game in Montreal and that of the Mi'kmaq.

I leave one more presentation of the ceremonial aspects to the various Native games. This comes from the information on the Maya ball game that is found in their sacred text the Popol Vuh "the lords of the underworld invited a mythical Mayan known as the First Father (Original celestial human) to a ball game. But the devious lords

109

withdrew their invitation and decapitated the First Father." [139] As such the Mayan game was linked to the first trauma humans suffered, which was entering this matrix reality for the first time. As such the ball game not only was presenting the story of the creation, but built into the game (and shown in the book Mayan Pyramids by Peter Tomkins) that the game itself was a teaching tool with how to exit this reality and return to our Original Homeland.

I will leave this examination now, but will come back to it in the final chapter, for there are some very co-incidental elements of the Mi'kmaqs (possible links to the Knights Templar and Ancient Egypt) that might indicate that whatever sports they played, though they were unique to North America, may have had their most ancient origins long away from North America.

---

[139] "Mayan Doomsday Prophecy" History channel, found in Anagnostou, Angeliki *Can you Stand the Truth* p68

5

IT'S A CARNIVAL
Montreal 1880's

Simple hockey continued in Montreal for the year 1876. Though they were still just games between fraternal friends at the Victoria Skating Rink. Three games are recorded as being played, on February 5 between Montreal HC and Victoria SC, on February 24 between Blues and Reds, and on March 29 between Montreal FC – McGill.[140]

The Montreal Gazette on February 7 1876 (discussing the game from the 5th) again lists all the players but now adds some positions (forwards, backs and half backs). What was important for me is that the article claimed that the game was *"conducted under the Hockey Association rules, Messrs W. Hutton President of the Rink, and Phillip Cross acting as umpires."* It is thus saying that the rules were in place in 1876, a year before they were published in *The Gazette* in 1877. This does not mean there was an association yet in Montreal, this could have been a reference to English field hockey, which did have an official association and rules that came out in 1875.[141] Interesting that two types of hockey were formed in both Canada and England in how in 1875. Just another of the many strange co-incidences out there with all of this. As any researcher knows, once or twice of something is a co-incidence. But after it becomes several, they become a plan.

The same 1876 *Gazette* game article also describes, *"A scramble, the puck is away and glides to the feet of two young*

---

[140]Found on SIHR website and the book *On the Origin of Hockey*
[141]EM Orlick "Origins of Hockey" *Montreal Gazette* September 15-18 1943

ladies..." The first instance of the block of wood called a "puck" in a Canadian newspaper.[142] And I wonder why the mention of the two young ladies in the comment? How does the puck slide between their feet, when the rink was surrounded by a plank of wood? This is indicating that the ladies had to be on the ice. Why would they be on the ice and not on the spectator side of the plank/boards? One of the new players to play in this game was Henry Abbot, whose father John was at the time a law professor at McGill and would later become the third Canadian Prime Minister.

*

1877

A lot will change in 1877, because for the first time a set of official rules will be published, However, they will just be the field hockey rules of 1875, mostly with the word "field" changed to "ice." The rules became a marker for EM Orlick in his series of four articles with the title "The Origin of Hockey"that he wrote for the *The Montreal Gazette* between September 15-18, 1943. He wrote at a time when Canada was attempting to find the "birthplace of hockey" to build its hall of fame, just as had been done four year's previous for baseball. That story (related in chapter seven) was how an obvious fake origin story of the sport surrounded Abner Doubleday, was seemingly happening in hockey. Col. James T. Sutherland was attempting to "pull a Doubleday" by making hockey' birthplace his home of Kingston, Ontario. Orlick's first article was written to present Montreal was the home of hockey by dismissing the other claimants, especially Kingston.

His second article disputed the claim of a Col. Weston from earlier in the year about something he claimed were "Halifax Rules," which were very different than what became the 1877 rules in Montreal. As mentioned, these Montreal rules were simply the adjusted field hockey rules of England, but that did not stop a number of former McGill rugby players later to claim that they had created ice hockey rules from rugby. The first of these claims began in 1908, that were still listed as true in several hockey books in the year 2000. This

---

[142] The research in *On the Origin of Hockey,* has revealed this term was used in England as far back as 1800.

story included three different McGill rugby players, each claiming that the three of them invented hockey and the rules in 1879. Those players were Dick Smith (who claimed to have created the rules to hockey in September 1878), FW Robertson (who claimed he watched field hockey games in England in 1879), and Chick Murray (who claimed to have combined lacrosse and rugby). This was supposed to be the reason there was no forward passing in Montreal hockey (as it had been adapted from rugby) by these three men. Orlick was clear that none of the three "rugby" players names are listed in any of the early *Montreal Gazette* player reports from the 1875-77 games, and that the rules for ice hockey were published in the *Montreal Gazette* in 1877, thus proving that the 1879 rugby claims were obviously false. So were these three men lying? Hard to say why three men would do that 50 years later, but there is nothing factual that can be proven for any of these men as having any connection to the origin of hockey, except as a self-created fable.

> *"With these refutations, the claims of Robertson, Smith and Murray, like those of the Kingston champions and the CAHA investigators- however sincere and well meaning they might have been- must be dismissed once and for all as figments of the imagination, or at the best, as conglomeration of historically incorrect statements."*[143] EM Orlick

But when you examine the 1877 rules closely (as historian Iain Fyffe did in his book and on his website[144] especially the field hockey and rugby offside rules), in hockey you could pass the puck forward, just that the player who would receive this forward pass had to begin behind the puck passer. The ice hockey offside rule is almost exactly the same as the recently published *Field Hockey Rules of England*. Fyffe claimed, "So you could pass the puck ahead of your winger, who could skate up to meet it. Indeed, in his 1899 book *Hockey: Canada' Royal Winter Game*, Art Farrell explained that this was the ideal method for making a pass."[145]

---

[143]*Montreal Gazette September 16, 1943*

[144]http://hockeyhistorysis.blogspot.com/search/label/Hockey%20origins(Iain Fyffe)

[145]Fitsell *Captains* .p 42,
https://mcgillathletics.ca/news/2015/5/22/MHOCKEY_0522155837.aspx?path=mhockey
and see the site http://hockeyhistorysis.blogspot.com/search/label/Hockey%20origins(Iain

The third article was to suggest a national committee be put together with participants from all relevant birthplace cities. The fourth article is by far Orlick's best. He goes on to list various elements of some of the newspaper articles he had found that related the early 1875-77 games in Montreal. He listed the already mentioned March 3 game from the *Gazette*, as well as several others. It was the start of digging into the true roots of early hockey.

McGill University played its first hockey game in 1877. A write up[146] can be found in the student paper "*The McGill Gazette*" regarding the second game (I bold the names that were found in the March 3 game):

> *"On Monday afternoon the 19th, the Hockey Club had their return match with the Montreal Club, which they had before beaten. The game began at 4.30, only six of the Montrealers being on the ice. These were* **Creighton** *(captain),* **Gough, Joseph,** *Kinghorn,* **C. Torrance and Esdaile.** *The College team were Abbott (captain),* **Campbell,** *Nelson, Redpath, F. Torrance, Howard, Caverhill and Dawson. After ten minutes of play, Kinghorn took a long shot at the goal, which bounced off one of the men's sticks and went over Campbell's Guard. First goal for the Montrealer's who were now reinforced by Geddes. The game soon recommenced, and from that time till the end of the match neither party secured any advantage.*
>
> *The Montrealers thus won by one to nothing. Although their captain had beforehand protested against any infringement of the rules, they began by playing "off side," their captain (Creighton) especially distinguishing himself. The play was very rough on both sides. For the College Campbell kept goal splendidly, stopping many very difficult ones. Abbott's pluck and skill gave a splendid example to his side. Of the rest, Redpath, Torrance and Dawson showed very*

Fyffe)

[146] *McGill Gazette* April 1, 1877 pg.4

*Illustration 19: Mcgill Hockey Team 1881, notice the very short
sticks in use (1881, George Charles Arless Senior, MP-0000.1589, McCord
Museum)*

So, we have several of the names from 1875 playing two years
later, though it seems the McGill team is completely new (except
perhaps for Campbell who seems to be a goalie). Interestingly, the
article indicated that Creighton's team began with only six players
(compared to the nine of McGill), and even with one more added
player to make seven, Montreal still won the game 1-0. Thus the
McGill players must have been very weak. An interesting fact is that
goalies were wearing no equipment at this time, yet in the entire game
only one goal was scored. That makes me question the style of play
and the sticks that were used. The photo from 1881 shown above,
seems to be the first photograph of a hockey team from McGill.
When you look at what they were using for sticks, they are very short
and with only partial flat blades. This would be very hard to control

115

the puck, as the players would have to be hunched over in the play. These look nothing like the much longer Mi'kmaq sticks we have documented and are supposed to be available. So why is the McGill team using something inferior, some type of hurley stick? Is that really the stick of choice in Montreal during this era? Could the university team not afford or obtain "real sticks"? Were Creighton and the other Montreal players using these hurley sticks? If this was a transplanted Nova Scotia game, as I contend, why not use the sticks that were in use there? It is too bad we have no clear photographs or drawings of any of the games of the 1870s in order to know clearly the type of sticks used. But if those are the sticks used by both teams in the 1870s, then the low scores make complete sense. But if Creighton was bringing a Nova Scotia game to Montreal, and was importing sticks from Nova Scotia that should be longer than the old hurley sticks, why is this McGill hockey team in 1881 not using them?

The Gazette article also seems to present that many players, especially Creighton, were playing off side. This has been suggested as proof that he was modeling hockey of his youth in Nova Scotia (where forward passing was claimed to be allowed). I am not so sure of that, as my guess is Creighton, as the organizer, writer and rule creator of all this, he would have known the rules. If he was continually going offside continually there must have been some other reason than his "forgetting" what city he was playing in. Why was he playing different from the very rules he is a part of creating?

Another point which the article makes is the first mention of "rough play" by both of the teams. One has to consider that the games up to this point tended to be by players of the same clubs and likely friends. As mentioned, the games were likely competitive, but there would be little reason to "roughhouse" with your friends. But here, the "older guys" may have been playing "new upstarts" from the College that the original players might have thought "needed a bit of a lesson" in the layouts of social class. Then again, the word "rough play" may not have been thought of in the same way in 1877 as it is today. My guess is that if the 1877 newspaper writer saw a Philadelphia-Boston or New Westminster-Victoria game in 1976, they would not think what was going on at the Victoria Rink in 1877 was all that rough.

The Victoria Skating Rink hosted more games in 1877. The most important, in terms of development, occurred on February 26. Creighton served as captain for the team from the Metropolitan Club, an exclusive men's organization of which Creighton was a secretary, against another high-end men's group, the St. James Club. In its report on the match on February 27, *The Gazette* published the first set of rules.[147] Something about this game, between these two "clubs," was important to have that as the official marking of the ice hockey rules. The Metropolitan Club is hard to get information on, other than it was located at a place called Beaver Hall Hill, founded by two of the original 1875 hockey players, and was the club that Dr. William Osler (one of the founding professors as Johns Hopkins Hospital) joined in 1875.[148] Meanwhile, the St. James Club, founded in 1857, is still in operation, and is presented on their website as, "the oldest private business club in Canada." Without question, these would be the two premier clubs for the elite in the city, so why exactly would these elite clubs want to be playing hockey against each other? The only reason can be that the game was in some way being "sanctioned," in a sense marking the sport as legitimate in eyes of the elite. I don't mean the players playing in the game, I mean those behind the scenes in charge of the decisions.

The Gazette newspaper report tends to discuss how the St. James' players fell constantly and made "somersaults" and acrobatic moves (not by choice). "*To an outsider the falls seemed to be an important part of the game. It was soon seen that the St. James' men were not sound on their legs, although the sound on their sticks could be heard all over the building. It was a good moral sight to see the disappointment which several shaky gentlemen experienced in falling to get at the ball.*" The players who are suggested by the newspaper as playing well tend to be the one's who were playing in the 1875 game (Henry Joseph and Creighton for example). "*In point of superiority the Metropolitans had decidedly the advantage as they were more active, better skaters, and played with some show of science. However, the next interesting point will be the dinner, which no*

---

[147] SIHR.org

[148] https://osler.library.mcgill.ca/exhibits/tour/tour.html

117

*doubt will be a good one and about which we presume there will not
be two opinions."*

As for the rules (which can be read in the appendix), they are
not grandiose, or even unique. They are pretty much the field hockey
rules from 1875, applied to the ice. The world field gets changed to
ice. The word face off is not there, but the English field term "bully"
is. So did the so-called Halifax Rules really exist, for if they did why
would the Montreal players need to change the obviously "Canadian-
made" rules of Nova Scotia for those of a field variety from England?
On the other hand, if there was a need was to "show" that hockey
came from England and not Canada, then anything that might point
to "unique" Canadian rules had to be eliminated. The new field
hockey rules might have been the way for Creighton, and his club
member backers, to invent a "new sport" by completing ignoring the
original Native rules.

There was another location in North America making ice
hockey rules around the same time, though not in Canada, but at St.
Paul's School, an elite boys boarding school in Concord, New
Hampshire. They became a hot bed of hockey in the 1870s, led by
their main headmaster James Potter Conover. As early as 1875 they
published a set of rules for hockey (likely meant as the field variety)
ad there seems to be no doubt that the school quickly shifted its focus
to the ice by the end of the 1870s. In 1883, they published a new set
of specific ice hockey rules. They did so as they claimed that they did
not understand the previous published Montreal Rules, and as such
wanted rules of their own. The only played intramural games within
the school, with teams named Delphia, Mohicans and Rugby. What
this shows is the same organization around the sport of ice hockey
was in parts of the North East USA before 1880.[149]

*

Carnival

Young Lawyer Robert D. McGibbon of the Montreal Snow
Shoe club is claimed to have wanted a festival to showcase Canadian

---

[149]Hardy, *Hockey a Global* pg 39, 85,86

sports and outdoor activities such as: snowshoeing, tobogganing and curling. Within a year (1883), Montreal was holding its first winter festival. These carnivals would last until 1889 (with 1886 moved due to a smallpox epidemic). Part of the purpose of these carnivals was to advertize the city of Montreal as a tourist destination (especially for Americans), and as a way to present the city as a good place for commercial investment. Class elements were found at the Carnival, as the British elite thought there should be limits to the upper class and the lower class mixing. This was "helped" due to the fact that most of the activities were priced too high for the lower class to participate in. Sylvie Dufresne points out in her article that most of the clubs also did not let Francophones participate, so the French mostly boycotted the carnivals. In 1885, the French started their own.[150]

Many Roman Catholics saw the winter carnival as a hedonistic activity. The idea of young women "promiscuously" moving on ice skates, or fearlessly "enjoying" toboggan slides with the "long skirts swirling and exposing lower limbs" was too much for the clergy. As one priest put it, the carnival was "Only a folly invented by the devil. Everyone remembers the throngs of lost souls who have come here seeking death in the pleasures of the carnival."[151]

The carnival was a giant spectacle, but none was as great as the Ice Palace. It was a castle 160 feet long and made from some 15,000 blocks of ice. "Viewed in the daytime, every block emitting its prismatic ray, dazzling and sparkling with crystal brilliancy as the sun lights on it, it presents an appearance which is completely fascinating, and has been visited, admired, and wondered at by hundreds every hour."[152] Then when the carnival came to a close, they would stage a "mock battle" at the castle between two armies that were wearing snowshoes. Fire-works would be launched from both sites,

'Sixteen hundred men, dressed in blanket coats, with their respective club colors in stockings, sash, and

---

[150]Kitchen Paul "Before the Trail", Poulter p282, Dufresne, Sylvie. "1883-1889: Quand Montréal avait son Carnaval!" Cap-aux-Diamants No. 64 (Hiver 2001): 10–14. https://www.erudit.org/en/journals/cd/2001-n64-cd1043766/8382ac.pdf. , Gillian Poulter, "Becoming Native in a Foreign Land" 1999 for York University https://www.collectionscanada.gc.ca/obj/s4/f2/dsk2/ftp03/NQ56261.pdf
[151]Shea 160
[152] *Harper's Bazaar* March 8,1884

*toque, surrounded it, and for half an hour rockets,
Roman shells, and balls of fire flew in every direction,
while red, blue, and green lights were burned at
intervals, each changeful rainbow hue giving some new
and brilliant effect. After the capitulation victors and
vanquished alike joined in one long line, and, with
torches high in air, marched toward the Mountain.
Taking a zigzag course they reached the summit,
where they again sent off fire-works, and turning,
wended their serpentine way back, looking in, the
distance like a thread of gold.*"[153]

The attacking army would eventually win. Many rightfully saw
the attack as a re-enactment of the storming of French-held Quebec
City by the English during the Seven Years War. The destruction of
the castle would then be celebrated with a giant "torch lit" snow shoe
tramp up Mount Royal, where more fireworks were set to end the
carnival. The "Harper's article" also discusses a fancy masquerade ice
skating party at the Victoria Rink. At the Grand Windsor Ball, it
seems that not only were the Governor-General of Canada, Lord and
Lady Lansdowne present, their "invited guests included (US)
President (Chester) Arthur and the Governors of all the States." The
US President was at the carnival, as was the governor of every US
state! Can you think of the amount of importance there was in having
pretty much every top member of the US leadership in Montreal for
the festival?

---

[153] *Harper's Bazaar* March 8, 1884

Hockey 1883[154]

Illustration 20: 1883 Winter Carnival Trophy, (Object Number M976.188.1, Transfer from McGill University, McCord Museum)

1883 is the year of hockey's first championship, as it was one of the sports added to the Carnival. It would be the first time that games would no longer be presented as "exhibition matches" between teams. The Bedouin Cup, also called the Birks Cup, was awarded to the champion of hockey at the Montreal Winter Carnival. Three teams arrived for the matches (Victorias and McGills from Montreal and a team from Quebec City).[155] The Quebec team is claimed to have arrived with only seven players, instead of nine as was the rule

---

[154]Research on the hockey 1883 includes, Fitsell *Captains* pp.44,47; Vigneault *Total Hockey* p.11 , Kitchen *Before the Trail*

[155] Interestingly the Montreal AAA (which later would win the first Stanley Cup in 1893) was the sports organizer of the carnival, but did not field a hockey team.

since 1877. As "gentlemanly ideals" of the times prevailed, the other teams played with only seven players against them. The play improved and created more excitement, and following the carnival seven man hockey became the new rule of team make up.

The 1883 games were outdoors on a shoveled off area of the Saint Lawrence River, for a very short round-robin tournament. On January 26, the Victorias tied Quebec 0-0, while McGill defeated the Vics 2-1. The games were played on ice that *The Witness* called "the worst possible conditions." Interestingly, and I did not see this mentioned elsewhere, but *The Witness* claimed that the ice was so bad for the next day's games that they were moved inside to the Crystal Rink. Not much gets said in the reports other than the game score or that there was strong overall play, but one sentence in one of the articles is hard to understand, "The beauties of the game were very well displayed in the course of this struggle, which were among the best of the whole carnival."[156] I have no idea what that means.

On January 27, the Victorias and Quebec tied 1-1, while McGill tied the Vics 2-2. McGills became the first Hockey Champions winning the Bedouin Cup (seen above) in a series of games in which only one game was not a tie. All of the winning players had their names engraved on the trophy, a custom that continues today on the Stanley Cup. One tradition from 1883 was eliminated; the referee also had his name engraved on the trophy. The cup and a replica of the original game puck are on display at McGill's Museum of Canadian History. The McGill winning roster: A. Low, J. Elder, T. Green, R. Smith, W. Murray, J. Kinlock (c.), P. Foster.[157] On this list is a very important name, T. (Thomas Daniel) Green, a man who will be examined more closely when he becomes the first president of Canada's first hockey league in 1886.

---

[156]*Montreal Daily Witness* January 27, 1883 pg 1, *Montreal Daily Witness* January 29, 1883 pg 3
[157]Wikipedia

Illustration 21: First hockey action photo, at McGill rink 1884 Winter Carnival. Notice the spectator turning oddly to face the camera. (Title: Playing hockey on the skating rink, McGill University, Source: Library and Archives Canada/Alexander Henderson fonds/c081683 , 3349908)

In 1884, the tournament moved to McGill's outdoor rink (won by Montreal Crystals), and it is here we get the first action photo in hockey history. The photo above is definitely from the 1884 carnival games played on the McGill rink. It is a wide angle photo of most of the rink, though the image was taken just as the play was moving out of full camera range. The outdoor surface can be seen as much wider than the 80 feet of the Victoria Skating Club. Again, the

---

[158] *Montreal Winter Carnival 1884* Gould (J. H.) & Co. (publisher), found in Toronto Public Library

sticks appear to be not overly long (causing players to bend over to play the puck), and the uniforms appear to be a bit "mix and match." Also curious is that a photograph expert shared his view that he felt this was a combination of a photograph and a painting, as the buildings have one type of direct light, while the spectators do not. I also draw your attention though to a spectator near the left goal post turning around to look directly at the camera. He just seems so "out of place," not only in his attire, but almost as if he "knew" the photo was about to be taken. I am not suggesting this is a time-traveling historian, but something just seems very unique about this person at the game.[159]

Quebec did not make the trip to the carnival this time, but a number of new teams did. From Montreal, the Crystals and Wanderers joined McGill and the Victorias. A new team entered, that from Ottawa, a team whose origin story claims to go back to the following year's carnival. The story claims that Jack Kerr and Halder Kirby had gone to Montreal for the 1883 carnival, saw the hockey matches, and decided to set up their own team. This is what a January 19, 1935 article in the *Ottawa Citizen* had to say about the start of hockey in Ottawa: "*Prior to that time hockey had been played by Ottawans on the Rideau canal. The players used sticks cut out of the trunks of small trees and the game resembled shinny more than hockey proper. Now however, that they had determined to play the game as it should be played, they abandoned the improvised sticks and procured a dozen real ones from Quebec.*"[160] Again this idea that anything prior to the British organized form was somehow "primitive."

The team had their first practice on March 6, 1883. Many of the players were from McGill who had come to Ottawa after graduation in 1882. They would soon be joined by two more McGill

---

[159] A second photo appears on page 12 of Paul Kitchen's *Win, Tie or Wrangle* book, that many sources claim to also be from 1884. However I noticed that the goalie looked like he is wearing some sort of cricket pads on his legs, which standard history indicated did not occur until used by Winnipeg goalies a decade later. Looking into it further, that photo is listed elsewhere as students from McGill playing in 1901. This would make sense given the goalie pads and also the type of sticks in use.

[160] *Ottawa Citizen* "Organized Hockey in capitol had beginning early eighties," January 19, 1935

players who had won the 1883 championship, Albert Peter Low and Thomas Green. Several of the grads also were part of the Geological Survey of Canada, which moved to Ottawa in 1882.[161] Low did not spend many years as a hockey player, as he became a key geological surveyor of the West and North, including commander of the famed 1903 expedition to the Arctic. Low later wrote a book about the trip called *The Cruise of the Neptune.* Meanwhile founder Kirby, who was a druggist in 1883, later went to McGill and became a doctor, eventually the Silver Seven's doctor for their Stanley Cup era after 1900.[162] As for a couple of other key players on that first Ottawa team, three are buried in prestigious Beechwood Cemetery. Frank Jenkins was the captain of the team, and was also the founder of Ottawa's first full orchestra in 1894, Nelson Porter would later become the mayor of Ottawa, and Jack Kerr who is claimed to have manufactured the first rubber puck in Ottawa.[163]

Here is the first anomaly in the Ottawa origin story. If all the players were mostly from McGill, why did they not go and get the new Ottawa resident James Creighton to help with the formation of the team? Everyone would have known he had moved to Ottawa in 1882 to work in the Canadian Parliament. I even think his appointment had been mentioned in the *Montreal Gazette.* Either way, his leaving Montreal would have been known due to his no longer attending events at the many city clubs he was associated with, nor any longer captaining hockey matches. When starting a new team, in a new city, would you not want the founder of the sport to be your guide or mentor?

Amazingly, Ottawa almost became the winner of the 1884 Carnival that year, and to declare a champion required a very odd playoff to be created. That playoff was won by the Victorias. Many games were postponed or canceled due to rain, and the Wanderers and Crystals did not even show up for their February 6 game (each

---

[161] Ottawa Citizen *March* 6 1883, Kitchen *Win Lose or Wrangle* p11-15

[162]*Ottawa Citizen* "Organized Hockey in capitol had beginning early eighties," January 19, 1935, Kitchen p16-18 Relevant Wikipedia pages,

[163] A photograph of the 1884 Ottawa team can be seen at, https://en.wikipedia.org/wiki/1884_Ottawa_Hockey_Club_season#/media/File:Ottawa-Hockey-Club-1883-84.jpg https://en.wikipedia.org/wiki/Jack_Kerr_(ice_hockey)

losing by default).[164] As such, I wonder how serious the players were for these games at the Carnival.

This year there was also a mention of hockey game in a Lewiston, Maine in *The Lewiston Evening Journal* newspaper on March 4. The match was between the Portland Polo Cub and Lewiston. The paper though made a very strange connection claiming the sport was "closely allied to the old-fashioned sport of purring." Purring is also called Shin-kicking, where people kick each other in the shins until they fall down. Obviously someone must have explained to the reporter that what they were watching was like shinny, which the reporter did not understand the ice game reference, thinking it was the shin-kicking event and not a stick-and-ball ice game. Portland won 3-0 and the paper commented, "everybody liked the conduct of both clubs during the game." Again, this idea of British gentlemanly behaviour had to be a part of the newspaper reporting of the era to make it seem "legitimate" for British eyes.[165]

Lastly, I want to briefly mention one of the most amazing historical documents I have come across. This is a complete listing given by the secretary of the Montreal AAA regarding all the winter sports events that took place in Montreal (and the rest of Canada) for the 1883-84 period. The first 80 pages are the records of all the snow shoe races. The hockey part begins on page 97, and runs for nine pages, and lists perhaps twenty other games that took place beyond the carnival, and not listed in any record I have seen so far listed as having occurred for this season.[166]

*

1885

This year's carnival was played at the Crystal Rink and won by the newly entered Montreal AAA/Montreal Hockey Club, which used the 'winged wheel' logo. The wings of the logo refers to the

---

[164]Kitchen, *Win, Lose* pp 23-26

[165]https://www.sunjournal.com/2022/08/21/in-1884-the-very-interesting-sport-of-hockey-arrived-in-lewiston/, https://en.wikipedia.org/wiki/Shin-kicking

[166]Becket, Hugh compiler. *Record of Winter Sports* 1883-84

winged feet of Hermes, or the winged disk of Horus. Originally this team was known as the 'Montreal Football Club,' and was captained by James Creighton before he moved to Ottawa. After he was gone, the club merged with the Montreal Amateur Athletic Association in November 1884, and the team took on the club's name. This would be the team that would be awarded the first Stanley Cup in 1893. As an aside, the famous owner of the Detroit Red Wings, James E Norris, was a player for the AAA in 1898, and once he took over the Red Wings in Detroit reused the wheeled logo of the AAA for his team. One could say that Detroit was in some way the NHL extension of the Montreal AAA club. A deeper overview of Norris can be found in the appendix.

*

1886

1886 is a key year for hockey, as the first true league would be formed in December. In the winter prior, the Montreal Carnival for 1886 was canceled over a smallpox epidemic in Montreal. When Burlington, Vermont heard of Montreal's misfortune, they decided to stage their own winter carnival, either out of pity for the loss of the great carnival or the hope of a big money windfall. Montreal offered to share their carnival information with the Americans. The carnival in Vermont would have many of the popular events from Montreal, including hockey. The Van Ness hotel in Burlington put together a local hockey team. Its players had never played before and had but a couple of practices before taking on the two great Montreal teams that arrived, the Crystals and the Montreal Amateur Athletic Association.[167]

Actually, the epidemic itself in Montreal has been interesting for me to read the newspaper reports of, and the historical views of it have great similarity to our recent 2020-23 insane experience. There had been a huge vaccination debate in Montreal as the British protestants regarded vaccination as necessary, while the Francophone Catholics saw smallpox as a judgment of God on the sins of his people- especially for what they called the "feasts of the flesh" that

---

[167]Kitchen, Paul "Hockey on the Lake" pp.20-21, *Hockeyology* pg 19

127

occurred at the Winter Carnival the previous years.[168] I won't go into more detail, but it is a fascinating historical read now in 2023.

Other hockey events take place in 1886. On a smaller note is the first documented hockey game in Kingston that was played between Queen's University and Royal Military College. The 1886 game is symbolically repeated today during the Kingston Winter Carnival.[169] Meanwhile the *Gazette* early in 1886 was calling for some changes to the sport. The first was that they wanted to get rid of the offside rule, "Do away with the offside rule and play hockey as lacrosse and there will be a better game." They also called for a true national championship. The paper also had negative remarks towards what they were deeming as unnecessarily rough play.[170] As the sport was moving from friends in elite men's clubs, to championships between sports clubs, the game's physicality increased.

Yet it was the end of 1886 (heading into the 1887 season) where the biggest hockey change of the decade occurred. On December 8, the first true league was formed, following on the success of the Winter Carnival tournament. The league included four Montreal teams in one division: Victorias, Crystals, AAA and McGill University, while two out of town teams, Quebec and Ottawa would be in the other division. The league was called the Amateur Hockey Association of Canada. This league would eventually become the Canadian Amateur Hockey Association. The AHA set up more detailed rules including naming the seven positions: goalie, point, cover-point (now defensemen), three forwards, and a rover (usually the team's best player who alternated on the rush and on defense). The most significant change determined the goal size, with the dimensions set at six feet wide by four feet high (its current size). Ottawa's Thomas D. Green was named the first president of the league. To be honest, this might be the biggest story of the entire early history of hockey, and yet it mostly seems to go unexamined. Don't let the very anglophone sounding name fool you, Green was a Native Mohawk.

---

[168]Shea p 158-59

[169] Fitsell *Captains* p.9; Vaughan *Puck Starts* p.60

[170] Kitchen "Before the Trail"

Thomas Green[171] was born in 1857 on the Six Nations Reserve near Brantford. Yes, that makes Brantford a link between hockey's first league president and its later all time scoring champion (Wayne Gretzky). His parents were Daniel Green and Mary Crawford (not very Native sounding names). His mother was a daughter of Peter Crawford, the Indian Missionary. His grandfather was Peter Green, a white man of Dutch descent who came to Ontario from Wisconsin as a 17-year-old. He soon married an aboriginal woman in her mid-30s, one of the "chief-makers," thus causing Peter to become a tribal chief. When the reserve began to be laid out, Peter had his home and land placed separate from the reserve itself, which meant that "though classified as Native by blood," his family would not be Native according to the laws. That meant that in the future, his children (like Thomas) were allowed to attend public schools in Brantford, rather than the horror that the Native children were forced to endure at the Mohawk Institute Residential School.

Thomas was called a gifted student, and had "his college tuition mostly paid for by the Church of England's missionary society and the Six Nations Council." With these stipends, he could attend McGill University, where he graduated with a Bachelor of Applied Science in 1882. It is claimed that while at McGill, he tutored other students to help raise extra money. To fit into a place like McGill, Green was going to have to not be acting as a Native, he was going to have to act British. And what was a good way to do that? Perhaps hockey was a door opener.

He played in the first Winter Carnival in 1883, winning the championship with his team McGill. He then moved to Ottawa, just in time to join up with the first hockey team in that city. After his graduation, Canadian Prime Minister Sir John A. MacDonald is claimed to have taken "a deep interest in him." Even so, he was often discriminated against due to his being a Mohawk by birth. A. M. Burgess, the deputy minister of the Interior, refused his work application. Even the recommendation of the Prime Minister mattered little with Burgess. Green would later take surveying work in the Canadian West, and later became friends with A.C. Rutherford,

---

[171]Biography on Green from http://www.landsurveyinghistory.ab.ca,
https://hockeygods.com/images/19668 a photo of Green (where he is in top row at the left)
at https://commons.wikimedia.org/wiki/File:Ottawa-Hockey-Club-1883-84.jpg

the first Premier of Alberta. How does someone from an out of the way reserve make such connections? And why when the first hockey league was formed, was he (now with the Ottawa club) chosen to be the first president?

I obviously never met Mr. Green, and he might have been a true genius. That would be the theory laid out by most writers such as Paul Kitchen, "He was obviously an impressive guy. His teammates elected him to be their representative in Montreal at the founding of the world's first hockey league. And those guys were so impressed, they made him president almost right off the bat."[172] That might be the answer. However Green is connected with some very unique people. Perhaps it is the connections that mattered?

Green winds up being connected with dinosaurs. Starting in 1896 he moved to Yukon for the Klondike Gold Rush as a surveyor. He then entered a partnership with J. B. Tyrell, forming the Tyrell and Green Mining Engineers and Surveyors. The name Tyrell might be recognized if you live in Alberta, as he is the man the famous Tyrell Dinosaur Museum in Drumheller is named after. He is claimed to have discovered the first dinosaur bones in the area in 1884. Tyrell was known as a geologist, mining consultant, and was a key surveyor of the Canadian West in the 1880s, but he received a law degree from the University of Toronto. He joined the Geological Survey of Canada in 1880, though I am not sure how his law background fit towards that appointment as surveyor.[173]

Green stayed in the Yukon until 1907. Also interesting was that one of Green's surveying clients was Joe Boyle, who would be the financial backer of the Dawson City Nuggets hockey team that partook in the famous 1905 challenge with the Ottawa Silver Seven for the Stanley Cup. Green had played on the first Ottawa hockey team in 1884, so he was perhaps the one who "brokered" a deal for Ottawa to agree to play what was an obvious inferior opponent, which was a series all about Yukon publicity. The life of Joe Boyle is strange to say the least. After fighting in World War One, he became the

---

[172]"How official Ottawa held back a 'great unsung native hero'" By *The Ottawa Citizen*, March 1, 2008

[173] https://www.brantfordexpositor.ca/2013/01/27/a-man-of-firsts

British direct communicator with Romania (some historians have suggested that he was the lover of the Romanian Queen Marie) while helping broker various cease-fires. He was also a key negotiator on behalf of Romania at the Paris Peace Conference in 1919, gaining the country a 25 million dollar credit from Canada.[174]

Green eventually moved to Alberta. When he died, he was buried in Edmonton with full "Masonic honours." Green was a Freemason, who belonged to several lodges including the Civil Service Lodge AF and AM, the Ottawa Lodge, and Tocheon Lodge No. 151 AF. That puts him in very elite company. Why do the doors of the white elite keep opening up for him? How did he make it into Masonry at a time when even the Canadian government was rejecting him for work? This was still a time when the remaining "free" native populations of the West were being subjugated, starved, Louis Riel executed, and those who surrendered, forced onto reservations.

Either Thomas Green was one of the truly great pioneers in hockey history (and would thus automatically demand a place in the Hockey Hall of Fame as a builder), or he was part of a giant smokescreen. This might have been a ritual way of officially handing over a Native sport to British control. They made a Native-by-blood the first president to legitimize this takeover. He lasted only one year (which again leads to the idea he was a token appointment for some sort of ritual purpose) before a new president took over, James Stewart, another "oddball" name in hockey history.

*

James "Jimmy" Stewart was a very interesting personality of the era. An orphan from Brockville, he moved to Montreal and became a star point for first the Montreal Crystals (a working class team he might have been instrumental in starting) then starring with the great Montreal AAA, and eventually he became the AHA president for several years. Morey Holzman wrote a book on him called *The Odd Fellow's Heart*. The title presents Stewart's link with another fraternal organization, the Oddfellows. According to Holzman in a message on the hockey website HFboards, "*Jimmy was*

---

[174] https://en.wikipedia.org/wiki/Joseph_W._Boyle

instrumental in starting the first working-class game, introducing the Montreal Crystals to the Montreal Carnival. He was instrumental in the organization of the first hockey organization. He helped introduce the concept of skating and positional play to the sport. He was the first to use a whistle to officiate games, he was the first to codify the size, weight and material of the puck, and he was the first to use sudden-death overtime in hockey to declare a winner. He also helped introduce the concept of the penalty box. He became president of hockey's first dynasty as well as the lead negotiator between Stanley Cup trustee Phil Ross and the Montreal AAA to allow the Stanley Cup to become the sport's most prominent trophy."[175]

I do want to add another strange coincidence as Stewart has a connection with James Creighton. Both were founders of the sport, Creighton organizing games, and Stewart organizing rules. Both were captains of the same Montreal club, just with different names over time. Both left for other cities and both seem to be almost unknown in the hockey world after they moved. Creighton had nothing about his hockey background in his obituary, while Stewart seems to have no interaction with the Pacific Coast Seattle hockey team that was playing in the city where he lived. And most oddly, both were placed in unmarked graves. How did the two seemingly key creators of hockey wind up in a cemetery the same way? It is one element of this story that I feel needs further examination.

The 1886-87 league was set up as a two division format, and at the end of round robin the two division winners, the Crystals and Quebec would meet in a one game final on March 19. The Montreal Crystals would become the AHA's first league champions, but not having to finish the champions game as, "*In what might have seen to foreshadow the ongoing laments about violent play, the visitors (Quebec) forfeited the title when they quit the game in the face of the home team's aggression. The moment the team left the ice, the referee awarded the championship trophy to Crystals.*" [176] The Montreal Gazette presented the game as,

---

[175]https://forums.hfboards.com/threads/the-odd-fellows-heart-by-morey-holzman.2818037/
[176]Vigneault *Total Hockey* p.13;

"The Crystal rink was crowded last night with lovers of the game of hockey in the hope of seeing a good game. In this they were disappointed, for after about twenty-eight minutes rough and very questionable play - the home team being very conspicuous - the game was stopped, owing to A. E. Scott meeting with an accident. The Crystal team refused to withdraw a man to equalize matters, and as these representatives of a so-called first class hockey team were the sole possessors of the ice when time was called, the referee declared the game ended in favor of the Montreal men." The following week the same paper added, *"We would refer to the recent match between the Crystals and Quebec team for the Dominion championship. It did hockey a great deal of harm in Montreal, a good many lovers of the game being disgusted at the miserable fiasco which the game ended in. The merits of the case have been given before and are simply: - The Quebecers came up all the way to play the Crystals a match and went on the ice to play a game of hockey. Roughness of the most barefaced and foul description was indulged in on both sides, men on either side who can play hockey when they choose, but who seem to prefer brute force, being noticeable. Soon one of the Quebec players, by accident, was thrown against the side of the rink and had his head badly cut. He had to leave the ice, and here came the trouble. The Quebec men said they had not a spare man prepared to play and asked the Crystals to drop one. They, however, refused to do this, as in fact they were not bound to do, and the Quebecers left the ice. Had the game proceeded it looked as if Quebec would now hold the championship, and very many people would rather see it go than be held here if Montreal had not it without a doubt. Still the Crystals think they were sure to win, and they had a chance to play Wednesday night and showed they were perfectly able to play the game pure and simple."*

Over time, the AHA did away with the round robin system and instead moved to the very strange challenge system where the champion had to be challenged directly by another club. As such, there would be no real league to speak of. Just constant challenges by teams to the cup holder, and the rest of the teams playing exhibition games. The league would continue like this until 1897, when a kerfuffle happened over the application of the Ottawa Capitals, and the teams moved to form an entirely new league, the CAHL.[177]

Meanwhile, the Montreal Winter Carnival did not last past 1889. However, there was one event that took place this final year that changed hockey forever. The new Governor-General, Lord Stanley, came to watch a hockey game. That story of the Stanley Cup and Ottawa is retold often in hockey books. However, I tend to show that the story of the creation of the Stanley Cup is anything but simple, weaved in quite a web of uncertainty.

---

[177]See Kitchen *Win Lose or Wrangle* p 77 for more information on this new league formation

6

WHOSE CUP IS IT ANYWAY?
Ottawa

Ottawa has quite a hockey background. A silver medal from 1852 was given to the winner of a shinny game (called shintie on the medal) on the Rideau River on Christmas Day. That medal is now in the Bytown Museum.[178] Yet we are told that Ottawa is not supposed to have formed its first team until 1883, then almost won the Winter Carnival the following year. How the team got so good, so quickly, has never been answered. However, the team ran into issues with rink closures and disbanded for a few years. The team restarted again in 1889, becoming a championship dynasty in the 1900s. However, it is another team, that did not play in any league nor have any statistics of its players kept, that becomes the real hockey story of Ottawa. That team linked to both Lord Stanley and James Creighton. Both would be directly involved in the creation of the most famous hockey trophy in the world, the Stanley Cup.

---

[178] Pat McGrath, *Ottawa Citizen https://ottawacitizen.com/news/local-news/capital-facts-the-early-origins-of-shinney-in-ottawa*

*

1889[179]

Illustration 22: Lord Stanley of Preston
(Title: Baron Stanley of Preston (Sir Frederick
Arthur Stanley), Source: Library and Archives
Canada/Topley Studio fonds/a027167, item id
3422367)

Frederick Stanley of Preston had become Canada's new Governor-General in May 1888. When the Montreal Winter Carnival took place, Stanley was there to take it all in. It seems one of the first things he did upon arrival was to be initiated into the Montreal Snow Shoe Club. Kevin Shea presents that "while watching the snowshoeing, Lord Stanley was summoned by the Montreal Snowshoe Club, and was somewhat begrudgingly tossed in the air by members in a custom known as 'the bounce'." The claim was that it

179 Kitchen *Win Lose or Wrangle*, https://www.nhl.com/news/how-stanley-cup-came-to-be/c-287700534v

was a custom given to winners of snowshoe races, new members to the club, or special guests to be tossed in the air by a dozen or so members, then caught as they fell. I showed this image in chapter two. This tends to be presented as happening to Stanley in 1889 because he was a special guest, but I am pretty sure this was a public initiation into the Snowshoe Club.[180]

The second thing Stanley did at the Carnival is a bit more famous; he attended a hockey game at the Victoria Skating Rink on February 4 between Montreal AAA and the Montreal Victorias. With him were his son Edward, daughter Isobel and a few aids. When he arrived, the game was in progress. It was stopped so that the band could perform "God Save the Queen." Then Victoria's Captain, Jack Arnton, led a three cheers toast for their new visitors. As for the game, *The Montreal Gazette,* which we now know is the personal promotion project of the sport of hockey described the match as "one of the finest exhibitions of Canada's national winter game" and wrote Lord Stanley "expressed his great delight with the game of hockey and the expertise of the players." 1889 would turn out to be the last year for the Winter Carnival, but it had moved hockey from small time exhibition to a full on spectator sport. Ottawa would now take it to the next steps. Upon returning to Ottawa, first Edward and Isobel, but then Arthur as well began to play hockey games on their outdoor rink that was alongside their Rideau Hall Ottawa residence.[181] Isobel is credited with organizing the first women's games, yet the brothers took another step. They formed a team, eventually calling themselves the Rideau Rebels. But first the city needed a new arena.

Of the previous indoor arenas, The Royal had been turned into a roller skating facility, and the remaining area (Deys) was in over-use. The new building was the Rideau Rink, which included the Rideau Skating and Curling Club. What is interesting is that Lord Stanley was a shareholder in the project. Sandford Fleming became founder and President of the Rideau Curling Club. He formed the club after he became upset when his old club (Ottawa Curling Club) stopped allowing the drinking of alcohol. The Rideau Arena opened February 1, 1889 and Stanley threw a fancy dress carnival.[182]

---

[180] Shea p 161, and McCord Museum portrait II 91495
[181] The first ice rink at Rideau Hall was built in 1878 for Lord Landsdowne. Shea 64
[182] Kitchen p 38

Another key figure connected with the arena was PD Ross, who re-started the Ottawa Hockey Club as their manager (and part time player), and brought back many of the old players to play. Ross is an important name in the early stages of hockey, who seems to have his hand in everything going on in Ottawa sports. He studied engineering at McGill (no surprise) and played football and hockey. He was working for the *Montreal Star*, then purchased the failing *Ottawa Evening Journal* in 1887. Ross also became the first president of the Ottawa Amateur Athletic Club (which would be modeled on the AAA of Montreal). It had a gymnasium, billiard area, and served as a hub for major sports teams. Like all "clubs" of its era, new appointees had to be submitted in by two candidates, their application carefully looked at, and then voted on. Basically meaning as Ross's own paper claimed about the Club "the new members are of the best class, including many well known city business and professional men." He wound up an influence of the newly founded Ontario Hockey Association, as well as appointed by Stanley as the first trustee for the Stanley Cup-, all of course tirelessly promoted via his newspaper. As you might expect, Ross was buried in our afterlife home of early hockey, Beechwood Cemetery.[183]

The first game played at the Rideau Rink seems to again be between two of the rich-man's clubs, the Rideau and the Ottawa. It was played on February 14 (Valentine's Day), an odd day for men to be focused on hockey and not their wives. But here comes the "catch," James Creighton was the Captain for the Rideau Team. Also playing was Lt. McMahon, and John Augustus Barron (MP) (who along with Arthur Stanley and Ross) would be a key founder of the Ontario Hockey Association. Ross captained the Ottawa team.[184] So the question I have to ask is, where exactly was Creighton since 1882? Hockey was being played in Ottawa, starting coincidentally just after his arrival, and the team was doing well. But he seems to have no connection to the new team. Should he have not been around in some capacity? Perhaps as a type of advisor? Why does he all of a sudden show up now in 1889, when we get the equivalent of a "ritual like" opening between two elite city clubs, in a brand new arena,

---

[183] Kitchen 38-44
[184] Kitchen p 40

which is directly linked to Governor-General Stanley and Sandford Fleming? Creighton just seems to re-appear like magic just at the moment a new direction for hockey is about to be taken. The next day another game takes place when a civilian team played against a military team. Ross was the referee and Creighton was an umpire. In the military lineup were three of Stanley's sons; Fred, Victor and Edward. Paul Kitchen rightly presents that it was these two games that were the origin of what would become the Rideau Rebels. Right away something just feels fishy about the whole thing.[185]

Before we go further with hockey, a look at the Stanley family is needed.[186] Biography writer P B Waite presented Stanley as:

> *"One of those quiet, careful proconsuls who are a credit to their class. Former prime minister Arthur James Balfour wrote to Lady Derby that her late husband had been one of his oldest and kindest friends, "a man who had a genius for inspiring affection among those who knew him." With wide interests, kind, retiring, and transparently honest and sincere, he was not altogether fitted for the cut and thrust of political life. Since he lacked flamboyance, the impression he left is misleading. There was a great deal of knowledge and experience in Stanley, but it was deployed modestly and tentatively. Canadians remember him more for Stanley House, Stanley Park, and the Stanley Cup. He would not have minded that recollection, imperfect though it is."[187]*

*

Frederick Arthur Stanley, 16th Earl of Derby, was the son of former Prime Minister Edward Smith-Stanley. After a long political career he became the new Governor General of Canada on May 1, 1888. While best known for the Stanley Cup, he is also remembered

---

[185] One more game should be mentioned, Brian McFarlane's book, *Proud Past, Bright Future* claimed that on March 8, 1889 the first indoor women's hockey game occurred between Government House (a team that had Isobel) and the Rideau Skating Club, Kitchen p 40, I have been unable to find the McFarlane book to verify the reference on page 9
[186] Information comes from such sites as
http://www.biographi.ca/en/bio/stanley_frederick_arthur_13E.html, as well as wikipedia
[187] http://www.biographi.ca/en/bio/stanley_frederick_arthur_13E.html

139

for many rail trips across Canada, and thus having several locations named after him, such as Stanley Park in Vancouver. His wife founded the Lady Stanley Institute for Trained Nurses, of which Dr Sweetland (one of the original Stanley Cup trustees) would be its first President. Not only was Stanley a high ranking Freemason, he was also a Knight of the Garter, the most senior order of knighthood in Britain. Interestingly, the oldest surviving audio recording is likely of Lord Stanley giving a speech in Toronto on September 11 1888 while attending the Toronto Industrial Exhibition.[188]

All of his children also obtained key positions. His son Arthur became a key politician in England, who also was a Grand Master Freemason, and even had a Lodge named in his honour. Edward Stanley was another high ranking Freemason and Knight of the Garter, was twice Secretary of State for War and also served as British Ambassador to France. He served as Honorary President of the Rugby Football League, and donated a cup for the French authorities, much as his father had done for ice hockey. Isobel married General Hardy (a son of the Earl of Cranbrook). Her name is now on two trophies for women's hockey in Canada. Victor became an admiral in the navy. George became Governor of Madras (India), interestingly the same location that the Theosophical Society would set themselves up in.

*

Rideau Rebels[189]

After having played a few February exhibition games, this group of parliamentary hockey players formed a team. They practiced on the rink outside the Governor-General's house, and thus called themselves the Rideau Hall Rebels (or correctly the Vice-Regal and Parliamentary Hockey Club). James Creighton was there. Lord Stanley biographer PD Waite commented that the team was founded with "James George Aylwin Creighton, as moving spirit."[190] Where

---

[188] Shea 126

[189] information on the rebels from Kitchen Win Lose and Wrangle, Shea Lord Stanley, and https://hockeygods.com/images/7101-
Rideau_Hall_Rebels___Ice_Hockey_Stick_Fun___1889, Puckstruck

[190] http://www.biographi.ca/en/bio/stanley_frederick_arthur_13E.html

does he get such a reference from? Nowhere have I seen a piece of information suggesting Creighton was the team founder...however I think Waite, whether he knows it or not, has likely hit on a key truth. The Stanleys were not the founders of this team, it was John Barron and James Creighton. And of course there is Sandford Fleming possibly lurking in the background at the Rideau curling rink.

The Rebels next exhibition game came in March 1889 when Lord Stanley invited the St. James Club of Montreal for a game in Ottawa. This was one of the clubs involved in the 1877 game in Montreal where the rules were published, a game in which Creighton was captain of the St. James opponent. The same would happen here, as Creighton was the captain of the Rebels. It is like 1877 happening all over again.[191]

The following season, the Rebels traveled for several games around Ontario in 1890, in the Governor-General's personal rail car. They now had a uniform of crimson sweaters, with white pants and caps. Starting around 1890, a new "leftist" political movement began in Canada which Ian McKay discussed in his book *Rebels, Reds and Radicals*. It may be a co-incidence that the parliamentary team chose to wear "crimson" jerseys, and use the name rebel in 1890. But the origin of hockey is a story is full of co-incidences, and all must be examined. This new movement actually had links back to the rebellions of 1837, and the working class of 1890 was calling for better and safer working conditions, more time off, unions, women's rights and connection to affordable medical care. It thus to me comes as no surprise that just as there was a sporting response after the 1837 rebellions, there was a possible sporting response in 1890 to "halt a rebellion in its tracks."

The Rebels did not have an easy time of it. They got into trouble before they left for their Ottawa tour for being caught practicing on Sunday, for this was still a time when sports was forbidden to played in many parts of Canada on the Sabbath. Not only did it become a major incident in Ottawa, with MP John Charlton along with several priests claiming that Stanley and his family

---

had desecrated the Sabbath with their Sunday hockey, the scandal hit the papers of New York, St. Louis, and Philadelphia.[192] Eventually it died down, but for a few weeks, some Sunday hockey practices at Rideau Hall in Ottawa were Continent-wide news.

In the first week of February of 1890, the team traveled to western Ontario. This trip is claimed to have popularized the sport in the province, which had only supposed to have began in 1887, after a magical origin story that will be found in chapter eight. This team included one of the Stanleys (Arthur) and Ross, but did not include Creighton who "backed out due to parliamentary duties." Their first stop was to first play a game in Lindsay, Ontario, where Barron had his legal practice and where he had recently formed a hockey team.[193] Barron would be the Chairman at the first OHA meeting in 1890, as well as the League's Vice-President its first two years. His son Frederic died in a 1901 game in Winnipeg, after taking a puck to the solar plexus and dying from what *The Winnipeg Tribune* February 2 article claimed was a weak heart.

From there, the Rebels played two games in Toronto on Saturday, February 8. In the afternoon, the Rebels beat the the Granite Club, 5-4. They were defeated in the evening game 4-1 by St. Georges. Originally the visit was highly anticipated as presented in the *Toronto Daily Mail* of February 7, "*The visit of the Parliamentary and Viceregal hockey team of Ottawa to Toronto has been looked forward to with great interest for some time. Hockey is one of the most popular winter games in Ottawa, Montreal and Quebec, and other eastern cities, while in Toronto the game has not been extensively played. The game is somewhat like lacrosse, but far quicker, and the excitement is at a fever heat all the time.*" Afterward the games became remembered for all the high sticks and fights that occurred. *Toronto Daily Mail* for February 10, 1890 wrote "*It is to be greatly regretted in a game between amateur teams some players should so forget themselves before such a number of spectators, as to engage in fisticuffs, and the action of some of the spectators in rushing on to the ice is also to be condemned.*" Shea and Wilson noted, "*Both games were littered with fights and high sticks, to the*

---

[192] https://puckstruck.com/tag/lord-kilcoursie/ and Kitchen pgs 44-45
[193] Shea p 360

point that hockey received its first appreciable coverage in Toronto, albeit through editorials denouncing the violence of the game."[194] Why exactly are exhibition games with a team of Canadian parliamentarians playing some elite club members from Toronto becoming games filled with fights and violent play? More had to be involved in the connections of the groups of players for these Toronto games. Was there some sort of Montreal-Toronto issue that was spilling over into the games?

Illustration 23: Rideau Rebels in 1890, with Mi'kmaq sticks. James Creighton is third from the left in the light shirt. (Title: Vice-Regal Hockey Team, Source: Library and Archives Canada/Topley Studio fonds/e008438039, item id 3422510)

---

[194] Shea 362, *Daily Mail* "The Granites defeated" February 10, 1890 page 2

143

Illustration 24: Rideau Rebels in odd photograph (Title: Rebel Hockey Group, Source: Library and Archives Canada/Topley Studio fonds/a204251, item number creator 58780)

At the end of their last Ontario exhibition series, in Kingston, they came into a photographer's studio. Creighton is in these photos (he missed the earlier games) but joined for the Kingston trip. The photos are weird. One of the photos (top previous page) has the team all seated, but with their sticks around and framing Barron's head. He is being singled out. Also in these photo Creighton (who is third from the left) is the only one not wearing a dark colour shirt, also standing out from the rest. Why? Another photo (bottom previous page) has this image of a different photo session, that included a dog, and has the players peeking under drapes that are placed on square wood supports, to make it appear if all of their heads have just been chopped off in guillotine. They are very strange photos.[195]

---

[195] In those photos are: Arthur Stanley, Edward Stanley, James Creighton, Captain HR Hawkes, Captain Aubrey McMahon, Lawrence Power, John Augustus Baron, Juchereau de St Denis Lemoine, Henry Ward. https://hockeygods.com/images/7101-Rideau_Hall_Rebels___Ice_Hockey_Stick_Fun___1889, Shea p 353

Creation of the Stanley Cup

The legend goes that in early 1892, Stanley's sons finally persuaded their father to donate a national trophy for Canadian hockey. What we do know is that at a dinner on March 18, 1892 honoring the Ottawa Hockey Club (and their recent AHA successes) Lord Kilcoursie read a letter on behalf of Lord Stanley:

> *"I have for some time been thinking that it would be a good thing if there were a challenge cup which should be held from year to year by the champion hockey team in the Dominion of Canada,"* it read. *"There does not appear to be any such outward sign of a championship at present, and considering the general interest which matches now elicit, and the importance of having the game played fairly and under rules generally recognized, I am willing to give a cup which shall be held from year to year by the winning team."*[196]

Later that year Stanley Secretary Capt. Charles Colville, took a trip to England and purchased a silver bowl for 10 guineas (approximately $50 at the time) from G.R. Collis and Company in London. One side of the bowl is engraved with the Stanley family crest under the words "From Stanley of Preston." The other side is engraved with the original name of the trophy: "Dominion Hockey Challenge Cup." The name "Stanley Cup" seems to have been first used as a title of an *Ottawa Evening Journal* article on May 1, 1893. Recall that the owner of the Journal was PD Ross, a trustee. When the Cup arrived in Ottawa from London, and a journalist asked Lord Stanley for his impression of the trophy he responded, "It looks like any other trophy, I suppose."[197] Recently, a silver historian, John Culme, was shown the original bowl of the Stanley Cup to determine its origin. He was able to recognize that the original Cup was actually a "run of the mill for the time" rose bowl. After reading the article (see footnote) I went on the internet myself looking for similar pieces for sale from the same time period. I could have bought an almost exact

---

[196] https://www.nhl.com/news/how-stanley-cup-came-to-be/c-287700534
[197] https://www.nhl.com/news/how-stanley-cup-came-to-be/c-287700534v

145

looking original 1905 bowl for around 500 US dollars. Of course it is not the bowl itself that is of significance but what this PARTICULAR one came to stand for.[198]

Just after the trophy's appearance, Stanley left for England in April (due to the death of his older brother) thus making him the new heir of Derby. He never returned to Canada, was never involved in the presentation of the Cup, nor with any Stanley Cup games. He made two trustees in charge of the trophy. One was PD Ross, and the other was Dr. John Sweetland. Sweetland was a coroner and surgeon for the Ottawa General Hospital, Carlton Jail and the Oddfellows. He was also the Sheriff of Carleton County, and President of the St. George's Society of Ottawa. Sweetland later became surgeon for the Ottawa Hockey Team (known at times as the Silver Seven) in the 1900s. He was also a founder and first President of the Lady Stanley Institute for Trained Nurses in 1890. He was a Freemason of Doric Lodge 58 in Ottawa, and of course was another burial at Beechwood Cemetery. Making this more unique is that Sweetland is also claimed to be the founder of Beechwood Cemetery.[199]

The trustees ran into a problem right off the bat in 1893. The trophy, being set up as a challenge trophy, had to have an initial winner for other teams to challenge. It seemed obvious that the winner of the previous AHA hockey season, the Montreal Amateur Athletic Association, be the initial holder of the trophy. While the team did finish first in the League, it was finalized on the last day only after a default win against the Montreal Crystals, who walked off the ice in protest of a referee allowing a previously ejected AAA player to return for an overtime period. This default angered Ottawa who, if Crystals had won, would have caused Ottawa and AAA tied for first, and required a playoff game to determine the champion. They were still demanding the playoff at the start of the following season. What is interesting in this affair is that the two trustees were from Ottawa, Ross was the manager of the Ottawa club, yet he refused Ottawa's demands for a playoff. Maybe they were trying to appear "neutral," or maybe there was some reason the Montreal AAA team was meant to hold

---

[198] https://www.thestar.com/news/2008/05/24/cup_runneth_over_with_cousins.html

[199] Shea 374, https://hockeygods.com/images/12565-Sheriff_John_Sweetland___First_Trustee_of_The_Stanley_Cup

the first Stanley Cup, as this club was a descendant of James Creighton and the first hockey players in the 1875 games.

Montreal was chosen, but even then it did not get easy, and in fact, when the players found out they could not "keep the trophy for good" after winning it several years, they (via team President James Stewart) refused it. Eventually the cup was given to the Club AAA President James Taylor, and that was the end of a long drawn out experience.[200]

*

1894

Illustration 25: 1894 Stanley Cup champion Montreal AAA. James Stewart is seated third from the left. (Object Number M2005.33.4.24, Credit Gift of Dr. J. Lawrence Hutchison, McCord Museum, Montreal)

The first Stanley Cup game occurred on March 17, 1894. At the end of 1894, four teams finished tied for the AHA Championship

---

[200] I recommend Paul Kitchen's essay "They Refused The Stanley Cup," which you'll find in the second edition of *Total Hockey* (2000). Kevin Shea and John Jason Wilson's book *Lord Stanley: The Man Behind The Cup* (2006) is also required reading on this 1893 experience.

with records of 5 wins and 3 loses. At the time no tie breaking system was in place. As such a three team tournament was decided upon that would happen in Montreal. Ottawa was given a bye to the final (why I am not sure) and on March 17 a semi final game was won by Montreal AAA over Montreal Victorias 3-2. *The Gazette* called it a very "clean game" and that the best hockey was obviously played in Montreal.[201] The Championship game would occur on March 22 at the Victoria Skating Rink, in which the AAA would hold onto the Cup with a 3-1 victory. *The Montreal Gazette* described the game:

> *"The hockey championship was decided tonight, and never before in the history of the game was there so large a crowd or so much enthusiasm. There were fully five thousand persons present at the match; and the tin horns, strong lungs and a general rabble predominated. The match resulted in favor of Montreal by three goals to one. The referee forgot to see many things. The ice was fairly good."* The Gazette also commented on the pro-Montreal crowd and their cheers *"There was 'siss-boom-ah,' 'rah-rah-rah' and several other audible tokens of imbecility and enthusiasm mixed ."* [202]

The Globe carried a different report of the game:

> *"Team play was marred by the softness of the ice. Rough and foul play was frequent, both defenses indulging freely in tripping and slashing. Young of Ottawa was injured by James in the second half and although he finished the game without apparent distress, fainted dead away at the end of it. After the match the victors were carried off the rink."*[203]

One other noted feature of *The Gazette* article was that, *"One of the pleasing features of the match was the display of ribbons. Every*

---

[201] *Montreal Gazette* "Montrealers Victorious" March 19, 1894 p.8

[202] *Montreal Gazette* "Montreal the Champion," 23 March 1894, p. 8. "Coleman vol 1, pg 14

[203] "Montreallers Champions" *The Globe*. March 23, 1894. p. 6

lady almost in the rink wore the favours of their particular club and never did belted knight in joust or tourney fight harder than the hockey men." Players were being compared to medieval knights, appropriate for the new ideology surrounding hockey that was being implemented on the Canadian psyche.

The legacy of the Stanley Cup on the psyche of Canada can not be denied. As Kevin Shea noted "the Vice-regal party gave its endorsement to hockey, and Canadians took notice. With the blessing of the Queen's representative, hockey rose from a child's game to an essential pastime that transcends every community of the entire nation."[204] In a sense one could think of it as the Queen sanctioning hockey as the sport of Canada. Trophies given for other sports by the Governor-General for football (Grey Cup), or lacrosse (the Mann Cup) did not come until after 1900. Hockey was thus being presented I 1893 as the "monarchy's choice" for athletic sport in Canada. It is no surprise that hockey on all levels exploded, similar to what had happened to baseball in the United States after 1871 and chose a professional direction. But that is another 1800s sport with a series of strange, and very obviously false, origin narratives.

---

[204] Shea p 49

7

BASEBALL
Doubleday Doubleplay

"It turned out that Spalding and Chadwick were not mere liars and blowhards, they were conscious architects of a legend, shaping a national identity, would-be creators of a useful past and binding archetypes...They were trying to create a national mythology from baseball, which they identified as American secular religion because it seemed to supply faith for the faithless and unify them, perhaps in a way that would suit other ends."[205] John Thorn

The key sport for this time period south of the Canadian border was baseball, and it has its own mess of an origin story. It needs to be briefly presented because the story is so outlandish that it was disproved right from the get-go. Then they came up with a second origin story, which turned out to be fake as well. However, 90% of people still believe the stories to be true. Neither of the supposed fathers of baseball ever knew that they would be paraded around as fathers. The story of baseball can be used to help us understand the story of hockey, and some other sports I will end this chapter with. For those interested in a more complete examination of baseball origin stories, I suggest John Thorn's *Baseball in the Garden of Eden*, David Block's *Baseball Before We Knew It,* and Brian Martin's *Baseball's Creation Myth.*

---

[205] Thorn, John *Baseball in the Garden* pxii

There are two lies when it comes to baseball. The first is where it originated from; the second is how. The second lie is that the sport just "evolved" out of old English stick and ball pastimes. We will come back to that. Suffice to say all North American sports are given the same M.O. Boys and girls play games with sticks and balls in England for fun. They come over as colonists to the New World, and although they play the same games in North America, something about this continent evolves those games into something else. But here is the catch everyone seems to miss in all of this. If children have been playing these stick-and-ball games for centuries, why does nothing new develop **until** they reach North America? Did England somehow destroy the creative mind for sport development? There is a clue, and as you may have guessed by now, it is that the First Nations people are the unique contributing factor to North America's sports. Just like Canada, the United States was a new country, and it needed elements that socially could be defined as its own. At the top of the list was a national sport. By the 1860s, the country had defined baseball to be that sport. However, no one had really looked into "how it came about" for another 40 years.

*

Doubleday

The former Civil War general Abner Doubleday (who was conveniently dead at the time of the decision) was designated as having invented baseball in Cooperstown, New York in 1839. That was because a commission in 1908 had presented this as the true origin story. As a result, the new Hall of Fame was built in 1939 at Cooperstown, the supposed home of baseball. Except, almost from the beginning, many key baseball people knew it was a lie made up by a key member of the Theosophical Society, Albert Spalding.

In 1903, sportswriter Henry Chadwick wrote another of his many articles over the years, presenting that baseball was the direct descendant of the English game of rounders. This was unacceptable to the star player from the 1870s (now sporting goods giant) Al Spalding. To him, baseball had to be an American game, with an American origin. So rather than finding true historical evidence to prove that, his decision was to make evidence up. He called for a

151

commission to look into the subject, which became in 1905 the Mills Commission (after Abraham Mills, the National League president). Mills had been the master of ceremonies in 1889 in Chicago after Spalding's worldwide baseball tour (we will come to that). As he was presenting an American origin of the sport, many in the audience (the prominent class of Chicago) chanted "no rounders" over and over. The commission was made up of seven men, all either loyal to Spalding or Mills. On April 1, 1905, the *Akron Beacon Journal* newspaper published an article by Spalding that asked anyone who had details on the beginnings of baseball to send a letter to Amateur Athletic Union president James Sullivan. Why exactly such an article needed to be placed in a newspaper in Akron, and not New York, Chicago or Philadelphia makes no sense. Something odd was already afoot.

Magically, just two days later on April 3, a letter was written and delivered to the newspaper by a former miner and real estate huckster, Abner Graves of Denver, Colorado. His letter claimed at first to have seen Abner Doubleday creating the game of baseball in Cooperstown New York, where they both lived in 1839. The claim stated that Doubleday modified a version of a game known as town ball, and used four bases. Graves claimed the first game had players from Otesego Academy and Green's Select School. Meanwhile, the play of the game was described as starting with a ball being tossed high in the air by the pitcher (which is very similar to the game played in Finland today called Pesapallo). The next day, April 4, the *Akron Beacon Journal* published the full letter with the headline "Abner Doubleday Invented Base Ball."[206]

Spalding wrote a letter back to Graves asking for evidence to back up his claim. Graves responded by sending a diagram matching one he said Doubleday had drawn, and added that the first game happened sometime between 1839 and 1841. Graves also changed his story to say that instead of watching the game, he was a player in that first game. This letter was enough for Spalding, who pushed the Mills Commission to make a decision. By the end of 1907, Doubleday was declared the official inventor.

---

[206]Graves letters https://ourgame.mlblogs.com/the-letters-of-abner-graves-8fc6a4694419

There are many problems with the story. The first is Abner Doubleday, who was born in Ballston Spa, New York but was later in his teens sent to Cooperstown, New York to live with his uncle. The city was founded in 1786 by William Cooper, father of the renowned novelist James Fenimore Cooper who wrote *The Last of the Mohicans*. Again coincidentally, Cooper would write large portions of the novel in, you guessed it, Ballston Spa. Which is indicating something is strange in the supposed histories of Cooperstown, Cooper and Doubleday.

The life of Abner Doubleday is one giant myth. When the Civil War started, he was a captain, "magically" posted at Fort Sumter, at the exact point from which the American Civil War would start. It was he who was supposed to have fired the first cannon shot on April 12, 1861. Starting both baseball and the Civil War is quite the resume. Eventually, he rose to the rank of major general and fought at the famous battles of Second Battle of Bull Run, Antietam, and Gettysburg. Even more "magical" is that he is also claimed to have ridden on the train with President Lincoln to Gettysburg when the Gettysburg Address was delivered.

Doubleday became a prolific writer after the Civil War, including articles for newspapers, magazines, letters and private diaries. In this mass of writing, the only time the word baseball appears is from 1871, when he was asking for some equipment. He wrote an amazing sixty-seven diaries; not one of them mentions baseball. John Thorn presented that Doubleday was considered short as a youth, and did not like to participate in sports, preferring instead to spend time at libraries and bookshops reading books on art, poetry and mathematics. Thorn also added that Doubleday had sent three dollars to James Monroe (editor of the Transcendentalism journal *The Dial*), and wrote a very detailed letter to Ralph Waldo Emerson in which he presented his deep spiritual pains and seeking.[207] Even more so, research shows that Doubleday was not in Cooperstown in 1839. He was a cadet at West Point and had been since September 1, 1838.

---

[207]Thorn p220

153

But there is more to the story. Doubleday, a lifelong spiritual seeker, joined the Theosophical Society soon after it founded in 1875. Madame Blavatsky (she of *Secret Doctrine* fame) tends to get most of the focus, but another of the three founders, Henry Steel Olcott is character as well. Most remember Olcott as one of the first Europeans to convert to Buddhism, but few know that he has quite an historical story. Olcott was a supposed to present for the execution of John Brown prior to the Civil War as a journalist, but the story seems like he was never there at all. He was one of three men on the Lincoln Commission to examine the assassination in 1865, doing much like the Warren Commission did after the 1963 Kennedy assassination, misdirect deep examination towards a chosen explanation. He then became a lawyer specializing in insurance and fraud, then came to a seance event of the Eddy Brothers, and began to write articles on it. Strange that someone who was an investigator of the Lincoln assassination) and then fraud examiner, would want to write articles about spiritual doings of what might have been a fraud. And in another oddity, Olcott was also a Freemason.

Blavatsky claimed her society was being guided by Ascended Masters who were attempting to help with the evolution of humanity and prepare for the arrival of the soon-to-come World Teacher (a sort of new Jesus). This organization was not just an early occult or spiritual movement (and there were plenty of those in the second half of the 1800s). Theosophy was set up in such a way as to appeal to a wide variety of spiritual seekers, from Freemasons to Transcendentalists, to those involved with the movement called "Higher Thought" (an original version of the law of attraction). Theosophy was the direct foundation of the 1960s New Age Movement. Almost everything spiritual since 1960 is linked directly back to the Theosophical Society, via the woman who became its key writer after 1900, Alice Bailey.

Some may wonder why I have devoted so much time to a spiritual organization the late 1800s. That is because when the main founders of Theosophy left the United States for India in 1879, Abner Doubleday became the new President. Again, it seems he was in the right place at the right time in history. And the one who proposed Doubleday as Baseball's founder, Al Spalding, was a also an important member of Theosophy. All not a coincidence.

Abraham Mills was also in the U.S. Army during the Civil War and became a longtime friend of Doubleday. It was Mills who organized Doubleday's memorial service at New York's City Hall and arranged for his burial at Arlington National Cemetery. Mills was also closely connected to Al Spalding, as Mills had tried to lure Spalding away from Boston while manager of the Washington Baseball Club in 1875. When Spalding chose to play in Chicago instead, Mills moved there as well to practice law and to assist in the start-up of the new National League. The three of them are interconnected. Spalding as well would become a member of the Theosophical Society and a principal donor. I would have to wonder if Mills was an underground Theosophist as well.[208]

If we look more into Abner Graves, cracks appear in the story. The biggest problem comes from when he shifted his story from watching that first game to playing in it. The problem is that Graves would have been five in 1839, while Doubleday was twenty. Quite a feat for a boy who'd be playing T-ball today to be part of a men's baseball game. Of course, a lot of twenty-plus-year-old men inventing a new sport want to try it out with a five-year-old unknown kid. One must also ask why Graves (who lived in Denver) was in Akron in the first place, at the exact moment the Spalding advert came into the paper. Why was a mining owner from Denver in Akron, Ohio at all? What are the odds he was there the very day Spalding had his search for baseball's origin article published? Was Graves sending this letter of his own accord for his own personal reasons, or was he somehow connected to Spalding right from the start? As a final note on Graves, in 1924, at the age of 90, he shot his 48-year-old wife to death, was declared insane and was committed to an asylum. Not presuming any more about him, just this life ending for him must be brought up.

Given that this story is almost a complete fabrication, the question becomes, why would Graves lie? Author Brian Martin has shown in his book that Graves might have been spinning a tale he

---

[208] Thorn pg 2

155

heard from someone in Denver about an early baseball game played in Ontario, Canada in 1838. John Thorn came up with the best quote, explaining the whole strange fiasco as "These letters may be termed the invention of the invention of baseball, as prior to this date no one had imagined that the game sprung from the mind of a lone individual at a specific point in time."[209]

A little extra information on Graves is required. To begin with, he not only became a Freemason in 1883 but was able to become a Shriner in 1889 as well, joining their lodge in Cedar Rapids. He was also a part of the 1849 "gold rush," which all baseball origin possibilities seem connected with, and he had mining prospects in Nevada, a place Spalding also heavily invested in. He married into the town founder's family of Dow City, Iowa, later having several businesses in town and even starting a bank. After the 1890s depression, he moved to Denver, where he would meet an odd doctor from Canada with a tale of his own.[210]

The letter Graves wrote to the Akron newspaper almost matches one sent by the former Canadian doctor, Adam Ford. He had been the mayor of St. Marys, Ontario —then possibly involved in a poisoning with one of the sons of a man he had a dispute with. After moving with his sons to Colorado, he penned a letter on April 26, 1886, to *Sporting Life* that was printed in the May 5 edition with the title "VERY LIKE BASE BALL: A Game of the Long-ago Which Closely Resembled Our Present National Game." This letter told of a game of baseball he witnessed as a boy in his hometown of Beachville, Ontario in 1838. He also listed the players in the game and gave basic rules. Yet in examining Ford and his son's behavior after reaching Denver, Brian Martin found that they often lied about their past, their achievements, the universities attended, and their careers. It just makes it hard to fully believe the story given the actions of the family. What we can say is that Ford and Graves must have known each other. Ford had rented office space in the new Masonic Temple Building in 1890, where Graves would have been for meetings. They both liked baseball so could meet at the local ball field, and both were drinkers so would have liked frequenting

---

[209]https://ourgame.mlblogs.com/the-letters-of-abner-graves-8fc6a4694419
[210]Martin, Brian *Baseball's* p. 22, 29,42, Thorn 278

Denver's many saloons. All in all, they must have known each other, and so one wonders (given their baseball background) if Ford had ever shown Graves his letter, talked about it, or given him a copy. If so, that is possibly how Graves could have got the outline sketch for his presentation that was sent to Spalding. It could also explain the need to put the letter in the Akron Paper, for had it appeared in Denver (or even a big paper from New York), Ford might have seen it and possibly known his story had been "lifted."[211]

*

Albert Spalding[212]

Al Spalding was one of the stars of early baseball in the 1870s, pitching for the Boston Red Stockings of the National Association starting in 1871, and he was a key component of forming the new National League in 1876. While still playing, he founded the Spalding Sporting Goods Company, which became the main supplier of balls, gloves, bats, and then the standardized baseball. Spalding also sold baseball rule books and annual guides. He even branched out into other sports, selling just about everything, and became a millionaire at a time when being a millionaire meant being incredibly rich.

He was a big part of the Doubleday lie, so we need to examine his life. First, he was sent on a tour of England in 1874 by fellow star player Harry Wright. He took the Red Stockings and Philadelphia Athletics. This was claimed so Wright could show the English people the differences between the game of cricket and baseball. Spalding would take a bigger tour in 1888.[213] This time Spalding took the Chicago White Stockings (today known as the Cubs) and a team comprised of other stars called the All-Americas. They left in October of that year along with a group of business people, sportswriters and wives on a worldwide exhibition baseball tour. The tour was not really to promote baseball, but to show off the new wealth, imperialism and power of the United States. They left

---

[211]You can read the letter in Martin 42-45,
https://protoball.org/Baseball_game_in_Beachville,_Ontario,_1838 North Andrew "The Beachville Game" https://sabr.org/journal/article/the-beachville-game/ Martin 77

[212] https://sabr.org/journal/article/the-guide-to-spalding-san-diego-1900-15/

[213]Chicagology gives a great detail and photographs of this 1888 tour.

157

Chicago and played across the Western US and then Hawaii. From there, it was on to Australia, across the Middle East, and to Egypt, where they played a game in front of the Sphinx at Giza on February 9, 1889. A baseball from that historic contest, kept by tour umpire and future Hall of Famer George Wright, was donated to the Baseball Hall of Fame in 1942. However, given the way they behaved on much of the tour, they were not really there to make friends, or connect with locals—but to revel in their "American superiority." They showed no reverence for the pyramids, as "many players tried punching at the Sphinx's eyes and ... throw[ing] baseballs ... over the pyramids. Spalding later [said the locals] were mortified, but he [explained] the distasteful behavior as mere fun."[214]

From there they played games in Rome (at the Villa Borghese), in Pisa, Genoa, Monte Carlo, Nice, Marseilles, and in Paris on March 8, just across from the incomplete Eiffel Tower being "built" for the 1889 Exposition Universelle. They then played all over the British Isles, including the Crystal Palace in London (site of the first World Exposition in 1851), before returning across the US to end back again in Chicago. It was at a dinner to celebrate the completed worldwide odyssey that the Mills' speech mentioned earlier occurred, with the crowd at the banquet shouting "no rounders." It is significant to discuss this tour because again there is a myth-making quality to it, presenting in a subconscious way to the world (and perhaps to themselves) that baseball had to be an American invention.

But the Spalding story goes on. His former mistress, Elizabeth Churchill Mayer and he were married in 1899. Mayer was a long-time Theosophist and was following the new world leader, Katherine Tingley (who took over after a split in the organization). In 1884 Madame Blavatsky's reputation had been damaged by charges that she had instructed some employees in the use of trickery to simulate psychic phenomena. It led to splits and struggles for control of the movement, both in the U.S. and internationally. Tingley established that she was the new leader in 1898 and presented that she was going to build a new "White City" that was to be the crown jewel of the

____

[214]More can be found in Thomas Zeiler's book on the tour, "Ambassadors in Pinstripes," form his article Zeiler, "Basepaths to Empire" p 203

158

Theosophical Society. Recall that the famous World Fair of Chicago in 1893 was called the White City, so that connection would have been understood by people at the time.[215] To make this (new?) White City, she selected the Point Loma area of San Diego, California, supposedly suggested to her by New York politician (and former Arizona governor) John C. Fremont.

The Spalding marriage took place at Point Loma where Mayer lived, and which was already becoming a giant Theosophical community. Spalding moved there and began to inject a lot of money into the area. The move by Spalding was originally mocked in various newspapers of the day with headlines such as "Leaves Baseball for Mysticism" and "Forsakes Baseball for Theosophy." When asked his views on Theosophy, Spalding generally described it in terms of his wife's passion and that he "married into it." The reading I have done does not indicate this, but rather that he was involved in such spiritual areas long before meeting his wife. The California community wound up with some spectacular buildings with massive amethyst domes and the largest Greek theater outside of Greece. Spalding himself built his own massive octagonal home with crystal on the roof that is now the administrative building of Point Loma Nazarene University. Controversy began to swell around Lomaland after the establishment of a Raja yoga school there.

Spalding built a $2 million cliffside Japanese garden (that later mostly slid into the Pacific Ocean), and a golf course, and was one of the business leaders that were involved in "building" the 1915 San Diego portion of the San Francisco Pan American Exposition. Just by luck, the man claimed to have helped Chicago get the 1893 Exposition over New York, Lyman Gage, "converted" to Theosophy after leaving the Secretary of the Treasury. He built a home close to Spalding. These World Fair connections of Spalding to this story I think are important, but this is a book about the origin of sports, so I will have to leave that for another project.

*

---

[215] You can read my book Exposing the Expositions for detail on all the bizarre lies that have been presented for years about these fairs- because I don't believe much of these expositions were "built."

Baseball Hall of Fame[216]

Truth be damned, the Baseball Hall of Fame was indeed built in Cooperstown. The story of getting the Hall there itself is as strange as can be expected. As early as 1920, there was talk of simply setting up a monument for Doubleday in the city, but nothing more. Then in 1923, the NL president helped the town buy the supposed location of the first game, where they quickly built a baseball park, named of course "Doubleday Field."

The hall eventually came to life via Yale grad Stephen Clark (he was a Freemason (Otsego Lodge 138).[217] He inherited a huge fortune from his Grandfather Edward, who was a partner in the Singer Sewing Machine industry. The family had already built several buildings in Cooperstown, but Stephen felt that tourism was needed to expand the city during the Depression. Then in 1935 came another "magical find." This time it was by a relative of Abner Graves. The relative claimed to have been looking through an old trunk in his attic when he found some books, pictures, and a baseball. He claimed these must have belonged to Graves. The ball did look to be old, and Clark bought what is now called the "Abner Doubleday Baseball." There is no proof of when this ball was from, who used it, or why. But it became added evidence for the proof of the Doubleday story.

Thanks to now having the ball, Clark decided it was time for a baseball museum. He assigned Alexander Cleland, of his estate office staff, to scour the country for baseball relics. The MLB owners liked the idea, a museum would help promote the game in the midst of the depression. So they had set up a 100,000 dollar fund to stage a 1939 baseball "centennial event" at Cooperstown. This is exactly the time a letter showed up on the desk of Baseball Commissioner Kenesaw Mountain Landis. It was from Bruce Cartwright, who claimed his grandfather, Alexander Cartwright, Jr., was the originator of baseball with the Knickerbocker Club of New York, and not Doubleday. He claimed to have diagrams, rules and diaries. Of course as we will see, this whole story is just as much a lie as the Doubleday story.

---

[216] https://www.americanheritage.com/man-who-didnt-invent-baseball

[217] https://www.scottishriteboston.net/en/page.php?id=501#.ZGHrgaXMJPY

Rather than bring up any further debate on baseball history, Cleland kept Doubleday as the founder but promised that a "Cartwright Day" would be included in the anniversary events at Cooperstown in 1939. On June 12, 1939, the National Baseball Museum opened, in honor of the 100th anniversary of the mythical "first game" that allegedly was played in Cooperstown on June 12, 1839. Cartwright was given a special plaque, one we will see that is mostly a series of lies. Doubleday himself has no plaque or enshrinement in the Hall. The word enshrinement is not used lightly, as the entire idea is right out of Theosophical ideology. A key tenant of Theosophy is that of the ascended masters, beings who are beyond the realms of this time, and are guiding humans to go from being mortal to immortal. The inductees of a hall of fame set up by are symbolically the same "ascended masters" of Blavatsky. They are people who have transcended the mortal world, to become the guiding hands of those humans that follow them (the new ballplayers) as they attempt to reach the state themselves of masters. Have you ever wondered why "character" should make any difference if a player makes a Hall of Fame or not? If you were a great athlete you should be in. Yet no Shoeless Joe, Pete Rose or Barry Bonds in baseball. Busher Jackson in hockey was not enshrined until 1971, who had been kept out by Leaf owner Conn Smythe (who we will see was the son of the founder and president of the Canadian Theosophical Movement).

I think today that various hall of fames of each sports do an excellent job of preserving the history and archives of the sport in question. Some excellent historians are associated with them, and perhaps my book will get a few of them to go looking into their extensive archives for more information that might locate a few more jigsaw puzzle pieces of information to help understand the real origin of the major sports.

*

Baseball's Second Origin Story[218]

There is a second origin story, this one surrounding Alexander Cartwright (1820-1892). Cartwright was also a Freemason

---

[218]Mostly taken from the biography of Cartwright at SABR site by **Monica Nucciarone** at https://sabr.org/bioproj/person/Alexander-Cartwright/

and had a very strange non-baseball life story. A lawyer in New York City, he later went west in the rather hard-to-explain California Gold Rush narrative of 1849.[219] Just one year later he showed up in Hawaii and became Honolulu's fire chief. It seems his only firefighting experience had been as a teenage volunteer in New York, which included time with the Knickerbocker Engine Company. Some think these firemen were the origin of the Knickerbocker baseball name. Cartwright rose to such prominence in Hawaii, that he became a personal advisor to then Queen Emma, and then her successor, King Kalakaua.

The Knickerbocker Baseball Club became a new team in the 1840s, breaking off from The New York Club. The Knicks chose to play games in Hoboken, New Jersey at a place known as Elysian Fields. We will come back to that name. The story claims that on September 23, 1845, a constitution, bylaws and twenty rules were adopted by the club. Among these rules are the supposed inventions of an out being recorded for a player touched with a ball (rather than hit by it as had been the previous rule), a foul ball decided, and a set distance between bases. These are now called Knickerbocker Rules and some call them "Cartwright Rules," but there is no evidence at all of Cartwright being a part of any rule creation or even that any such rules were invented. The 1845 Knickerbocker Club gets the "first baseball team" nod for the same reason that Montreal does for hockey: they were an organized team, they created a written set of rules, and they made innovations. Yet when deeply researched, they were clearly not the first organized baseball club, nor the first to write down rules, or even create any rules. They more or less formed a new club and then borrowed, or as Thorn wrote, "consolidated" into one place, various rules used all over the country that they thought were worthy.[220] They were not inventors, but packagers.

The team's first game was played against their former New York Club on June 19, 1846. The New York Club won 23-1. So how good was the "first" baseball club when the team they played in the first game defeated them by 22 runs? Few seem to remark that the New York Club, which had been an active club for much longer, and

---

[219]See the Chapter on San Francisco in my book *Exposing the Expositions*
[220]Thorn p 26

from where all the Knickerbocker players emigrated, must have had more of the original baseball players. Thus the "myth" places the focus for determining origin on rule classification and club structure, not on where players were playing baseball.

Cartwright claimed to be the umpire of the first game played on June 19, but the score sheet from that game is missing from the New York Public Library. A photograph of it was taken by James M. Khan in 1953, and it shows the umpire signature line blank. Cartwright is not on the list of players. For the second game of the day, J. Paulding (very close to the last name Spalding) signed the umpire's signature line. Cartwright's name is again missing.[221]

Cartwright, like Doubleday, wrote a lot in his life, but alas no baseball appears in his writing. There is claimed to be an original handwritten diary of Cartwright's westward journey, now in the Bishop Museum in Honolulu. Bruce Cartwright Jr, (who sent the letter in the 1930s) typed up what he claimed to be the text of these diaries sometime after 1920. His transcription claimed an entry on April 23, 1849, as "During the past week we have passed the time in fixing the wagon-covers, stowing away property etc. varied by hunting and fishing, swimming and playing Base-ball. I have the ball and book of rules with me that we used back home." Monica Nucciarone examined this diary carefully, and she claimed that there is no mention of baseball. Furthermore, she added that certified document examiners looked over the diary and suggested Cartwright could not be the author. Nucciarone wrote, *"DeSoto Brown, archivist and collections manager at the Bishop Museum, states that handwritten items of high importance to families were sometimes transcribed by someone with excellent handwriting. Even if this were the case for the alleged Cartwright Gold Rush journal, why would anything to do with baseball be left out if it was in the original writings?"* Bruce claimed the original diary had been burnt in 1893, and he worked his transcriptions from pieces presented by his cousin Mary. Meanwhile, it was Mary who donated the very diaries that are in the museum. Other men who are supposed to have accompanied Cartwright out West in 1849, Charles Gray and Cyrus Currier, also made diaries but likewise have no baseball mentioned in them.[222]

---

[221]https://sabr.org/bioproj/person/alexander-cartwright/
[222]https://sabr.org/bioproj/person/alexander-cartwright/

As an aside to again get us asking deeper questions, the first masonic ceremony in Hawaii happened in 1860 for the construction of Queen's Hospital, funded by Queen Emma and King Kamehameha IV. Beyond just advising, Cartwright was also the executor of the Queen's will. King Kamehameha V was the first native Hawaiian to become a Freemason, of a lodge built with the help of the acting Grand Master, one Alexander Cartwright Jr. "The king, together with Cartwright, spread cement beneath the Cornerstone for what would become the Judiciary Building."[223] When Cartwright died, his obituary in the key Hawaiian newspapers listed a lot of information about his life, but nothing about any involvement with baseball. How much does that remind one of the omission of hockey in James Creighton's obituary?

As mentioned, Cartwright is in the Baseball Hall of Fame, though some now believe that was done as a means of deflecting the growing controversy over Abner Doubleday. But what is written on his plaque is incorrect. It lists him as "The Father of Modern Baseball," and attributes three rules to him: "Set Bases 90 Feet Apart. Established 9 Innings as Game and 9 Players as Team." The Knickerbocker Rules were not anything like that. Bases were set at forty-two paces; a game was won by the first to reach twenty-one counts (what we now call runs); and each team was to have an equal number of players (not a specified number). So why did the Hall of Fame put the rules as they did on Cartwright's plaque? Were they putting a clue out in the open for anyone with enough historical knowledge to see the pointing to a fraud?

John Thorn pointed out that there were in fact five early baseball clubs in New York: the Gotham Club, New York Club, Eagle Club, Brooklyn Club and a forgotten team, the Magnolia Ball Club. The latter was formed in 1843 and was made up of working-class men. Thus to keep the elite-only origin tales, it was written out of history. Certain interviews with others in the late 1800s have been found, with men such as Daniel Adams, Duncan Curry, and William Wheaton. All were with the Knickerbockers, and their interviews

---

[223]https://sabr.org/bioproj/person/alexander-cartwright/

provide controversy over Cartwright's alleged pivotal role. When reading them, they remind me very much of the rugby player articles from Montreal that began to appear after 1908, in which people seemed to be making statements long after the fact toward their importance in the sport's origin story. Wheaton was a lawyer and, yes, another Freemason among the many people of this story who went West with the 1849 Gold Rush. He claimed in an 1887 interview with *The San Francisco Daily Examiner* that he was the one who developed the "Knickerbocker Rules" in 1837. Meanwhile, Doc Adams was a graduate of Yale, who then got a medical degree from Harvard. He became a practicing doctor in New York and started playing baseball in 1839 as part of the New York Club before he and several others decided to split and form the Knickerbocker Club in 1845. Adams said it was he who developed the position of shortstop in the late 1840s.

A key component of the baseball from England theory is David Block's 2005 *Baseball Before We Knew It: A Search For the Roots of the Game*. "Block traces back the near and distant relatives of baseball to Europe, and England in particular. His hypothesis is that the direct lineal ancestor of baseball is an English game called stool ball which by the early 1700s had evolved into base ball which was a very rudimentary form of what became today's game. Carried to America by colonists a variant of base ball was played in the encampments of George Washington's Continental Army."[224] That of course sounds very familiar to the story of the origin of hockey. English origin, North American transformation, British colonial elite organizing and "patenting" it. Early mentions of baseball in England can be found in Jane Austen's 1798 novel *Northanger Abbey*, the 1755 English novel *The Card*, a diary by William Bray also from 1755, and the book *A Pretty Little Pocket Book* by John Newbery in 1744. All of these references seem to be about boys and girls playing a game, but whatever it was, it had the name baseball.[225] Did baseball exist in England prior to coming to North America, or was it a game played long before colonization and taken "back to England" in the early 1600's, but only catching on with the youth— the upper class adults still preferring their games of football (soccer) and cricket.

---

[224]https://havechanged.blogspot.com/2017/12/madame-blatavsky-and-beginnings-of.html
[225]Thorn p23

Esoteric Layouts

I mentioned I would come back to the myth of the first baseball being founded at a place called the Elysian Fields, in Hoboken, New Jersey. A student of Greek mysteries will notice the name instantly. The Elysian Mysteries were the worship of the goddesses Demeter and Persephone, and the rites of immortality that would come from them. To place the myth of the first baseball game in a location with this name is indicating an attempted presentation of the "first baseball ritual." There is much that could be presented when it comes to the esoteric and mathematical nature of baseball. You are more than welcome to delve deeper into that area if you so choose.

Baseball, unlike any other sport, is made up of countless parts of sacred and esoteric geometry, and occult precepts built into the game. Those that have come across this have thus tried to explain that it must have been invented by Freemasons, given that it tends to be the only group most authors know of that has an esoteric base. I even found a photo of a very odd MLB "Masonic All Star Game" that was played in Trenton, New Jersey on October 12, 1935 and sponsored by the Tall Cedars of Lebanon.[226] I do not in any way think this organization invented baseball, but similar to what happened to hockey and lacrosse in Montreal, they were the ones who were a part of taking perhaps a "lost" sport and repackaged it. When more help was needed to present a plausible origin story, Spalding and his new Theosophical friends were brought in.

Other Sport Origins

---

[226] https://www.fidelitylodge.com/allstargame.php

While I could do the same deep dive into other sports, just a short overview showing the strange questions surrounding their origin claims may be enough to pique your interest and prompt further investigation.

Basketball is a sport claimed to have been created by Freemason James Naismith, in Springfield, Massachusetts. He had been born in Almonte, near Ottawa, in 1861, and then attended, (surprise!) McGill University. The basketball invention has long been presented as his way to keep his students in shape during the winter. He wanted a sport that was indoors and involved limited contact. The claim goes that he used a childhood game he played called Duck-on-a-Rock as a model. This is said to have involved the tossing of stones very high to knock another stone from a boulder. The problem is that there is another 1891 origin story, that of 16-year-old Lambert Will of the Herkimer YMCA of New York. He is claimed to have invented the sport while tossing cabbages into peach baskets at a local general store in 1890. Historian George Fosty looked into this subject and found three photographs of the Herkimer basketball team, the earliest with the date of Fall 1891. The problem is that If Naismith invented a new sport in December 1891, and the first real game happened in January 1892 as claimed, then how could a basketball team have been photographed several months previous to the sport's invention?[227] Then there are the issues that the game has many similarities to the famous Olmec-Mayan ball game of Mexico, which used stone "hoops" and rubber balls. I disagree fully with the anthropological suggestions of how this ancient Maya sport was played, or that the people who lost matches were sacrificed. I wonder what the real connection to the mythology of the sacred text *The Popol Vuh* is. I visited several of these ballcourts in 1999, and there is a deep sense of sacred geometry and architectural magic associated with them. As an aside, Naismith lived in proximity to key Mayan archaeologist Le Plongeon, who was one of the first to make detailed photographs of the Mexican sites, and often traveled to New York for selling artifacts and fundraising. It puts the key Mayan archaeologist of the day in the same geographic vicinity of the two men claimed to be possible inventors of basketball. Le Plongeon was also a Freemason

---

[227] https://boxscorenews.com/inventor-of-basketball-lambert-will-nominated-for-basketball-hall-of-fame-p167737-240.htm

https://freemasonry.bcy.ca/biography/naismith_j/naismith_j.html

and thus could have met Naismith at meetings. He is oddly connected to the baseball story by also being a part of the 1849 Gold Rush, and his theories of the Mexico-Egypt connection were admired by Helena Blavatsky.[228]

Naismith made a very odd quote in 1936 while attending an Indiana high school championship game and said, "While the game was invented in Massachusetts, basketball really had its origin in Indiana, which remains the center of the sport."[229] What does that really mean? Is it a type of code? Perhaps he did not really mean Indiana as a state, but perhaps Indians as a Nation?

The sport of football (soccer) is said to have been created at a meeting in London at the Freemasons' Tavern in 1863, even though it has a history well back into the Middle Ages in England, as well as to the Italian city of Florence. Wikipedia states that "Calcio Fiorentino (also known as calcio storico "historic football") is an early form of football that originated during the Middle Ages in Italy. Once widely played, the sport is thought to have started in the Piazza Santa Croce in Florence. There it became known as the giuoco del calcio fiorentino ("Florentine kick game") or simply calcio, which is now also the name for association football in the Italian language. The game may have started as a revival of the Roman sport of harpastum."[230] The Florence version was an extremely violent combination of soccer and rugby. So was soccer a sport developed by Freemasons in the 1860s, a sport created during the early stages of the Italian Renaissance, or a sport that was played by the Ancient Romans (and perhaps taken from Ancient Egypt)? Once you dig into sports origins, it all starts to get muddled.

Many elements of the Freemason ritual can be found in sport as the website of the Scottish Rite describes *"Masons created two categories of football: association football and rugby football. There are even aspects of soccer and rugby that are mirrored in Masonic*

[228] https://www.masonrytoday.com/index.php?
new_month=5&new_day=4&new_year=2021,
https://en.wikipedia.org/wiki/Alice_Dixon_Le_Plongeon
[229]https://blog.history.in.gov/the-first-state-basketball-champs-crawfordsville-high-school-1911/
[230]https://en.wikipedia.org/wiki/Calcio_Fiorentino

rituals and traditions. For example, the signal used by a soccer referee to indicate a successful goal is also used by the Master Mason during meetings. Even the leadership structure and meeting rituals of the Football Association incorporate many key practices associated with Freemasonry."[231] The American football sign for a touchdown is also linked to be a Freemason gesture, claimed in *Duncans Ritual and Monitor* of 1866 to be the "grand hailing sign of distress."[232]

The claimed "father" of American Football was Walter Camp, who was a Yale Skull and Bones member from 1880. He is the one who is claimed to have brought organization and rules to a more primitive sport (early rugby).[233] As we saw in the Native chapter, various tribes had soccer-like games, stick-and-ball games similar to golf, while a game played by a tribe in California that involved running with the ball and avoiding being tackled to the ground. So even is American football a game from rugby, or from the California Native Peoples?

I know this might have seemed like a strange chapter for a hockey origins book, but the point was to show that the sport of baseball has a very strange origin story as well. This is to provide a foundation that no sports origin has ever really been properly defined. Part of that might be because the photographic record of the 1800s has been taken so far on face value. Like all elements of this research, that too requires a complete re-examination.

---

[231] https://scottishritenmj.org/blog/sporting-gold-masonic-athletes

[232] Duncan, Malcolm C Duncan's Ritual and Monitor of Freemasonry p 18 https://sacred-texts.com/mas/dun/dun02.htm and
https://www.gnosticwarrior.com/freemasons-created-the-game-of-football.html,

[233] https://surreyfreemasons.org.uk/football-and-it-connections-with-freemasonry/,
https://www.scottishgolfhistory.org/origin-of-golf-terms/fairways/freemasons-in-early-golf-history/, https://www.businessinsider.com/most-powerful

8

FABRICATED HISTORY
Toronto and Winnipeg

Now we come to a bit of a key crux to the whole story of the evolution and movement of hockey across Canada, a story that very much needs to be up for questioning. In the standard narrative, Toronto had no hockey before 1888. The story of hockey's magic trip to Toronto first appeared in print in the 1893 *Dominion Illustrated* magazine article titled "Hockey in Ontario" by W.A.H. Kerr. The article claims that in 1888 Montreal AAA goalie Tom Paton visited Toronto on business, and was shocked that no one had even heard of hockey there, "With characteristic energy, he telegraphed Montreal that day for 18 sticks, a puck, and a few copies of the rules. When the equipment arrived the next evening, Paton organized a scrimmage with ten keen skaters."[234] Supposedly, this first real game was February 16, 1888 between the Granite Curling Club and the Caledonia Curling Club. How much skating had the curlers done in their life? What sort of hockey skills would they have had? Three years later in 1891, not only were women playing hockey, the University of Toronto had a hockey team, and a provincial hockey league had been formed.[235]

Here is the part that makes this origin story so unbelievable to me. The Montreal Winter Carnival had been taking place since 1883, with people in attendance like the President of the USA, as well as "elite club members" from all over Canada. So in all those years, no

---

[234]W A H Kerr "Hockey in Ontario" *Dominion Illustrated Monthly* March 1893, https://www.thecanadianencyclopedia.ca/en/article/tom-paton
[235]Kotylo "The History of Hockey in Toronto", *Total Hockey 2000,* W A H Kerr "Hockey in Ontario" *Dominion Illustrated Monthly* March 1893

170

one from any of Toronto's curling, lacrosse, or snowshoe clubs ever came to Montreal and saw a hockey game? None of them who had been supposedly playing shinny their whole life in the winter, were not curious to check out a new updated version of their favorite pastime? That is beyond far-fetched that so many could be at the carnival and all just miss seeing a hockey game. More far-fetched is that hockey had a league operating in Kingston in 1885, and was supposed to have started in Winnipeg in 1886. So no one from the Toronto sporting community also never made a trip to Kingston, or bumped into a player who was telling them about the new sport? There is no way that Toronto in 1888 could be ignorant of hockey in Montreal as the standard narrative suggests. Besides, the sports of shinny, hurley and bandy are supposed to have been widespread all across Canada at the time (as will be shown to be in several Toronto newspapers in the 1860s), so this "new version" would have just been just a slight adjustment to a sport they should already knew. If the Paton story was in any way true, the Toronto sportsmen would have already had hurley-shinty sticks at home, so could have started playing the game with Paton's having to send for a rulebook (I mean there were only ten, he should know what they were) before new sticks were even needed to be shipped for. Again, this whole story seems fishy to me. Either the story is a lie and players in Toronto had been playing hockey for a long time, or the story editors who wrote the newspapers wanted the history of hockey to only originate from Montreal.

The article claims that Paton had been in Toronto on business, and was in the office of J. Massey when he found out about the lack of hockey in Toronto. The Massey family was one of Ontario's wealthiest, a key manufacturer of farm equipment. The family name still stands on such Toronto buildings as Massey Hall and Massey College. So again we have the foundation of the sport tied to the elite. When looking through the genealogy of the Massey family, it took a long time to locate one that had the first initial J., alive in 1888. The only one I could find was a James Massey, to whom the current town of Massey Ontario (far in the Canadian north near Sudbury) was named after.

James was born in New York City to William Massey, but seemed to live in Toronto after that. The historical website of the Massey town suggested that James often traveled to this small

171

community in between his two marriages, then bought a farm in the area. Not much else is known about him, nor is much known about his father William, other than that he was born in Canada in 1829.[236] The article claims there was a second person in the office, that being C. McHenry. Historian Len Kotylo has suggested that both men were members of the Granite Curling Club, and such was the reason the "first game" in Toronto took place between the Granite and Caledonia Curling Clubs. The *Toronto Globe* on February 17, 1888 referenced this game "The play was very exciting and this sport is sure to become popular. "C.G. Crawford scored the first goal for the Granites five minutes after play began. J.E.B. Littlejohn and D. Donaldson also scored for their side before half-time closed. In the second half, the Caledonians scored their only goal."[237]

As for the long origin of hockey in Ontario, is this a very strange quotation at the start of the 1893 *Dominion Illustrated* article:

> *"It would be quite the proper thing to be able to trace the game back to the good old days when all Hamilton used to play all Toronto on one end of Lake Ontario, and the winner used to go to the other end of the Lake to play all Kingston for the championship of the Province, with no bother about gate receipts and on the 'grand old game' principles of no referee nor umpires, but alas history and truth prevent any such touching reminiscence.*[238]

So who was playing these massive hockey games on the Lake between cities prior to 1888? Why would something this large, which even claims to have been played for a Provincial championship, not be listed in any newspaper of the day; either Toronto, Hamilton or Kingston. This could be a veiled clue, as this type of game sounds much more like the Native games mentioned where entire villages would play each other. There would have been no newspaper reports,

---

[236] https://www.masseyareamuseum.com/james-henry-massey.html

[237] Hornby, Lance "First hockey game in Toronto history" Toronto Sun Feb 14, 2015

[238] W A H Kerr "Hockey in Ontario" *Dominion Illustrated Monthly* March 1893, https://www.thecanadianencyclopedia.ca/en/article/tom-paton

as the English papers would not be following what sports the Natives might have been pursuing.

Kerr's article then goes into a long discussion of the first games played in Kingston, including the use of Halifax sticks and a bandstand that was in the middle of the hockey surface making it challenging for players to determine which side of it the puck carrier would emerge from. Kerr then goes on to discuss how "shinty had been played on Toronto Bay away back into the seventies, when annual matches between the Federal and Commerce banks used to be one of the events of the winter, as far as we can learn." Again this idea that it is bank employees who are the first hockey players (as we will see is the same in Winnipeg), wanting to associate elite and finance with those who played a stick game on ice. Yet Kerr states of shinty as far back as the 1870s. Why would people not be playing such games in the 1860s or 1840s? He provides no detail as to his statements.

Kotylo also found references in newspapers to ice games long before the 1880s in Toronto, usually called "shinty." In 1863 the mayor James Smith caught two boys playing shinty on Clara St. on a Sunday and wanting them arrested, while two Sundays later was a similar occurrence on Simcoe St. Another from 1862 suggested young boys on the lake would trip up skaters with their shinty sticks for fun.[239]

Who is the mystery writer, W. A. H. Kerr? Well it seems he was a hockey player for Toronto, listed as playing in a game for Toronto Osgoode Hall against Ottawa on March 2, 1892.[240] Kerr had been one of the original attendees for the first OHA formative meeting in 1890 (led by PD Ross of Ottawa) though Kerr at the time was listed as being a part of Royal Military College.[241] Beyond that I can find no other mention of this player-writer, and that includes on the very complete SIHR player database. As for Paton, again, this is another player with an odd obituary. When he died in 1909, his obituary appeared in several newspapers calling him "a great

---

[239] Listed newspaper and dates for the references: October 12 1863, December 27, 1862 *Toronto Globe https://torontosun.com/2015/02/14/first-hockey-game-in-toronto-history*
[240] *"The Ottawas Are Champions". The Globe. March 3, 1892. p. 6.*
[241] http://pointstreaksites.com/view/oha/about-us/oha-history-8683

173

sportsman" or expert, but only at lacrosse. Only *The Gazette* stated that he was a hockey player, with no mentions of him being a Stanley Cup winning star goalie, nor the founder of the Montreal AAA team, nor even the father of hockey in Toronto. That is strange. Some might suggest that this is because lacrosse at the time was viewed as Canada's national sport, but hockey had overtaken it by 1909 to be the defacto number one sport of the country. So why omit something so obvious of such a key hockey player from the obituary record?[242]

Illustration 26: Barrie Womens Team 1889 (Copy located in Simcoe County Archives, Minesing, Ontario, and also be seen at Barrie Hall of Fame website)

The image above is claimed to be the oldest photo of a women's hockey team in Barrie, late in 1889. Recall that the first woman to play hockey is supposed to be Isobel Stanley in early 1889 (with a photo of her on the ice with female friends on their outdoor Ottawa rink). That means in just a few months, Barrie had also put together a team. The question becomes, who did they play? There seem to be no other teams listed in Ontario. This team continues to have photos taken over the next decade, but in subsequent years, the ladies in the photos look much older. They do not appear to be these

---

242 https://www.thecanadianencyclopedia.ca/en/article/tom-paton

young women who have aged, but different women entirely. So where did these, all seemingly very young women, come together from to play on this first team, and where did they go after the season of play?

Another important element of this image is the sticks they are using. These are very clearly Mi'kmaq sticks, longer and flat bladed. This should have been standard issue for every hockey team in Canada in the 1880s. These women had them, and I don't think they had the money to go out and get top of the line sticks. So why then do we have photos of the men's teams from Montreal in the 1880s using short hurley sticks (such as the 1881 McGill team photo, or the 1884 Carnival action photo). Or did at some time in the mid 1880s someone figured out a new stick to use?

*

Winnipeg

An article by former NHL player turned Brandon University sports history professor Morris Mott outlines some of the history of hockey in Manitoba.[243] In 1893, there were articles in *The Manitoba Free Press* and *The Brandon Mail* that discussed how new hockey was to the province, claiming that the sport was only three years old. The articles placed the beginning of hockey in Winnipeg at 1890, when two clubs; named The Victoria Hockey Club and The Winnipeg Hockey Club originated. However further research shows newspaper reports of hockey games going back to 1886. Also, there were presentations showing hockey games being played on the Red River as well as hockey games being played on ice indoors at roller skating rinks. Most of those games were between teams called the "Bankers" and the "All-Comers."[244] Again it is the bankers are the ones who are "championing" the rise of hockey.

So that then takes us to the story of the person who is supposed to be the "founder of hockey" in Manitoba, and of course we have another superman-like story. This is P.A. MacDonald,

---

[243] Mott, "An immense hold in the public estimation: the first quarter century of Hockey in Manitoba, 1886-1911."

[244] Mott and *Manitoba Free Press* Dec. 23, 1893, pt. 1, p. 6, *Brandon Mail,* March 9, 1893, p. 8.

175

supposedly born in 1857 in Gananoque, Ontario. He became a lawyer (just like Creighton) and moved to Winnipeg in 1880. The claim, with no proof, is that he took a trip to Montreal in 1886 and returned to Winnipeg with some hockey sticks. He is supposed to be one of the players in the "Bankers" vs. "All-Comers" games. He soon becomes one of Winnipeg's leading citizens and references to him over the years in the city's newspapers often state that he had introduced hockey to Winnipeg. So at least this has some sort of credibility, as someone traveled to Montreal, saw the games in person, and then brought it back with them. The big problem here is that Winnipeg is about five times farther from Montreal than Toronto is. Toronto had a railway linking it to Montreal, the Grand Trunk, so the 500 km could be traveled in less than a day. But with no railway linking Toronto to Winnipeg, and with up to 10 days of wagon travel required, you can begin to see my problem with the Toronto stories. If Winnipeg can have hockey, why does Toronto get hockey until two years after Winnipeg? Moreso, is that it seems that Winnipeg had only recently been hooked by rail to the East in November 1885, linking it to Montreal via Sudbury and Ottawa.[245] How convenient that a key hockey player from Montreal seems to show up on one of the first trains from the East to Winnipeg.

What more can we know about Patrick Anderson MacDonald? According to his biography, after graduating with a law degree from Queen's University, he moved to Winnipeg. Being a lawyer, I find it odd that he was also in the cavalry to fight in the North West Rebellion of 1885. He became chairman of a board of a conciliation between the Canadian Pacific Railway and its machinists in 1908, and was also the Public Utilities Commissioner for Manitoba. In the sports field, beyond bringing the first hockey stick to Manitoba (which then immediately discounts all of the sticks used in shinny and hurley and Native America stick games), he is also claimed to have founded; the Assiniboine Curling Club and the Winnipeg Rowing Club. He was also a canoer who paddled to Hudson Bay. He was also a member of the two Winnipeg elit clubs;

---

[245] However the Manitoba Historical Society informed me that a bridge had been built over the Red River in 1881 suggesting a rail link to Montreal could have happened at that time. https://churcher.crcml.org/candate/candate.htm
http://www.mhs.mb.ca/docs/mb_history/58/firstrailway.shtml

the Manitoba Club and the St, Charles Country Club.[246]   I am surprised he is not also credited with starting the first MacDonald's franchise, bringing Bobby Hull to the region, and even personally sculpting the Golden Boy statue while paddling the St. Lawrence River. This is how it is with any of those proclaimed as a "founders" in any way of the sport. It is like they get scripted with a myth of perfection around them. OK, it might be true that he "did everything," and "founded everything," but it seems to me much more likely that he just became one of the a "chosen ones" to explain away how so many new things just starts to appear in this era.

Back to former NHL player Mott, he presented his thesis as to why hockey took so long to form in Manitoba, which was due to there not being a proper indoor arena, thus no good skating ice in the city. The claim is that once an outdoor skating rink was finally built, MacDonald formed some kind of club. However the next year, 1890, which is when The Victorias and Winnipeg clubs formed, there seems to be no MacDonald connection with either team. The founder of the Victorias team in 1890 is supposed to be another Ontario transplant, Jack Armytage. He would have been 18 at the time, pretty young to be the one forming a brand new hockey club, right?. Not only that, but he was also a figure skater, a golfer, a rower, a lacrosse player, but he also scored 80 goals in 50 Manitoba hockey league games. Quite the sports resume! He was also well connected, being a member of the Manitoba Club, the St. Charles Country Club, the Pine Ridge Golf Club, and he was a Freemason.[247]

After 1890, several new rinks were being built in Winnipeg for both curling and hockey, and hockey was being said to explode. *"In Winnipeg, by 1898-99 there were well over a hundred teams. There were the highly competitive "senior" or "intermediate" or "junior" teams--intermediate teams were not quite as good as senior ones, and usually junior teams were composed of younger members of a senior or intermediate club. There were teams from different banks in a Bankers' league, teams from the denominational colleges in an Intercollegiate league, teams from firms such as G.F. and J. Galt and*

[246]Manitoba biographies, http://www.mhs.mb.ca/docs/people/macdonald_pa.shtml

[247]SIHR website, http://www.mhs.mb.ca/docs/people/greenarmytage_jc.shtml

Company (groceries) of George D. Wood and Company (hardware) in a Wholesaler's league, and teams from large establishments such as the Canadian Pacific Railway in a Mercantile league. There were two teams composed of Icelandic-Canadians, and another two teams composed of lacrosse players. There were teams formed by public school students, by newspaper carriers, and by residents of boarding houses."[248] Again, the speed of the rise of the sport of hockey in Canada in this time period is staggering. Unless of course hockey had been around much longer, just in "non-club forms," and thus not suggested as a proper sport, and thus not to be written about in papers. It ~~has~~ had to be presented as a British invention.

*

Stanley Cup

Winnipeg "all star" teams were already making exhibition tours of the East as early as 1893, winning the majority of their games.[249] Not just being seen as equals from the standpoint of talent, but also teams from Manitoba and Winnipeg were making innovations. Some of these included a pre-game warm-up, the development of the wrist shot (as opposed to a more field hockey like smack of the puck), goalies wearing cricket pads to protect their legs, the development of different sticks for goalies, and the adoption of lacrosse-style face offs.[250] Winnipeg finally was accepted to challenge for the Stanley Cup in 1896, which would be held in Montreal on February 14. That, too would create several innovations, mostly the way in which the game was "covered."

So for the 1896 cup, the Winnipeg Victorias traveled east to play the other Victorias from Montreal. It was the first East-West Canadian sporting showdown...that would later get placed into the way the playoffs for football's Grey Cup would be set up. This 1896 match would turn out to be a "one game challenge" played on Valentine's Day. Winnipeg goalie George Merritt turned out to be the focus of the news reports, partially for his wearing of cricket pads (the

---

[248]Mott

[249]Mott, *Winnipeg Free Press* February 1893 and 1895

[250]Fitsell, Hockey's *Captains*, p 94-96, Vaughan *Puck Starts* p.67-68, Mott

first time a goalie had done this in Stanley Cup play), and for shutting out the AAA team 2-0, "Merritt was a phenom, there were 20 times in this half when under ordinary circumstances the Victorias would have scored." Three Winnipeg hotels, (Manitoba, Queen's and Clarendon) were getting telegraph reports sent to them from reporters at the Montreal rink. From there, people were phoning their family and friends at homes and the Free Press related that every single telephone in Winnipeg "was never idle."[251]

A second 1896–Stanley Cup match took place on December 30, 1896 back in Winnipeg, at the Granite Rink, where the Victorias from Montreal won back the trophy 6-5. The arena was sold out, and scalpers were said to be getting over $10 for $1 tickets. Again, the telegraph was used to send play by play reports back to Montreal. *The Gazette* announced, "For weeks it had monopolized all conversation...and ordinary business pursuits have been neglected in the excitement over the impending struggle."

> "For weeks it had monopolized all conversation...and ordinary business pursuits have been neglected in the excitement over the impending struggle." Winnipeg got off to a 3-0 lead in the game, and led 4-2 at the half. After the third goal Montreal captain Graham Drinkwater protested an umpire Clarke's claim, and demanded to have him replaced by Heubach. Later in the game it would be Winnipeg's captain Army who objected to the call of the other umpire, Shearer, and he was demanded to be replaced by Shaw of Ottawa. Shirley Davidson and Ernie McLean scored twice for Montreal, who along with Winnipeg's Dan Bain also with 2 goals led to a tie game at 5. McLean scored his third of the night, on a pass from Drinkwater to win. Eric Zweig included it in his book *Twenty Greatest Hockey Goals.*[252]

Dan Bain and his teammates played by a strict code of behavior. In 1899, their challenge for the Stanley Cup was lost on a

[251] Gazeet and Jenish p18, http://www.mhs.mb.ca/docs/people/merritt_gh.shtml
[252]*Montreal Gazette* December 31, 1896

technicality; team members were outraged when one of their players was injured by a Montrealer who received what they perceived as an inadequate penalty. The Victorias left the ice in protest and forfeited the game (and the Cup). They lost again in 1900. But in January 1901, the Winnipeggers again won the elusive Cup, defeating the Montreal Shamrocks in two games at Montreal. Bain scored three decisive goals in those games.

The star player for Winnipeg was Dan Bain, a Manitoba athlete to excelled at everything. "Virtually every Manitoban of the day would recognize Bain on sight, or at least knew him by reputation, because he was widely admired or hated—depending on one's disposition. Described as one of the most broadly talented athletes in Manitoba's history, as well as one of its wealthiest businessmen and most eligible bachelors." His story is actually quite bizarre and at times somewhat troubling (when looking behind the scenes). I don't want to go too deep on this person, but if you are interested I leave a few articles for you to check out in the footnote.[253]

He was born in Ontario (Belleville, 1874), and moved to Winnipeg with his family when he was six. His father was wealthy, and added to that wealth by buying farmland and horses "on behalf of the British government." Dan Bain was also one of the great athletes of his generation. He won a roller skating championship in 1887, a pairs figure skating championship, a speed-skating championship, was Manitoba's all-around gymnastics champion, one of the province's first bicyclists, and a lacrosse and golf star. Yet he became best known for hockey, when he decided to give that sport a try in 1895. He played for seven seasons and won the Stanley Cup twice, in 1896 and 1901. The SIHR website has him scoring 93 goals in 41 Provincial games, and another 8 more in 11 Stanley Cup games. He stopped participating in 1902, still the best player in Canada at the time. As he aged, he had very little good to say about hockey, either the changes to the game, its professionalization, and the conduct of the players who were playing it. He was inducted into the Hockey Hall of Fame

---

[253]Manitoba History: "Dan Bain: The Squire of Delta Marsh" by Gordon Goldsborough Number 80, Spring 2016 http://www.mhs.mb.ca/docs/mb_history/80/bain.shtml, and the SHIR website for stats on Dan Bain

in 1949 and responded that, "the honour gave him no great thrill, because the quality of the other players in whose company he was enshrined was so low." Yet he did keep skating, winning another Canadian pairs figure skating championship in 1930 at the age of 56.

Bain became a grocery and food king, operating Donald H Bain Ltd, in the city that was the hub for all goods going to Western Canada. He bought the famous Waghorn House at 69 East Gate of Winnipeg. Though large, he immediately renovated it to add such things as a spring-mounted dance floor and a trophy room to display his extensive collection of sports and hunting memorabilia. Described by a friend as "salty in speech and strongly opinionated," Dan Bain was tough and individualistic. He felt justified in forcing his strict, moral code on everyone with whom he interacted, going so far as to fire one of his nieces when she used a swear word while working at his company. Later in his life, Bain would often tell a typical visitor to his Delta hunting lodge that, to be successful in life, he should avoid three things: women, liquor, and politics. He never seemed to drink. In fact, visitors to Bain's lodge recalled having to sneak alcoholic drinks in their bedrooms because Bain refused to let them drink in his presence. Bain also had an abiding love of dogs and often had at least a couple with him at all times. It was widely claimed that he treated his pets better than members of his family. He also purchased a secluded hunting lodge (Mallard Lodge), that to add privacy, built a wall around its entirety.

Dan Bain was a Freemason, a Khartum Shriner, and an Odd Fellow. He was also a Life Governor of the Winnipeg General Hospital, President of the Niakwa Country Club and the Winnipeg Winter Club, and a founding member of the St. Charles Country Club. He had his hand in everything in Manitoba. Though a lifelong bachelor, he had several women around to look after his house, or at least that was the way it was presented. There is much more strangeness surrounding his life that I do not want to get into here, but you are welcome to follow the footnoted references and look into it yourself.[254] There will also be quite a bit of strangeness surrounding the many hockey photos of the 1890s that Bain appears in.

---

[254] http://www.mhs.mb.ca/docs/mb_history/80/bain.shtml

181

Theosophical Society

Back to the Toronto story. One more person in the 1890s must be considered, though he himself did not seem to have that much of a direct interest in hockey. That is Albert Smythe, who was the founder of the first branch of the Theosophical Society in Canada in 1891. He was the father of Conn Smythe, who would later become the owner of the Toronto Maple Leafs, changing their name from the St. Patricks, and their uniforms from green (to blue). During the depression he built Maple Leaf Gardens, known at the time as one of the "cathedrals" of hockey. Conn Smythe was known for having a very physical fighting team (known for the phrase "if you can't beat them in the alley, you can't beat them on the ice"), and was perhaps the key driving force within the NHL owner meetings and league decision process for several decades until he sold the team in 1964 to a group that included his son and Harold Ballard.[255]

Back to Conn's father Albert, Albert was said to have met one of the Theosophical founders William Judge in 1884 while on a boat emigrating from Ireland and immigrating to North America. Albert Smythe was a journalist for both the *Toronto Globe and Toronto Star*, as well as being a well-known poet. Some biographies suggest the death of a young lover might have been the cause to send Albert emigrating to America in the first place. Such an emotional state would of course make his mind "ripe" to be filled with any organization offering promises. Interestingly, Smythe's 1891 charter would be the last one personally signed by world Theosophical co-founder Helena Blavatsky before her death later in the year.

*

Photographs

I want to end this chapter with a discussion of some very strange photographs of hockey players or teams from 1885-1900.

---

[255]Information on Smythe can be found at History of Theosophisty in Canada
https://www.Theosophistycanada.com/history-of-Theosophisty-in-canada.php
and https://www.Theosophistycanada.com/files/albert-e-s-smythe-bio.pdf

Many have a "doctored" aspect about them. Often there are heads that are cut out and pasted in, other times entire people or objects are added or removed, as well as extremely odd sexually suggestive posings. There are clues in these photos, and I will share a couple of obvious oddities to peek your curiosity about this line of research.

Illustration 27: Suggested to be the Montreal Victorias in 1895, but the odd V on the shirt questions that. (Object Number MP-0000.257.1.1, Gift of the Estate of Mrs. Graham Drinkwater, McCord Museum)

The first odd photo comes from the McCord Museum and is listed as the Montreal Victorias playing in 1895. The closest player to the camera is suggested to be star Graham Drinkwater. It was given to the museum in the 1930s by Drinkwater's widow. I would agree that the photo is genuine and was part of his personal collection. What caught me as odd is the first player has an obvious V drawn on the front of his white shirt with a black marker. None of the other players have this black V on their shirt. The Victorias of the era did not wear white shirts in games, instead dark sweaters with a white V (see photo below).

183

Illustration 28: Montreal Victorias of 1898 with the Stanley Cup (Photography studio Wm. Notman & Son, Object Number II-124120.0, McCord Museum)

So why does the black V need to be put on the player in the first photo? Is that really the Montreal Victorias playing in 1895? If it was any type of league or Stanley Cup game they would be wearing the sweater above. By the way, that is Drinkwater seated to the left of the Stanley Cup for comparison to the first player in the previous photo. Secondly, the match would not be on the open ice as this is (which seems to be the McGill Rink, see final photo in chapter nine), but would have been played inside the Victoria or Crystal Arena. There are also no people here watching the game, seeming like a few passers by who just stopped to see what was going on. That would not be the case in a key game in the 1895. And what of the person walking across the ice in the background, looking as though he is climbing stairs? Obviously whatever this picture was, by placing the black V on the shirt, it is attempting to trick people into thinking they are seeing a photo of the 1890s Montreal Victorias. Why? My guess is that this photo could be from one of the early carnivals, or perhaps some sort of practice game. But this is a perfect example of how it is easy to make mistakes with photographs without looking at them very carefully.

As for star rover Graham Drinkwater. Of course he graduated from McGill, yet is listed as only playing seven seasons, from 1893-99. Even with so few games he was considered the star of his era (along with Winnipeg's Dan Bain). After retiring he became a referee, a trustee for the Allan Cup, and a key stockbroker with his own firm in Montreal. He, along with his wife, also became key supporters of the Montreal Orchestra.[256]

Illustration 29: Winnipeg Victorias 1894-95, notice the heads of the two young players on the right. (Victoria Hockey Team, Winnipeg, 1894-95. "Champions of the World" Courtesy Hockey Hall of Fame / PA-050667)

------

[256]Wikipedia Drinkwater page and http://www.greatesthockeylegends.com/2012/02/get-to-know-hall-of-famer-graham.html

Illustration 30: Winnipeg Victorias 1896. This is the same photo as above, notice the two heads pasted in on the the right (credit Manitoba Archives, Manitoba Sports Hall of Fame)

Here are two more odd photos. The first is of the Winnipeg Victorias of 1894. The second appears to be the same photograph, but this time listed as the team in 1896. If you look closely you will notice two of the younger players to the right of the 1894 photo, have had their heads pasted over with two much older players. Of the original players, the one seated was goalie Jack Shepard, pasted over in 1896 is the man with the mustache- the famous goalie George Merritt. Both at times in the 1880s played goal for the Victorias, but Merritt was the one in goal for the Stanley Cup games. The other young player replaced is Ford Thomson, who played up and down between senior and intermediate hockey for the Victorias in the 1890s. Obviously, in 1896 they wanted a new updated photo of the winning team, but rather than take a brand new one, they just pasted in the two heads into the old photograph. You will notice this strange photo shopping of pasted in heads, and even people, again and again in this era.

Also odd is that to the left in both photographs is the star Dan Bain. Bain's head seems to have been "added in" already in the first photograph. The colour and texture of his head seems off compared to everyone else (it is too bright as if light by a different source). What is even more odd is how the photographer placed his right arm suggestively over the leg of cover-point Higginbotham. Every one of these team photos of the era was very staged, as you will notice by seeing some players looking one direction, others straight on, others somewhere else. All have been carefully posed. Why does the photographer want Bain in this position? In the second photograph from 1896 you notice that is darker, and the bottom of the image has been cut off, making it harder to notice the suggestive layout of Bain's arm.

There are often some of the hockey sticks positioned to look like extended penises of the players. I have found this "penis stick placement" in at least twenty photographs of the era. One is the Montreal Victorias of 1888 (shown above, illustration 28) occurring with the two players sitting closest to the Stanley Cup. Other examples of this stick placement are the photos of the 1891 Ottawa Hockey Club, and the 1897 Winnipeg Victorias (see at footnote).[257] Why have the photographers done this? Again this is not accidental, the photographers have posed the players this exact way. If you look at the Winnipeg 1899 photo that appears in Art Farrell's hockey book of that year[258] it again appears that Bain's head seems to be "doctored" into the photograph. Almost photo of Winnipeg from this era seems that there is always something wrong with Bain's head, and often he is the only oddity in the image. Another is a dressing room photo where Bain is not in uniform, but is standing on the left side of the players wearing a long coat, with most of his face covered by a bandage.[259] Yes, he might have taken a stick or puck to the head and had to leave the game, but it is constantly odd that there is something about his

---

[257] https://en.wikipedia.org/wiki/1890%E2%80%9391_Ottawa_Hockey_Club_season#/medi a/File:OttawaHockeyClub1891.JPG

https://hockeygods.com/images/13205- Winnipeg_Victorias___Victoria_Hockey_Club___1896___1897_Season

sihrhockey.org/2020/columns/article.cfm?aid=705

[258] https://no.wikipedia.org/wiki/Fil:Victoria_Hockey_Club,_Winnipeg,_1899.png

[259] https://hockeygods.com/images/11866-Winnipeg_Victorias___1896

face in all of the photographs. I mean he was on those teams, wasn't he?

If these few photographic oddities have peeked your interest, I encourage you to take a look at other hockey team photos from the 1880s and 1890s. Some of the strange images likely have a simple explanation for the appearances, but not all. I have just begun to look into the images of the other sports during the 1880s and 90s, and am finding similar questions about them. I have no specific answers, but something is very strange that is going on with the photographic record of this time period.

But there are more strange links in the story that will be presented in the final chapter. This includes the possible ties of the Mi'kmaq Peoples to Ancient Egypt and the Knights Templar, Sandford Fleming's very odd life, and the possible pointers within the first hockey book published in Canada.

9

SANDFORD AND SON
The clues to the origin

"There is a season for every thing, and we do not notice a given phenomenon except at that season...Boys fly kits and play ball or hawkie at particular times all over the state. A wise man will know what game to play today, and play it. We must not be governed by rigid rules, as by the almanac, but let the season rule us...You must live in the present, launch yourself on every wave, find your eternity in each moment."[260] (H. D. Thoreau)

Now we come to the final chapter of the book, and one where we must look at the varied pieces of evidence in a new light. There will be no definitive answers here, but likely a lot of new concepts that you have likely not seen presented before.

*

Mi'kmaq

There are two very unique areas of examination when it comes to examining the Mi'kmaq People.[261] The first is with their tribal council flag. I cannot post images of flags due to copyright rules, but it can be seen at[262]. To anyone who has studied the Knights Templar, the Mi'kmaq flag will look identical (with just the position of

---

[260] Found in Isaacs, Neil David *Checking Back* p.18

[261] I reached out to several elders of the Nation, but none responded to my emails for conversation and discussion prior to publishing this book.

[262] https://en.wikipedia.org/wiki/Grand_Council_(Mi%27kmaq)

189

the star and half-moon reversed) to the Knights Templar battle flag.[263] Why? There is supposed to be no contact between North America and Europe until 1492, and certainly not with the group of knights from Southern France that were attempted to be exterminated by the Church of Rome in 1307.[264] However it is clear that many Templar Knights escaped the slaughter in France, as did their "treasure." One of the suggestions of what that treasure was is the Holy Grail. Some theories link the escaped Templars directly with Nova Scotia. Perhaps the identical flag is not a coincidence as current scholars maintain. The connection to Scotland is important as the province is named "New Scotland."

One suggestion is that the Templars went to Scotland, helped Robert the Bruce defeat the English at Bannockburn, and helped build Rosslyn Chapel. Why Scotland? That would be links that exist between France, Normandy, the Norwegian Vikings and Scotland (specifically the Orkneys), which were controlled by the Norwegian kings well into the 14th century. There are many similarities between the two areas including stone circles, and the ogham and rune languages. Some historians connected the Templars with Henry Sinclair (St. Clair), the Earl of Orkney, who was confirmed in 1379 by the Norwegian King Haakon at Marstrand, now a small island-town in Sweden, though close to several of Sweden's largest stone circles. For some reason Wikipedia has listed this town as being near Tonsberg, Norway (which is on the other side of the Fjord). Tonsberg has ruins of an old Templar round church, so perhaps there is a sly comment being made for those who can figure out the clue.

The St. Clair family has its roots in Norway, with the Earls of Møre on the West Coast near modern day Ålesund. These earls were related to the Earls of Orkney in Northern Scotland through two Norse brothers in the late 800s. After 1206, there becomes an unknown period of rule in Scotland (similar to the unknown Hyksos period of Ancient Egypt) upon which came the first Scottish named

---

263 The two flags can be seen side by side at

    https://mysteriesofcanada.com/nova-scotia/the-curse-of-oak-island-season-4-episode-2-always-forward/, http://www.danielnpaul.com/Mi%27kmaqFlags.html

264 The Church of Rome first exterminated the Cathars from Southern France in the late early 12th century, and these two crusades are without question linked, and as I suggest in my book *Exit the Cave.*

king Henry Sinclair in 1379. Henry is the grandfather of William Sinclair, the one claimed to have built Rosslyn Chapel. Where did Sinclair get his name from? A treaty was signed by the Viking leader Rollo with King Charles of France in 911. This treaty created the Duchy of Normandy. These new Viking rulers became known to history as the Normans, who originally were called Nordmans (the European name of the Northern Vikings). Rollo and his group of conquerors changed their surnames to that of the place the treaty was signed Sanctus Clarus (holy light) Sur Epte, which in time became St. Clair then Sinclair.[265]

Henry Sinclair connects to our hockey story as he was identified by Johann Reinhold Forster in 1784 as a possibility for the person described as Prince Zichmni by the Zeno Brothers of Venice in their personal letters written around the year 1400. These brothers described a long voyage throughout the North Atlantic with their captain, Zichmni. Many historians claim the letters are a hoax, but part of such rejection is due to what that truth would mean to the standard historical narrative of Christopher Columbus being the first European to North America (which is another narrative full of holes). Several possibilities of proof for this contact do exist, from plants depicted in Rosslyn Chapel that are only native to North America, or the Westford Knight Rock Carving in Massachusetts that some researchers have claimed to depict one of Sinclair's travelers (Sir James Gunn). Native historian Evan Pritchard attempted to claim that the famous mythological hero of the Mi'kmaq, Glooscap, was Sinclair. I do not believe this is the case as the myth is obviously very old in its origin. However, the Mi'kmaq could have incorporated Sinclair and his Knights Templar into an already existing myth.[266]

Another suggestion is that the Templars sailed to Canada to bury their treasure in the famous pit on Oak Island, Nova Scotia. Yes, we can not ignore that one of the world's great mysteries lies less than fifty miles south of the supposed birthplace of hockey. There have been millions of dollars spent, and several deaths, in the last century

---

[265] Can this treaty be a reason for the Allied forces invading Normandy in 1944 when other areas seemed much better for an amphibious landing?

[266] More Sinclair information can be found at the following sites,
http://www.orkneyjar.com/history/historicalfigures/henrysinclair/princehenrytrip2.htm
https://jamesonfamily.org/Sinclair_Gunn.html

exploring what has come to be called "the money pit" on the island. As to what this hidden treasure is, runs the gamut from the Holy Grail, to the lost works of William Shakespeare, to the body of Jesus. What is really interesting is that there are no oak trees in Nova Scotia. But they grow only on this particular island, and another island on the opposite side of the province, both of which are linked by the Gold River. It is as if the two oak islands that are marker points to this river of transportation. Books such as *Templars Across the Atlantic* suggest that Sinclair built a castle in central Nova Scotia along the Gold River (now just a ruin). Recall that the name of the river "gold" is also the symbolic name of the final work of the alchemic process.[267] Keep in mind, that the Stanley Cup became known as "hockey's holy grail" at a very early stage in history. Did people place a subtle clue about the origin of this sport into this trophy's nickname?

*

Then we come to the Mi'kmaq hieroglyphs, a written language of over 5000 individual symbols.[268] Actually, they are more like ideograms, one symbol stands for entire concepts as opposed to sound to picture correspondence. As such, they are similar to Ancient Egyptian and Mayan hieroglyphs. The Europeans try to take credit for this language, the early French missionaries claiming that they updated some early drawings the Mi'kmaq would make on trees and birch bark. The most famous claimant to be the inventor is Pierre Maillard, a French Jesuit preacher in the early 1700s. He claimed to have made the glyphs so that the Mi'kmaq could read the Bible. Today there is even a statue of Maillard in front of a church in Nova Scotia honoring his invention. If Maillard really gave the Mi'kmaq a language to use and to read Biblical texts, why would he not give them Latin, the very language texts of Christianity would be written in, or French, that the missionaries would be using? It is obvious that

---

[267] https://www.historyscotland.com/history/the-knights-templar-and-scotland/,

http://www.glastonberrygrove.net/reference/history/micmac/templars.html
https://templars.fandom.com/wiki/Colony_Of_Templars_In_Early_America
[268] Details on the glyphs can be found at https://www.starmythworld.com/mathisencorollary/2011/07/case-of-micmac-hieroglyphs-powerful.html , https://www.muiniskw.org/pgCulture4a.htm , https://en.wikipedia.org/wiki/Mi%EA%9E%8Ckmaw_hieroglyphic_writing

Maillard did not invent anything; he tried to take ownership of something that already existed.

These glyphs are listed by other missionaries long before Maillard. In 1652, Father Gabriel Druillettes, another Jesuit missionary, reported seeing the Mi'kmaq use ideograms to record his teachings, "*Some of them wrote out their lessons in their own manner. They made use of a small piece of charcoal instead of a pen, and a piece of bark instead of paper. Their characters are novel, and so individual that one could not know or understand the writing...they carried away this paper with them to study in the repose of the night.*" In 1677 Father Chretien Le Clercq, a Franciscan, made notes in his journals of observing Mi'kmaq children taking notes using charcoal and birch bark as he was teaching them prayers. He also claimed to have learned the language and then expanded it with new symbols to help explain the Christian ideology better. In 1691, he published *Nouvelle Relation de la Gaspésie,* wherein he discusses his development of this writing system. This at least is more plausible, for Le Clercq acknowledges that the written language existed before him, and he merely added a few extra symbols. This is similar to what was done with Coptic in the Middle East that took the older Egyptian language and then added some Greek letters for sounds specific to Ancient Greek. In 1866, Father Eugene Vetromile (Society of Jesuits), published *The Abenakis,* where he discussed that the Native Peoples had written manuscripts held by medicine people: *"Several Indians possessed (in the time of the first French missions) in their wigwams, a kind of library, composed of stones and of pieces of bark, and the medicine men had large manuscripts of these peculiar characters, which they read over the sick persons... The Indians assert that by these signs they could express any idea with every modification, just as we do with our writings.*"[269] Other tribes across North America, such as the Ojibway, also had glyph-like writing systems that they placed on birch bark. The Mi'kmaq have a slightly different twist.

The twist revolves was first presented in the work of Barry Fell, who was a marine biologist at Harvard, but also was an expert in

---

[269]https://www.muiniskw.org/pgCulture4a.htm

ancient languages.[270] He wrote the book *America BC,* in which he attempted to claim that Celtic and Egyptian visitors came to the Americas long before Columbus, based on pieces of ancient languages he found in the Americas. When examining the Mi'kmaq hieroglyphic language, Fell noticed that the glyphs used to depict the Lord's Prayer in Vetromile's 1866 book, were similar in appearance to Ancient Egyptian hieratic (a faster, simpler form of hieroglyphics), but also were similar in meaning.[271] What seemed interesting to Fell was that the Native language was definitely Native in spoken sound, yet they appeared Ancient Egyptian in their written form. Fell claimed other artifacts from across North America also depict the Ancient Egyptian language (and early Libyan), such as the Davenport Calendar Stone found in 1874 in Iowa, and the Shell Stone found in 1888 in Long Island, New York.

These of course are Fell's personal opinions, and from my own knowledge of hieroglyphs, I can see he made many errors of correspondence. Yet some word-glyphs do seem to be a perfect match. Many scholars and archaeologists discredited Fell, many claiming that by being a marine biologist he could not have understanding of languages. The reason this thesis gets un-examined is because of the possible implications it could have on the "Columbus finding North America" myth. An interesting website was looking into the work of Dr. Fell and presented this overview of standard history and I wanted to share it here,

> "Archaeologists, anthropologists and ethnographers work hand in hand with historians. Their job is to present information that protects and preserves political history. As a unified group these folks soundly condemn the work of Dr. Fell. They do so without basis in fact and a vengeance undeserved. His revelation that the Celtic, Arabic and other People visited, emigrated and traded with Native Americans, is

---

[270]Fell's real name was Howard Barraclough Fell, and his father was a railway engineer and inventor in England., who created the Fell Mountain Railway System.

[271] Fell, *America BC* pg 253, pgs 254-55 present the Mi'kmaq glyphs and Egyptian glyphs side by side for comparasin. This book can be found at archive.org , Good work in Italian with useful diagrams by Alberto Arecchi titled *Il mistero dei Micmac* http://www.liutprand.it/micmac.pdf

simple truth. History hides these facts from the general population. They would rather keep the idea that the Native Americans were illiterate savages, incapable of civilized behavior. Nothing could be farther from reality."[272] (Equinox-Project)

As for Barry Fell, his real name was Howard Barraclough Fell. His father died in a fire on ship while working as a seaman. Barry's grandfather was a railway engineer and inventor John Barraclough Fell, who created the Fell Mountain Railway System in England. John later built railways in Italy, Malta and over the Swiss Alps. As a "railway genius" of his time, he would have been known, and possibly met, Sandford Fleming. It is just interesting how easy it is to connect the people in this story to Fleming.

There is not much of this hieroglyphic language that can be found in modern Mi'kmaq culture. Over the last one hundred years the language has mostly been lost. The reason scholars generally provide as to how the language was lost is that a "written language was not that useful to the Mi'kmaq, being a primarily oral culture."[273] It does make one wonder, if the Mi'kmaq seemed to have a very unique ball-and-stick ice game compared to the rest of the continent, and they had a very unique hieroglyphic language that might have connections to Egypt, then could the unique ice/field game be so unique because it was a game shared by their Egyptian/Viking Trans-Atlantic contacts in the distant past?

*

Freemasonry

I must present a short overview of Freemasonry itself. A Freemasonic writer, writing for the masses, described the organization as *"Freemasonry is a strange topic. It's not a religion, but it's religious. It's not a political movement, but its members are some of the greatest political and social reformers in history. It's not a charity or service club, yet its various organizations operate outstanding*

---

[272] http://www.equinox-project.com/DRFEL.HTM
[273] https://www.muiniskw.org/pgCulture4a.htm

195

charities." So then, what is it? This of course is a secret society, full of oaths, initiations, and secrets. Hoddap claims, *"Masons like to say that Freemasonry is not a secret society; rather, it is a society with secrets."*[274] Thus a secretive answer about secrets. That is the Freemason side, that they are a fraternity of men (women have their own lodge) who are bound by oaths, with a focus on charity and helping one another. Sounds harmless.

Other examiners of Freemasonry present that it is the organization that is behind everything that goes on in the world, and which at the highest level, is looking to exert complete control over this entire realm and everyone in it. Francine Bernier commented, *"Secrecy was the golden rule of Freemasonry. Very few people today know how deeply involved Freemasons were with the politics that defined Modern Europe and North America."*[275] They have had their hidden hand in the layout of key cities like Washington DC, their members hold the highest of positions of power, and if one looks closely they have had their hand in just about everything in the last 200 years. So why not have a hand the origin of sports as well?

Readers Digest put out an article in 2022 that tried to explain why so many key historical figures were photographed (or portrait painted) with one hand in their jacket. The claim made was that there is a belief that in Ancient Greece it was disrespectful to speak with your hands outside of your clothing. The article claims that this is reason why photographers and painters wanted a hand hidden, to imply "a noble, calm comportment and good breeding."[276] However, the other hand is always visible. Why only one? Just to show that they were only half-noble, or there was only good breeding on one side of the family? This is the kind of misdirection that is thrown around. The reason for being photographed with a hidden hand is clear. The gesture shows that they are a Freemason, and are in living in line with Freemasonic ideals. It is a message, and is not accidental.

I am not presenting this topic to force you to believe one side or the other, or to try and present any person connected with these

---

[274] Christopher Hoddap *Freemasons for Dummies* p 2, 16

[275] Bernier, *Templer's Legacy* p.15

[276] https://www.rd.com/article/historical-figures-hand-in-jackets/

organizations today in any specific light, only to show fully that this group (and other similar secret societies) were deeply involved in the creation and growth of sports in the 1800s. My research for this book has shown that that is not in doubt. The question people need to ask themselves is, why? Why do these esoteric and secretive groups want to manufacture sports during this time period? Those sports eventually turned into "sporting empires" that they themselves would wind up in the ownership and administration of? But I do not think what sports has become, was the reason for its creation. It was about the seeming connection of the "top" of society with the "bottom."

There is one more part to this puzzle that takes us back to the city of Montreal.[277] That is because the formation of Montreal was not just done of a whim. Montreal was originally named Ville Marie, a site where a group of what can only be called "mystics" were sent by the Compagnie du Saint-Sacrament and its leader Jean-Jacques Olier (aligned to the mystic St. Sulpice Cathedral in Paris). They were sent specifically to start a New Jerusalem. I do not say that lightly. That was the real founding plan of 1640.

Jacques Cartier first explored the region of Quebec in 1574, then Samuel de Champlain in 1608. He set up the city of Quebec, and put the Jesuits in charge. That was another thing Olier was trying to do, bring his vision of a new world (related to the worship of the divine feminine) and create a new city away from Jesuit control. There is even talk that the "mystic visions" claimed by the founders were really a code that they were bringing with them, the Holy Grail. Perhaps not an object per sey, but the wisdom that was the basis of what it stood for. 1642 Paul de Maisonneuve, Jeanne Mance and others landed and formed a city, with what became a series of ritual, ceremonial and mystical activities. This city is linked by all sorts of connections to Southern France, the Holy Grail, the Cathars, the Knights Templar, and the Grail initiation cave at Montreal De Sos. Some have also suggested that the painter Poussin's famous 1640 painting *Et In Arcadia Ego,* depicts the four initial founders of Ville Marie.

---

[277] *See Berneier's Templars' Legacy* for information on the founding of Montreal, the story of Rennes Le Chateau and Southern France can be examined in my 11 part series on my social media channels

The strange mystical founding of Montreal is too much detail for this examination, but it cannot be ignored that just about every major North American sport's origin is tied to McGill University in the city of Montreal. Given that the city was set up, and run for over a century as a New Jerusalem and that all of the early city's architecture was filled with esoteric and alchemic symbolism, it must be acknowledged that there is a connection between the place (Montreal), the esoteric wisdom behind its foundation, and that which happened there (the founding of various sports). There is a reason Montreal was chosen as the birthplace of North American sports. The question is, who might the father of those births be?

*

Sandford Fleming

Illustration 31: Sandford Fleming in 1903 (Object Number II-147485, Notman Photographic Archives, McCord Museum)

It is time to return to the story of Sandford Fleming and look more deeply into his possible connections to the hockey origin story. Recall that he is connected directly with James Creighton in Nova Scotia, getting him the very job that takes him to Montreal. Fleming was likely also the one who let Munro Grant know that Creighton was an historical writer. I would likely guess that Fleming was also very influential in getting Creighton his job at Parliament in Ottawa (not far from Fleming's own estate that included his private skating rink). Fleming was also connected with Lord Stanley via their role as investors in the new Rideau Ice Arena in 1889. So who was Sandford Fleming?

Sandford Fleming's early life (born in 1827) is a bit of a mystery before he steps on a ship at age 18 headed for Canada. Most books and articles about him gloss over this 1827-1845 period. We know very little of his parents, generally only that his father was named Andrew and his mother Elizabeth. With a bit of digging one can find that Andrew was a successful building contractor, and the family lived in "considerable comfort." Other than that we are told his family was Presbyterian, that Sandford was noticed at an early age by engineer John Sang, to whom Fleming at aged 14, dropped out of school to apprentice with.[278] Beyond that, there is nothing else about his parents, even though several books about Sandford have been written. Even the father's birth and death dates can not be found on genealogy sites, odd for someone with such a famous son. As for his trip to Canada, the story is claimed that his father had heard stories from his cousin, a Dr. John Hutchison who had emigrated to Peterborough. Sanford and brother David were "shipped" to Canada by their father to strike it rich as their doctor relative had. That also sort of makes no sense. Sandford was just apprenticing to one of the key engineers of the day, even dropped out of school to do so, yet he is shipped to Canada to live as Hutchison's guest in his large house in Peterborough.[279]

Sandford, in his own diary, puts himself at the site of one Canada's most important events pre-1850, that being the fire of the parliament buildings in Montreal on April 25, 1849 (mentioned in chapter two). Not only was he in Montreal, at the fire, but also

<hr>

[278]Greene. Lorne, *Chief Engineer* p 2
[279]Green 3-8

199

claimed that along with three others, he rushed into the building to save a giant portrait of Queen Victoria that was hanging over the speakers chair. It is now hanging in the parliament in Ottawa. I mean you cannot make this stuff up...oh, apparently you can.[280] What he wrote in his diary about the aftermath of the event, but what is wrote is odd. "Very little was saved. I assisted to save the Queen's picture and saved the crown which was on top of the flames, took it home....I had the honor of sleeping last night with the crown in my bedroom-wrote to Father.""[281] He took home the crown from the parliament and slept with it? Why would he do that? No further information can be found on what became of this crown. Did he keep it? In Chapter four I revealed how he was the final recipient of the 1606 Masonic Stone. Is this crown another of his "gifts"?

We know he was a Freemason, being initiated in Toronto in 1854. I went looking for photos of Fleming for a clue, and found one from the early 1890's, during in his time as Chancellor of Queens University in Kingston. In that photo,[282] his right hand is hidden within the Chancellor robe. Fleming is making the Freemason gesture. Also one might find it odd that a man who dropped out of school at age 14 was made Chancellor of a prestigious university. This is mentioned in his biography that he was very reluctant to take the position because of his previous school issue. I get the sense that might be a cover for something else, as the above referenced photograph suggests.

A science website describes Fleming as "a Scottish-born Canadian engineer and inventor. He proposed worldwide standard time zones, designed Canada's first postage stamp, left a huge body of surveying and map making, engineered much of the Inter Colonial Railway and the Canadian Pacific Railway, and was a founding member of the Royal Society of Canada and founder of the Royal Canadian Institute."[283] He formed the Institute in 1849 when he was just 22 years old, and had been in Canada for less than six years. Is

---

[280]Greene p 11, 29

[281]Cole, Jean Murray, *Sir Sandford Fleming* p 148

[282] http://www.sandfordfleming.ca/en/photo.php?f2032_27_queens_uni
          Source *Sandford Fleming Empire Builder* by L.J. Burpee

[283] https://rasc.ca/honorary-member-sandford-fleming

that not a bit young to create Canada's first Science Institute? Just two years later, he became the first person to design a Canadian postage stamp.

In 1851 when Britain moved control of the postal service to Canada, they needed new stamps. The one to do the reorganization of the post office was James Morris. The claim is that just two days after his appointment, Morris met with Fleming on February 24, 1851 to discuss stamp creation. Why would Morris meet with Fleming, who was at the time a land surveyor? Would you not meet with an artist? The claim is that Fleming suggested using the beaver on the stamp, instead of the usual image of the Queen. "Fleming felt that the beaver was totally appropriate, since this characteristic specimen of Canadian wildlife, known for its industriousness, its building skills and its tenacity, was the perfect representative of a young nation occupied with building its future in a land that was still virtually undeveloped. The beaver was also evocative of the colony's beginnings, since beaver pelts were one of the first articles of trade between Amerindians and the French who disembarked in New France." The stamp was issued just two months later on April 23, 1851.[284] What was really happening was the making of an image for Canada , and Fleming for some reason was the one chosen to do this.

---

[284]https://www.historymuseum.ca/cmc/exhibitions/cpm/chrono/ch1851ce.html

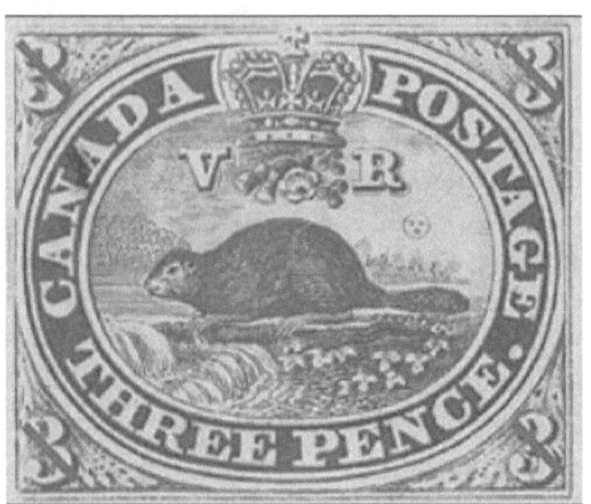

Illustration 32: Canada's First Postage Stamp, (Canada Post © 1851. Reproduced with Permission.)

Take a close look at the stamp above. Notice how the 3's sit at every corner thus make a 33 on top and a 33 on the bottom, the key number of Freemasonry. Secret societies meet in "lodges," which have been claimed to have been named after the secretive home of the beaver. On the stamp the beaver is in fact building its lodge, indicating that the lodge system in Canada was being built. There is a field of trilliums (often symbolically representing spiritual embodiment with consciousness). The British crown exists in the center underneath which was a rose (secret societies were often claimed to meet and discuss "sub rosa" or under the rose). There is also a Scottish thistle and Irish shamrock (indicating that Canada is only for the English). There is no French or Native symbolism. A very "face-like" sun (which would be symbolically the all-seeing eye) is in the upper right to view it all. I cannot think of a more symbol of Freemasonry than this stamp.

To look into the stamp issue further, I went through Fleming's diary for 1851. In the diary was a listing for Monday February 24 as, "Breakfast at Elsaps Hotel with Mr. Ruttan and Honble Jas Morris Postmaster General- Designing postage stamps for him- 3d Beaver stamp."[285] The "honble jas" means Honorable James in shorthand. First of all, what is a 3-d stamp? Does he mean it like as we would mean it today, 3-dimensional? Because the currency of the day was a pence, and if he was short handing the note it should have been written "3-p." What is Fleming referring to by 3-d?

Next comes an odd insert in the diary, added by the book's editor, which claims that the what was supposed to be the following page had been removed from the diary by a Fleming descendant, and given to H. Borden Clark, book dealer, with proof of stamp). What exactly does that mean? Why would a page from the original diary be ripped out and give to a book dealer? If anything, a page would be removed by a descendant to hide something. What needs to be hidden at the exact moment he is supposed to be designing a postage stamp? Perhaps he does have a design, but it is nothing like the one we have come to know. I mention this removal of a page, as it seems to me the only time it appears in the 331-page diary.[286] Sandford Fleming created two other postage stamps in 1851 for international mail, and they are equally as covered with symbolism.

Sandford Fleming continues the historical question marks as his life goes on. The next deals with the "building" of the Crystal Palace at the 1858 Toronto Exposition. It was two stories high (55 ft.), 256 ft. long, and 96 ft. wide. Opaque glass appeared in the ceiling. There were 47,000 sq. ft. of space between the main floor and gallery. The building was said to hold up to 8,000 people. The claim is that it took just 90 days to construct. When it was dismantled and moved, they added a third floor to make it 185 feet.[287] Anyone who has read my book *Exposing the Expositions* will know why I put quotation marks around building, as my research into these fairs tends to indicate that none of the main structures were actually built. I have been questioning the story of these fairs for four years, massive events built in record impossible times, without machines, often used for

---

[285] Jean Murray Cole ed, Sir Sandford Fleming p 189

[286] And to note, Public Archives in Ottawa has Felming's complete diaries through 1914. Given the importance he may play in the origin of hockey, someone in that region might want to go to the archives and look carefully at the entries between 1870-1875, and again between 1885-1890 to see what other links could be found in the diaries to the hockey narrative.

[287] https://www.torontojourney416.com/crystal-palace/,
https://www.thecanadianencyclopedia.ca/en/article/toronto-feature-the-crystal-palace

only a few months, then dynamited and thrown in to landfills. As such any connection of a person to a World Fair is a red flag to me, as one of my suggestions is that nothing was built but "refurbished" to hide a deep historical truth; that there was once an ancient civilization across North America that had been wiped out prior to/or along with, the colonial arrival.

The structure, also known as The Palace of Industry, was originally located near King St. W. and Shaw St. In 1878, it was dismantled and moved to the Exhibition Grounds, where it was enlarged and stood until 1906, when it was destroyed by fire. All of the world's Crystal Palaces (from London to Montreal) were destroyed by fire. The two architects of this building are claimed to be Fleming and Collingwood Schreiber (another CPR chief and a Knight of the Order of Michael and St. George). They are supposed to have won the bid by deciding to copy the 1851 Crystal Place of London. You mean no one else but them decided that copying the great new building of the century was a good idea?[288]

Was Fleming really the architect? Every historical book and website seems to say so. However, I came across one book that I would call the most historically accurate on the subject. That is the official 1858 Exhibition booklet. It provides the details of all of the exhibits, items for sale, restaurants and the like. The early part of the booklet gives an overview of the Crystal Palace. It gives all the building's measurements, the location were all of the materials came from (such as the glass from England), and even who the construction company was (Smith Burke and Co.). Yet nowhere in this entire discussion was there any mention of who the designers or architects were.[289] That is a huge oversight, as the architect is an important discussion of any new incredible building. They list where ever part of the building material comes from, but not the architects. Is that a clue?

---

[288] The buildings original location was just south of the Provincial Lunatic Asylum (another massive building). As always they questions comes, why are there needed to be so many mental hospitals having to be built after 1850, and why do they need to be opulant and bigger and more amazing than Medici Palaces of Florence?

[289] Booklet, Provincial Exhibition Toronto 1858 at Toronto Public Library site
https://digitalarchive.tpl.ca/objects/343566/provincial-exhibition--toronto-1858

Looking in Fleming's story further, in the early 1850s he became a key engineer on various railways being built in Canada. This began in Nova Scotia, and eventually he worked as the key engineer for the link to British Columbia. Fleming was in Manitoba in 1879 to investigate Red River flooding in order to determine where to place the CP bridges. That puts him in Manitoba prior to the start of "organized hockey" there.[290] Perhaps a coincidence. He proposed the idea of time meridians at a meeting of the Canadian Institute in Toronto on February 8, 1879. He lived and worked in Toronto since the 1850s. That puts him in Toronto just before hockey is in its development stages there. In 1880. he became the Chancellor of Queen's University in Kingston, at the exact same time period that the first hockey teams were being formed in that city. As we saw in chapter six, he was in Ottawa as a financier of the new Rideau Arena with Lord Stanley- thus connected in some way with the Rebel hockey team, which directly led to the Stanley Cup. Everywhere hockey is having an "origin" he tended to show up. As an added bonus, Fleming is also credited with the design of what might be Canada's first inline skate in 1850.[291] Either we are dealing with Leonardo Da Vinci reincarnated, or something else is going on with this man's entire biography.

---

[290]http://www.mhs.mb.ca/docs/people/fleming_s.shtml

https://www.gov.mb.ca/chc/hrb/internal_reports/pdfs/railway_stations_intro.pdf

[291] http://www.standrewsottawa.ca/heritage-biographies-fleming

Art Farrell's book

llustration 33: Montreal Shamrocks, Stanley Cup champions in 1899. Art Farrell is to the far right, standing. (Object Number II-133942.0, Notman Photographic Archives, McCord Museum)

With that I examine briefly, *Hockey: Canada's Royal Winter Game,* a book that came out in 1899, written by Art Farrell (as mentioned earlier the player directly connected to George Meagher through marriage). Many claim this to be the first hockey book. This is true only for Canada, for a book came out in in the United States by Beverly Bogert in 1893.

Much of Farrell's book is dedicated to long lists of rules in various organizations, and a section on what he calls the "science of hockey," which could be considered the first "how to play your best" guide. However, I want to look at his first couple of chapters, which are on the origin of hockey, and are quite strange. In the book's introduction:[292]

> *"To realize the necessity of a book that explains rules and the intricacies of the play of our glorious sport, one has but to travel to some town where the game is just developing from its infancy, where the players are scarcely able to appreciate its scientific points, and he will readily perceive that it is a long-felt want. Situated at a distance from the hockey centers, a young team cannot, by their own interpretation of the rules— without hints or instruction, without seeing the more practiced men at play—arrive at a thorough appreciation of these rules, or grasp with sufficient clearness the idea, the objective point of our noble sport, until they are grown old and stiff.*
>
> *They need, too, a guide to help them to the more quickly perfect themselves in their favorite pastime, and to avoid the dangers to which every player, however careful, is exposed."*

Farrell claims that without explanation of the rules, there is no chance for players in the various cities and villages to figure out the game for themselves. Only with standardization can boys and girls actually be able to "play" hockey. He also says they lack the ability to "grasp with sufficient clearness," or another way of saying- the players need Farrell to explain hockey to them. Remember this would be the ONLY book on hockey available in Canada at the time (and for several years going forward). As such, its influence in the minds of the early hockey players in the 1900s was very strong.

The following chapter first discusses how snowshoeing and tobogganing have *"slid itself into insensibility, and unless promptly revived will fade, like the memory of a pleasure enjoyed, into regions of the past."* This is important message to the elites, that the focus on snowshoeing and other winter sports that were presented at the winter

---

[292]Farrell, Art *Hockey: Canada's* all quotes come from this source

207

carnivals of the 1880s are now past, except hockey. It now is the official sport going forward. *"...in every city in the Dominion, the game will boom. Every athletic club will have its teams, and universities, colleges and schools will buzz on the ice at their favorite sport, while hundreds and thousands, eager to enjoy the sight, will flock to the rinks and cheer their sides to victory."*

Farrell then moves toward a strange examination of the past with a quote to Ancient Egypt,

> *"To trace back the sport to its very birth is not within the province of this little work, besides, its earliest history seems lost in a background of Egyptian darkness. Of all the games that developed from the old Roman sport the British hockey alone shaped the destiny of ours. There can be but little doubt, but that "shinny," the forerunner of our scientific hockey, is the Canadian interpretation of the game played across the water, adapted in its application to the climate of the country. Hockey in England is played in the winter on the frozen ground. It consists in driving a ball from one point to another by means of a hooked stick...it bears but little reference to hockey as played in Canada. Suffice it to say that in the shape of the sticks, not limited in their proportions, in the nature of the object that was used as a ball, in the unlimited numbers of the players, and in its principles, it is the parent of "shinny on the ice.""*

There is a lot to unpack in this section. He makes a key focus here to bring up specifically that the link to hockey is directly to Ancient Egypt and Rome, though he makes no specific comments as to why he is saying this. Then goes into a long description as to why field hockey of Britain is not ice hockey of Canada, but that it was the very thing that "shaped" Canada's sport. In other words, if you are looking for the origin of hockey you turn only to England. Next comes an even more bizarre paragraph.

"Shinny, so called, perhaps, on account of the frequent danger to which a player's shins were exposed, was a grand exhilarating sport. It had a hold upon us that the chilly atmosphere, or "the love we bore for learning," could not unfasten. Boys swarmed to the lakes in battalions and rattled along on old iron or wooden skates tied to their feet with rope. A few broken bones, a few frozen fingers, but, never mind, there were plenty of men to replace the dead. What a sight did a shinny match present! Hundreds on the same sheet of glare black ice, all eagerly engaged in one glorious game. What laughing, calling, cheering and chasing, there was to be sure! With their bright eyes and rosy cheeks they dart now in one direction, now in another till the great congealed bay roars and cracks with its living weight. The ball is in all directions in seconds of time, till finally the vast struggling crowd surges towards the goals, surrounds them, and a fierce lucky swipe knocks it through, while a hundred lusty voices cry their loudest Game! Game!!...As time wore on, the gradual development of rules and regulations wrought, in this warlike pastime, the important changes, that were, in time, to give birth to the science that characterizes hockey as the peer of clean, exciting, fascinating games."

Notice how often he is using military and war terminology to discuss hockey in Canada: battalions, plenty of men to replace the dead, and that it is a warlike pastime. He also is very clear to use the word ball here, and not puck, which by now should have been most commonplace in all outdoor hockey-type games in Canada- thus indicating that those using a ball in an ice game are playing the "old game" not the new game he is presenting in this book.

This last section of the book gives an overview:

"Twenty-five years ago, hockey, as played to-day, was an unknown sport. Shinny was played on the lakes, rivers and canals throughout the country, but only a discerning eye could discover in this crude, but

infatuating amusement, the grand possibilities that a refined game could offer. Without restrictions as to the proportions of the stick, the nature or quality of the puck, the size of the playing space on the ice, or the number of the players, the sport could not develop into a scientific game, until such time as it would be discussed and regulated, by those who sought its advancement."

This is the very nature of the argument of my book, which states that the elite took control of native sport, and in Montreal shaped it by adding British rules and organization. This was usually described as "science" in the time period. Just what Farrell is describing here. Science was now presented as the answer to every question, every problem, every issue. The presentation is the answer to any sport should be the same British science.

He finishes his overview with the explanation of how hockey provides great effects for the body and mind, how to overcome fears, and create a good moral character. But includes a very odd paragraph,

"Without comparing it to an oil painting of a chariot race, an Indian buffalo hunt or a fierce battle, what is prettier than the spectacle that a good game presents, of four stalwart, shapely forwards tearing down the ice, playing their lightning combination, of a brilliant rush stopped by an equally brilliant defense play, of a quick dash through a struggling mass of excited players, or a ziz-zag, twisting, twirling, dodging run to score a deciding goal?"

What is this supposed to mean, comparing hockey to an oil painting, chariot races and buffalo hunts? What is the meaning of such odd symbology? The book by Farrell is extremely odd, especially considering that this is the first book of hockey published in Canada, and stayed that way for almost a decade. I suggest that his sly references to buffalo hunts and Ancient Egypt are not as far off the mark as one might initially think. Perhaps he should have included Greek philosophers in his statements.

*

Philosophers?

The book *On The Origin of Hockey* presents information from a very strange 1873 event known as the Tichborne Trial. It was the O.J. trial of its day in England. Simplified, a man named Roger Charles Tichborne was born in Paris in 1829, and then was sent in the 1840s to a specialized boarding school, Stonyhurst College in England. In April of 1854, his ship was lost near the coast of Jamaica and he was considered dead. His mother would not admit to her son's death, and sent queries around the world looking for him. A letter arrived from a Sydney Australia lawyer in 1865 claiming a local butcher in New South Wales was her son, now named Arthur Orton. Orton was immediately sent to Paris by the grieving mother. Even though there was only passing similarity, and he did not speak French, she agreed this was her child. He was given a lavish monthly stipend, which lasted until his mother died. Then the other children took Orton to court to determine rightful heirs to the rich mother's estate.

There were various trials that lasted several years. In one of them was a long exchange by the lawyer to Orton for him to remember his time playing hockey and bandy while at Stonyhurst School. The lawyer set the questions as a trick, getting Orton to indicate the he did know what bandy was, claiming it was a part of the school and not a sport.

However, the part of the trial I want to share came on May 31, 1873 where a John Lawson was asked about the sport of bandy at the school. Some of his answers are a bit odd. He claimed that bandy "was played by the philosophers only." He was also clear that hockey was played on the ice, and bandy on the field, but the bandy sticks were longer. Lawson also mentioned that the ice hockey game was played with a cork bung, but bandy with a leather ball. A later witness though responded that he thought hockey and bandy were the same. When Lawson was asked where the bandy games took place he said

211

that "when the philosophers were at St. Mary's Hall the bandy-ground formed part of the garden in front of the seminary."[293]

While there is some interesting detail here of sticks and cork bungs, and if hockey and bandy were the same thing- my focus is, why are the philosophers the only ones to play bandy? How does the playing of bandy help with philosophy? I say this as a philosopher myself, and I am not sure that hockey would be any more or less helpful to my research than golf, football or eating a cheese sandwich. Does the original form of hockey-bandy have some sort of built in philosophical tool within the structure, geometry and rules of the game? Baseball does, so why not hockey?

*

Epilogue

Illustration 34: Hockey on the McGill ice rink in 1900 (Artist / Unknown, Object Number MP-0000.2241, McCord Museum)

---

[293]Giden *On the Origin* pgs 146-151

Have I found definitive answers to any of my questions that began this book? Why Montreal, 1875 and James Creighton? Perhaps partially, but there is still a long way to go. What has come about for me has been the realization that another narrative in history needs a complete re-examination. What I have done in this book is just a small step on that pathway. Even after 200 pages of research, it will require even further research to answer the question fully of why they created hockey in the 1800s." The first step was to find the "who" was behind the origins, the next stage of the research would be to determine exactly "why" and "how."

Anyone who wants to find truth has to ask very deep questions, questions that the majority is either unwilling, or afraid to ask. While I have set out some ideas of a possible thesis; Mi'kmaq game, appropriated by British elites, modified to create an identity for themselves and the country, with Sandford Fleming perhaps the main cog in that wheel, it cannot be proven. I was not there in 1875 to ask questions of the participants at that first game in Montreal. I wish I had been. Without a time machine all I can present are possibilities. However, if Sanford Fleming really were behind all of this, he would be the real Father of modern hockey. That would make James Creighton the Son, and the Victoria Arena the Holy Spirit. Thus even if one thinks this research is somehow tarnishing Fleming's "name," the end result would make him the father of modern hockey. The examination in this work was to find a better understanding of what the game in 1875 was, and why it happened.

I hope that my work might inspire other researchers to go down another rabbit hole of exploration in sport origins. To build on what I have done. As always with my research in any historical or

---

[294]David Lowenthal *The Past is a Foreign* p.xvi

213

philosophical subject, I am bringing one jigsaw puzzle piece of information. Others before me have brought other pieces. There is still more to locate and be brought to light. The hope is that as various people study different segments of a problem, and find a new "missing" part, then one day all of them could be pieced together to re-make the jigsaw puzzle whole again. Then, and only then, might we really know the truth about anything in history.

Lastly, I would like to offer my thanks to the many Native men and women of the past, and their various ice games that likely were the true origin of a sport that encapsulated a large part of my life. Without them, there would have been no Lafleur, or Gretzky, or Yakushev, or Lidstrom for me to watch for over fifty years.

APPENDIX 1

"Ice Hockey in Nova Scotia" 1859

This article is from the *Boston Evening Gazette* from November 5, 1859.[295]

"In Nova Scotia the time for ice is during the months of December, January and February. The lakes are then frozen and the ground generally covered with snow, although but seldom is there snow enough before Christmas to make sleighing. Skating is the favourite pastime during December, and, indeed, all through the winter, if – as is sometimes the case – there has been a great deal of snow.

There are some excellent skaters in this province, particularly in Halifax. I have seen young men who could cut their names in German text, or write the Lord's Prayer with skates on the ice easier than most skaters could cut the "outside edges." I don't like to be uncharitable, but I have known some skaters who, I think, would not be able to do it without a written or printed copy before their eyes. Throwing a somersault on skates is almost an impossibility yet I have seen it done successfully.

Fancy skating is not so much practiced now in Nova Scotia as formerly; more attention is paid to games on ice. Ricket is the favorite pastime, and is played thus. Two rickets are formed at about the same distance, one from the other, that cricketers place their wickets. If there are many players, the rickets are further apart. A ricket consists of two stones – about as large as the cobble stones with which some of our streets have been lately paved – placed about three of four feet apart and frozen to the ice. Sides are then formed by two persons –

---

one opposed to the other – tossing or drawing lots for first choice of partners.

choosing-sides

Choosing Sides
One team captain would place his hand on the stick, the other team captain would place his hand on the stick above the opposing captains hand, and so on up the stick till one captain holds the top of the stick. The captain holding the top of the stick gets to choose first from the group waiting to play.

The one who obtains the first choice selects one from the crowd, the other party then chooses another, and so on alternately, until a sufficient number is obtained on each side. Any number can play the game, and generally, the "more the merrier". Each ricketer is provided with a hurley (or hockey, as it is termed here,) and all being ready a ball is thrown in the air, which is the signal to commence play, previous to which, however, a ricket is chosen by each side and placed in charge of a man whose duty it is to prevent the ball from passing through. The game maybe 10, 15 or 20, or any number agreed upon, the side counting the number first being the winners. The counting consists in putting the ball through your adversary's ricket, each time counting one. From the moment the ball touches the ice, at the commencement of the game; it must not be taken in the hand until the conclusion, but must be carried or struck about the ice with the hurlies. A good player – and to be a good player you must be a good skater – will take the ball at the point of his hurley and carry it around the pond and through the crowd which surrounds him trying to take it from him; until he works it near his opponents ricket, and "then comes the tug of war," both sides striving for the mastery. Whenever the ball is put through the ricket a shout "game ho!" resounds from shore to shore and dies away in hundreds of echos through the hills. Ricket is the most exciting game played on the ice"

Editor's Note:... "It might be well if some of our agile skaters would introduce the game. It would be a fine addition to our winter sports,

and give a new zest to the delightful exercise of skating. We have sent
down for a set of hurleys preparatory to its introduction."

FIRST PUBLISHED ICE HOCKEY RULES
Feb 27, 1877[296]

1. The game shall be commenced and renewed by a Bully in the center of the ground. Goals shall be changed after each game (goal).

2. When a player hits the ball, any one of the same side who at such a moment of hitting is nearer to the opponents' goal line is out of play and may not touch the ball himself, or in any way whatever prevent any other player from doing so, until the ball has been played. A player must always be on his own side of the ball.

3. The ball may be stopped, but not carried or knocked on by any part of the body. No player shall raise his stick above his shoulder. Charging from behind, tripping, collaring, kicking or shinning shall not be allowed.

4. When the ball is hit behind the goal line by the attacking side, it shall be brought out straight 15 yards, and started again by a Bully; but, if hit behind by any of the side whose goal line it is, a player of the opposite side shall it out from within one yard of the nearest corner, no player of the attacking side at that time shall be within 20 yards of the goal line, and the defenders, with the exception of the goal-keeper, must be behind their goal line.

5. When the ball goes off at the side, a player of the opposite side to that which hit it out shall roll it out from the point on the boundary

---

[296] https://www.degruyter.com/document/doi/10.3138/9781442657496-015/pdf, Wong, John Chi-Kit, Lords of the Rinks- The Emergence of the National Hockey League 1875-1936 (U of Toronto Press 2005)

line at which it went off at right angles with the boundary line, and it shall not be in play until it has touched the ice, and the player rolling it in shall not play it until it has been played by another player, every player being then behind the ball.

6. On the infringement of any of the above rules, the ball shall be brought back and a Bully shall take place.

7. All disputes shall be settled by the Umpires, or in the event of their disagreement, by the Referee.

JAMES NORRIS

James E. Norris can be thought of, not as a founder of hockey, but one who took what the founding fathers were doing, and marketed it for decades.

Born in 1879 in Montreal, he would up being a rich businessman in the grain and cattle industries, and owner of the Detroit Red Wings of the National Hockey League. He was also owner of the Chicago Stadium, where the Blackhawks played and after 1944 became the "owner behind the scenes" with Bill Toban standing in as the defacto owner. Meanwhile he had loaned the Bruins enough money in the 1930 that as a high stakes creditor one could say he had a say in the affairs of that club, then in 1950 bought a huge stake in Madison Square Garden thus being a major controller of the New York Rangers. In a sense he was the actual owner of all four US based teams, but in reality only openly owned a more than 50% share of one (the Red Wings). A joke at the time was that NHL stood for Norris House League. After his death his son Bruce took over the Wings, while his other son James D was an owner of the Chicago Blackhawks and at the same time the key shareholder in the New York Rangers.

James Sr had been a defenseman for Montreal AAA Hockey Club, mostly playing for its Intermediate team but getting into three games for the senior team in 1898 while attending McGill University (as seemingly every key organizer or founder of early hockey did). His father was rich from mill, shipbuilding and land ownership. The family moved to Chicago around 1900, and James played hockey with the Kenwood Country Club and Chicago Wanderers. In business he began buying grain elevators in the 1910s and was the largest cash grain buyer in the world in the 1930s.

When the NHL announced in 1926 that it would place a team in Chicago, Norris made a bid for the team, but lost to Frederic McLaughlin. Norris thus decided to become a key financial backer of the Chicago Stadium, which opened in March 1929. He tried to get a second team in Chicago, then to even try to make the American Hockey Association a rival league to the NHL. By 1932 he bought the financially insolvent Detroit Falcons and the Detroit Olympia. It was here he changed the name to Red Wings, and gave them their current winged wheel logo, which he used the old Montreal AAA logo as a template.

I have presented this here just again to see how much of what became hockey in the NHL era, was all linked by people (and thus the thought process) of the 1880s and 1890s hockey foundations, specifically in Montreal and Ottawa.

Thank you with photo help

Thank you to direct help received with permissions from:

Hockey Hall of Fame Resource Center
The Martin and Osa Johnson Safari Museum
Canadian Library and Public Archives
Canadian Museum of History
Canada Postmaster
Manitoba Sports Hall of Fame
Simcoe County Archives
Glory Days Sports Cards
Amno Domkirkeodden

Thank you for hosting public domain images:
McCord Museum
Yale University Art Gallery
Smithsonian Art Museum
British Museum

BIBLIOGRAPHY

BOOKS

Cole, Jean Murray ed. *Sir Sandford Fleming: his early diaries 1845-1853* (Natural Heritage Books 2009)

Culin, Stewart. *Games of the North American Indians.* (1907)

Diamond, Dan ed. *Total Hockey.* (Total Sports Publishing New York 2000)

---------------- ed. *Total Hockey.* (Total Sports Publishing New York 1998)

Farrell, Art. *Hockey: Canada's Royal Game.* Cr Cornell Montreal 1899

Fell, Barry. America BC: Ancient Settlers in a New World (Pocket Books New York, 1978)

Fitsell, JW. *How Hockey Happened.* (Quarry Press 2006)

-------- *Hockey's Captains, Colonels and Kings.* (The Boston Mills Press, 1987)

Fosty, George. *Black Ice: The Lost History of the Colored Hockey League of the Maritimes 1895-1925.* (Nimbus Publishing 2008)

Giden, Carl, Houda, Patrick, Martel, Jean-Patrice. *On the Origin of Hockey.* (Hockey Origin Publishing 2014)

Grant, George Monro ed. *Picturesque Canada: The country as it was and is,* vol 1 and 2. J Clarke New Hampshire 1882

Green, Lorne *Chief Engineer: life of a nation builder Sandford Fleming* (Dundurn Press 1993)

Gruneau, Richard S and Whitson. David Hockey Night in Canada: sport, identities and cultural politics. Garamond Press 1992

Hardy, Stephen; Holman, Andrew C; *Hockey A Global History* (University of Illinois Press 2018)

Isaacs, Neil David *Checking Back: A History of the National Hockey League* (Norton 1977)

223

Jenish, Darcy. *The Stanley Cup: One hundred years of hockey at its best.* (McClelland and Stewart 1992)

Kitchen Paul. *Win Lose or Wrangle: The Inside Story of the Ottawa Senators 1883-1935.* (Penumbra Press Manotick 2008)

Klein, Jeff Z, Reif, Eric. *The Klein and Reif Hockey Compendium.* (McClelland and Stewart 1987)

Loewen, James. *Lies My Teacher Told Me.* (The New Press 2007)

Lowenthal, David. *The Past is a Foreign Country* (Cambridge University Press 1985)

Martin, Brian. *Baseball's Creation Myth: Adam Ford, Abner Graves and the Cooperstown Story.* (McFarland and Company 2013)

McKay, Ian. *In the province of History: the making of the public past in twentieth-century Nova Scotia.* (McGill University press 2010)

McKinley, Michael. *Putting a Roof On Winter: Hockey's rise from sport to spectacle.* (Greystone Books 2000)

Metcalfe, Alan. *Canada Learns to Play: the emergence of organized sport 1807-1914.* (McClelland and Stewart 1987)

Oxendine, Joseph B. *American Indian Sports Heritage.* (Human Kinetics Books 1988)

Poulter, Gillian. *Becoming Native in a Foreign Land.* (UBC Press 2010)

Poulton, J Alexander. *A History of Hockey in Canada.* (Over Time Books 2010)

Raddell, Thomas. *Halifax: Warden of the North.* (1948 Doubleday 1948)

Routledge, Edmund ed. *Every Boys Book: A Complete Encyclopedia of Sports and Amusements.* (George Routledge and Sons 1869)

Sable Trudy, Bernie Francis. *The Language of This Land, Mi'kma'ki* (Cape Breton Press 2012)

Shea, Kevin and Wilson, John Jason. *Lord Stanley, The man behind the Cup.* (Fenn Publishing 2006)

The Sagas of Icelanders : a selection. (New York : Viking 2000)

Thorn, John. *Baseball in the Garden of Eden.* (Simon and Schuster 2011)

Tuthill, JA. 1898 *Ice Hockey and ice polo guide.* (American Sports Pub Company 1898)

Wong, John Chi-Kit. *Lords of the Rinks- The Emergence of the National   Hockey League 1875-1936.* (U of Toronto Press 2005)

----------. *Coast to Coast: Hockey in Canada to the Second World War.* (University   of Toronto Press 2009)

*

ARTICLES

Becket, Hugh W compiler. "Record of Winter Sports 1883-84: Snowshoe   and skating races, hockey and curling matches." *Becket Brothers*   Montreal 1884

Bennett Paul W. "Reimagining the Creation: The 'Missing Indigenous   Link' in the Origins of Canadian Hockey."

D'Arcy Jenish "Hockey's Forgotten Pioneer." January 18, 2008 Legion   Magazine

Dufresne, Sylvie. "1883-1889: Quand Montréal avait son Carnaval!" Cap-   aux-Diamants No. 64 (Hiver 2001): 10–14.

Eveland, Timothy R.J. "Did Vikings Play Ice Hockey?" (timothyrjeveland.com)

Fitsell, Bill. "Kingston" *in Diamond, Dan (ed.) Total Hockey,* 1998 New   York: Total Sports Publishing,

----------, The Rise and Fall of Ice Polo in Diamond, Dan (ed.), *Total Hockey,* Kingston, New York: Total Sports Publishing 2000

Fyffe, Iain "Hockey Origins" (hockeyhistoryasis.blogsport.com)

Goldsborough, Gordon "Manitoba History: Dan Bain: The Squire of Delta Marsh" (mhs.mb.ca)

Grant, Mark." Hockey Hall of Fame Nomination : MI'KMAQ FIRST   NATION." (hockey-stars.ca)

"Hockey on Ice" *Harper's Young People* 1884,

Hornby, Lance "First Hockey Game in Toronto History" *Toronto Sun*   February 14, 2015

"How Official Ottawa Held Back a 'Great Unsung Native 'Hero'" *Ottawa   Citizen* March 1, 2008

Humber, Bill "What was Early Canadian Hockey and What does it owe to others?" (SIHR.org)

Kitchen Paul "Hockey on the Lake" Diamond, Dan (ed.) *Total Hockey,*   Kingston, New York: Total Sports Publishing 1998,

-----------, "They Refused the Cup" chapter 3 in Diamond, Dan (ed.), *Total Hockey*, Kingston, New York: Total Sports Publishing 2000

----------- "Before the Trail for the Stanley Cup," chapter 3 in Diamond, Dan (ed.) Total New York: Total Sports Publishing, Hockey 2000

Kotylo, Len "The History of Hockey in Toronto", chapter 7 in Diamond, Dan (ed.) Total New York: Total Sports Publishing, Hockey 2000

Marie, Denise. Crystal Palace – The Beautiful & Ornate Building Once at the Exhibition (torontojourney416.com)

Martel, Jean-Patrice "Origins of Ice Hockey" thecanadianencyclopedia.ca

Mickoski, Howdie Being a Hockey Fan in 1900 in Diamond, Dan (ed.), *Total Hockey*, Kingston, New York: Total Sports Publishing 2000

Mott, Morris "An immense hold in the public estimation: the first quarter century of Hockey in Manitoba, 1886-1911." (mhs.mb.ca)

Morrow, Don, "The Knights of the Snowshoe: A Study of the Evolution of Sport in Nineteenth Century Montreal" *Journal of Sport History* v 15 n 1, 1988, p.5-40 (jstor.org)

_______ The Institutionalization of Sport: A Case Study of Canadian Lacrosse 1844-1914 (Jstor.org)

"Organized Hockey in capitol had beginning early eighties," *Ottawa Citizen* January 19, 1935

Outing : an Illustrated Monthly Magazine of Sport, Travel and Recreation 1893-01: Vol 21 Iss 4 Publication date 1893-01

Owen, Gerald The Origins of 'Hockey' n Diamond, Dan (ed.), *Total Hockey*, Kingston, New York: Total Sports Publishing 2000

Pessati, Alessandro. "Stewart Culin and the Study of Games."

Potter, Mitch "Cup Runneth Over With Cousins" *Toronto Star* May 25, 2008

Poulter, Gillian and Don Morrow "Knights of the Snowshoe" (jstor.org)

Robidoux, Michael A "Imagining a Canadian Identity Through Sport: A historical interpretation of lacrosse and hockey. (spring 2002 *Journal of American Folklore* v 115, 4556) (Jstor.org)

Schmidt, David L and Marshall, Murdena. *Mi'Kmaq Hieroglyphic Prayers*, 1995 Nimbus Publishing (naig2023.com)
Society For International Hockey Research Database (sihrhockey.og)
"The Montreal Winter Carnival" *Harper's Blazer* March 8, 1884
Vigneault Michael "Out of the Mists of Memory," *Total Hockey* 1998
________ "The Cultural Diffusion of Hockey in Montreal 1890-1917" (University of Windsor thesis 1986)
Zukerman, Earl, "Today History: McGill hockey team played first game   on Jan. 31, 1877" January 31, 2014 (reporter.mcgill.ca)
-----------------, "McGill University" in Diamond, Dan (ed.), *Total Hockey,*   Kingston, New York: Total Sports Publishing 2000

BASEBALL ARTICLES
North, Andrew "The Beachville Game" (sabr.org)
Souder Mark, "The Guide to Spalding: San Diego, 1900–15" (Sabr.org)
Sullivan, Ted. "Humerous Stories of the Ball Field" (1903: MA Donahue   and Company)
Zeiler, Thomas W. "Basepaths to Empire: Race and the Spalding World Baseball Tour." The Journal of the Gilded Age and Progressive   Era Vol. 6, No. 2 (Apr., 2007), pp. 179- 207 (29 pages) Published   By: Society for Historians of the Gilded Age & Progressive Era

Other Website articles found at

https://birthplaceofhockey.com/hockey-history/origin/
http://www.biographi.ca/en/bio/creighton_james_george_aylwin_15E.html,
https://sihrhockey.org/__a/public/creighton.cfm
http://www.hockeyshome.ns.ca/index.htm
http://www.traditionalsports.org/traditional-sports/europe/la-soule-a-la-crosse-france.html
https://www.rollerskatedad.com/history-of-ice-hockey/
http://www.hurstwic.org/history/articles/daily_living/text/knattleikr.htm
http://www.mhs.mb.ca/docs/people/macdonald_pa.shtml

https://skateguard1.blogspot.com/2015/01/george-alfred-meagher-champion-figure.html
https://hockeygods.com/images/7101Rideau_Hall_Rebels___Ice_Hockey_Stick_Fun___1889
https://www.nhl.com/news/how-stanley-cup-came-to-be/c-287700534
https://www.onondaganation.org/culture/sports/longball/
https://havechanged.blogspot.com/2017/12/madame-blatavsky-and-beginnings-of.html
https://www.Theosophistycanada.com/history-of-Theosophisty-in-canada.php
https://www.Theosophistycanada.com/files/albert-e-s-smythe-bio.pdf
https://www.Theosophistycanada.com/history-of-Theosophisty-in-canada.php
https://www.Theosophistycanada.com/files/albert-e-s-smythe-bio.pdf
https://healthahoy.com/ancient-sports/native-american-shinny-hockey/
https://www.hokejovysen.cz/en/ipha/history/
https://www.americanheritage.com/man-who-didnt-invent-baseball
https://theunexpectedcosmology.com/the-sacred-geometry-of-baseball-a-masonic-ritual/
chicagolgy for world tour
https://theunexpectedcosmology.com/the-sacred-geometry-of-baseball-a-masonic-ritual/
https://sabr.org/journal/article/the-guide-to-spalding-san-diego-1900-15/
https://www.npr.org/2011/03/16/134570236/the-secret-history-of-baseballs-earliest-days
https://www.americanheritage.com/man-who-didnt-invent-baseball
https://sabr.org/bioproj/person/Alexander-Cartwright/
https://www.npr.org/2011/03/16/134570236/the-secret-history-of-baseballs-earliest-days
https://www.masseyareamuseum.com/james-henry-massey.html

VIDEO
The Game of Hockey- A Mi'kmaw Story By April and Cheryl Maloney, 2023 Version

ABOUT THE AUTHOR

Howdie Mickoski is an historian, philosopher and researcher. He has written several books, as well as given hundreds of interviews and created a similar amount of video content. A former hockey player and coach, he has an honors degree in history, and has studied hockey history for over forty-five years.

More information can be accessed at:

howdiemickoski.com (click on "hockey portal")

Howdietalkssports at Youtube

OTHER BOOKS BY THE AUTHOR

Exposing the Expositions:1851-1915

Exit the Cave: Ending the reincarnation trap

Falling For Truth: A spiritual death and awakening

The Power of Then: Revealing Egypt's lost wisdom

Hockeyology: Digging up hockey's past

Thanks for reading.